# What Really Matters?

*A Collection of Lectures in the L. D. Johnson Series*

Edited by
## Thomas O. Buford

Furman 175th *Anniversary*

SMYTH&HELWYS
PUBLISHING, INCORPORATED   MACON, GEORGIA

Smyth & Helwys Publishing, Inc.
6316 Peake Road
Macon, Georgia 31210-3960
1-800-747-3016
©2001 by Smyth & Helwys Publishing

*Library of Congress Cataloging-in-Publication Data*

What really matters? : a collection of lectures in the L.D. Johnson
series / Thomas O. Buford
p.    cm.
"Book written to commemorate the 175th year celebration of Furman
University"
ISBN 1-57312-368-4
1. Christian life—Meditations. 2. Johnson, L. D., 1916-
3. Furman University.
I. Buford, Thomas O., 1932- II. Johnson, L. D., 1916-
BV4501.3 .W45 2001
378.757'27—dc21                                    2001049157
                                                        CIP

# What Really Matters?

॥⁄⁄

## *Lectures*

# Background

The guiding purpose for publishing these essays is to raise the question "What really matters?" and to learn from various faculty of Furman University some answers to the question. Also, it is our purpose to encourage a broader audience to consider the question and their answers. These lectures are not about L. D. Johnson. He would have been quick to direct the focus to the important question they raise, not on himself. We focus on what he focused on, the question and the search, and encourage each person to join in the search alongside him, though now only in memory for many of us.

Each essay expresses deeply held personal beliefs that form the character of the author. They also portray the author's working through the question "What really matters?" Confronted with a common question in a context of freedom of inquiry, each person reveals the basis of a way of life and gives answers that come slowly.

Those insights guided the organization of the book. Instead of headings or a common lecture title, we provide the names of the essayists, the departments or areas in which they work, and the dates of presentation. In the case of faculty who are also administrators, we have included the title for which they are best known. In these ways we preserve the individuality of the essayists. Believing that Furman's way is found in the individual persons who live and work here, we let each individual person speak.

Each essay was originally delivered as one of the L. D. Johnson Memorial Lectures. The series was established by the Watkins Center to honor the life and work of the late Dr. L. D. Johnson, Chaplain, Furman University, February 17, 1967–December 20, 1981. It is an appropriate honor since for many years we were so richly inspired by his example, leadership, love, and support. One of L. D.'s most outstanding contributions to Furman was the development of the university's Characters and Values Statement. He often called us to stop and look at who we are and what we are about. Therefore, the theme for the lectures is always the same: "What Really Matters?" The lecturers are chosen from the Furman faculty, with selection being rotated among the departments. Most of the lectures are printed as prepared for delivery and later for publication. Some have been updated for inclusion in this volume.

These lectures were supported and encouraged by the determined and tireless effort of Miss Betty Alverson. Through her years at Furman her persistent challenge to each of us was to face the question "What really matters?" and to find an answer that called from each of us our best.

Our thanks to Mrs. Debra Corvey, Secretary to the Philosophy Department, who cheerfully and enthusiastically saw the manuscript preparation through from its inception to its final publication. Thanks also to Smyth & Helwys, especially Cecil Staton and a behind-the-scenes person, these essays will find a broader audience. The editorial assistance by David Cassady, Erin Smith, and the staff at Smyth & Helwys combined to make this work a pleasure of cooperation.

We also appreciate the support of Smyth & Helwys, as the text deviates from established publishing policy. The format for citations varies from essay to essay. This is intentional. Prepared for a general university audience, these essays were originally lectures that express what really matters and not developed for publication or for the audience of a particular scholarly discipline. Keeping the format of that lecturer's discipline or personal preference, we attempt to maintain their personal character.

Finally, the idea for publishing these essays originated in the office of the Vice-president for Academic Affairs and Dean. He noted that Furman celebrates her 175th anniversary during the 2001–2002 academic year. As we take stock of our stewardship of what has been handed to us, we wonder how well we have done. One insightful indication is found in these lectures. Among these pages one finds serious people grappling with the question that binds us into an academic community. We place these personal essays before you for your judgment and to invite your participation. This good idea could have languished for lack of support. Thanks to A. V. Huff, this good idea materialized. Without his encouragement and the financial support of his office, this would have been another good idea lost.

Thomas O. Buford
Editor
May 1, 2001

# L. D. Johnson Knew What Mattered

Dr. L. D. Johnson was the kind of man a parent could point to as an example of a decent human being. That may not be the highest praise of a mortal man, but it comes close. It is praise that would have made L. D. Johnson, an unpretentious man, uncomfortable.

As a human being and as a preacher, L. D. Johnson was remarkable. There are not many among us capable of coming away from charmed circles, from places of wealth and power, without somehow wanting to occupy them. L. D. Johnson was capable of looking beyond the temporal to the eternal. He simply knew what mattered. And his faith was so sincere, so unadorned by flashy ornaments of so-called modern religion, that he escaped being sidetracked from his journey.

L. D. Johnson, like all sincere people of faith, believed he had a purpose for living. If he could somehow make this cradle of cruelty a little more humane, a little more Christlike, then L. D. knew that his trek would amount to something greater than his own life.

This man, this preacher, this believer in the Prince of Peace did not fail. Through his Sunday columns in the *Citizen-Times* and other newspapers, he touched the lives of tens of thousands of people — people he did not know. There also were congregations, students, and just ordinary folks who turned to him for advice.

His Sunday column, which masterfully meshed religion with the humanities, modern problems, and just plain Oklahoma horse sense, became a household fixture in the Carolinas and beyond.

Like other readers, we had our favorite L. D. columns. One of the most memorable offerings dealt with L. D.'s tour of a Virginia maritime museum. The preacher had been accompanied by an old salt who did not like the shoddy workmanship of today's merchant fleets. The old mariner touched that reservoir of decency in L. D. Johnson, and the preacher delivered a stirring column on the dishonesty of doing a job poorly. And if that piece could touch the heart of a cynical newspaperman, we reasoned that it touched others far removed from the ink-and-type crowd.

Had L. D. Johnson never written another word, we would have held him in high esteem. But he wrote more, and we got to know the man behind the Sunday morning mug shot.

He was everything we had imagined him to be — and more. We asked him to speak on world hunger to a Warren Wilson College seminar. We did not think he would accept. After all, this chaplain and professor of religion at Furman University surely had a thousand excuses why he couldn't come.

We were wrong. He merely asked how long he should speak and when he should arrive.

That said a lot for L. D. Johnson. But he had been answering the call for help for years, in little churches and big mainline congregations, in classrooms and in lecture halls.

Watching him stand before that Warren Wilson audience on a Saturday morning and talk without notes on human need, we knew that here was a man and preacher touched with Christ's compassion, gentleness, and, yes, moral fire. He pulled no punches that morning. You do not forget such eloquence in an age of fence-straddlers.

L. D. Johnson did more than talk about hunger. He acted. He helped raise money to build windmills so starving people could irrigate their lands and raise crops.

Through it all, the uses of wealth in his university, in his South, and in his nation troubled this Christian gentleman. His best column this year, in our view, was the one he wrote on this subject the week of Thanksgiving.

This Southern Baptist minister not only understood the folly of the arms race and the outrage of hunger, but he understood grief. He had been there and back. He helped many a parent through the darkness of a death in the family.

On the afternoon of December 21, 1962, Carole Johnson, daughter of L. D. and Marion Johnson, was traveling home to Greenville, South Carolina, to spend Christmas with her family when another motorist pulled out onto the icy road and ended her short life.

Some of the things L. D. Johnson learned about life that Christmas were passed on in a beautiful book titled *The Morning After Death*.

The tall Oklahoman told a reporter, "You don't know what life is about until you consider not having it. So it is important to ask yourself the meaning of your own death, to understand it and face it. Then go on."

On a Sunday, nearly nineteen years to the day after Carole Johnson died, death came to L. D. Johnson. Those of us who knew and loved this Christian man and are crushed by his passing can take comfort in knowing that our friend was a man's man. And we know, too, that we saw Christlike qualities in this wonderful human being called L. D. Johnson.

# Theron D. Price
## Religion
*October 25, 1982*

## *By Way of Introduction*

Such a title as "Some Things That Matter" invites attention to virtually any-thing in the cosmos. Some of the baser element in the faculty here present will probably say, "That's just the kind of thing that Price would undertake." Actually, I'm not undertaking all that. So many, many things are important. Perhaps few finally matter.

It is important whether there be a good harvest, whether the recent dis-covery of a jumping gene may lead to a control that would prevent healthy cells from becoming cancerous, whether there be full employment, stable family life, quality education — or that we not appear gauche in public, not lose our cool in a crisis, even that we not get run over by a truck. These things do matter, but it is not to these that I turn.

For me to speak now of the few things that decisively matter is not to minimize any of the things just mentioned. It is a way of seeking out the ulti-mate ground on which stand all things that pertain to the human good. The one theme of this address is personhood, as that pertains to ourselves, to oth-ers, and to that Being who is the source and end of all being, the ground and rationale of all that really matters.

If that theme is as broad as the cosmos, this is what you would likely expect from a theologian of sorts. I take refuge in the conviction that any subject that can be fully covered is probably not worth talking about. I am even willing to have said of my speech what Dorothy Parker is reported to have said in her review of a book by Henry James: "He chewed more than he bit off." But, now, let's move on.

We are born into a physical world we did not make, into a mortal exis-tence we did not choose. We are conscious of an uncertain future we cannot control. It is in such an awesome setting that we come to personal self-aware-ness, that is, to awareness of our selves as selves.

Years before we ever learn to discern a value or choose a good, we become aware also of others — others like ourselves. People, that is to say, of similar mortal existence, similar questions and problems, similar fears and conflicts, similar needs and drives, similar hopes and dreams. These people touch, affect, sometimes penetrate our lives so as to become a part of our self-understanding, even of our existence.

Also, for as long as we have been people on this planet — and the temporal backdrop of this keeps being moved farther and farther back — our human kind have been convinced that we are dealing with what is more than human, i.e., with the Transcendent. It is documentable, with certainty I believe at least as far back as the Mousterian, that people have entertained ideas and observed practices, which in our language it is customary to call "religious."

These facts provide the structure for what follows, for I wish to speak, in order, of ourselves, of others, and of the Transcendent Mystery as the things that finally matter. Of ourselves, I shall stress that it matters.

## That We Become Who We Are

Putting it this way implies some sort of distinction in things human between the actual and the real. To make such a distinction is hazardous in an age when many appear to have turned science into scientism. Nonetheless, the distinction is given credibility by impressive intellectual and moral traditions. The distinction is so commonplace in Buddhism and Hinduism as to require no explanation, much less defense. Platonism and all forms of Romanticism rest upon it. All who take seriously the biblical perspective on our human existence recognize its importance there. All these, I think, would say that the real or true human person is the actual plus the potential.

By "person," I mean that human center of self-awareness and purposeful intent that identifies one as what he is and may become. Man is a self, but "no man is an island." We exist in relation — in relation to others, to a society of others, composed of individuals indeed, but also in some sense prior to the individual and in measure determinative of him. The outermost ranges of this personal community, and indeed its ground, are part of what Father Teilhard de Chardin meant by his phrase "the divine milieu." All this together is the real, and in it we have our true being. But we are not just out there loose in the divine milieu.

Our actual concrete existence is experienced within limitary conditions, which both bound and challenge us. The late Karl Jaspers of Basel described these conditions as *Grenzsituationen*, "boundary situations." Let this claim our attention for a few minutes as one way of reflecting upon how we become who we are. And I give the answer before delineating the ideas. We become who we are; i.e., we turn our actual existence into our true being, through humble and courageous coping with the boundaries.

What are these boundary situations? Jaspers names five. There are many more situations than five, and they are often important for us. "We are always in situations," he says. "Situations change, opportunities arise. If they are missed they never return. I myself can work to change the situation. But there are situations which remain essentially the same even if their momentary aspect struggle, I am subject to chance, I involve myself inexorably in guilt." These are boundaries that we cannot evade or change: death, suffering, conflict, chance, and guilt. On the one hand they are, along with wonder and doubt, a profound source of philosophy. On the other they are the potential evokers of our personhood. These are not merely concert situations, which we may master to our profit. These are ultimate boundaries, not to be prayed away, from contention with which there results in us either indifference, or despair, or else rebirth. "We become ourselves [vis-à-vis these boundaries]," says Jaspers, "by a change in our consciousness of being."

Nowhere more than in this setting does the human person reveal his actuality and move either toward or away from his potential. To fail to cope bravely with these boundaries, as cope the Stoics saw we must, is to diminish our personhood and the possibility of its freedom. To cope with integrity and courage is not only to enhance the measure of what we are and may become; it is to begin to learn the meanings of joy.

On this point, I believe the existentialists are correct. Certainly this was true for Kierkegaard. It appears congenial with other things Jaspers has said. And, if I have read him correctly, it was true even of that devout atheist Camus. This particular angle of vision was true also of Jesus, no existentialist I think, but "who for the joy that was set before him, endured the cross" (Hebrews 12:2).

Perhaps that last word is a clue. The cross as a physical fact is one piece of wood intersected by another. As the New Testament symbol of moral reality asserted as moral redemption, it is the undertaking, out of free goodwill, of a course of action whose essence is self-giving for the sake of other — a course of action that could not be demanded of one nor enforced upon him. On a cross one makes no escape from the boundaries — from conflict, suffering, guilt, grief, death. The cross does not produce, all in a swoop, peace of mind, prosperity touted as a chief sign of God's favor, nor even escape from what appears to be a streak of absurdity in the universe. This kind of joy and our kind of pleasure have little in common. But in such an awesome act, an act of response to the situation, which it was his distinctive vocation to manage, Jesus of Nazareth is revealed as the Christ.

To be a person in a biblical way means, in part, to find this out for oneself. Or, to put it in existentialist terms, it is in such acts of true being that one attains awareness of freedom and certainty of God. This is what a genuine realism would describe as joy.

It is surely this realistic encounter with these rugged facts of life that makes possible our discovery that the truth lies not in but beyond them. We find the truth of our being through engagement with the boundaries, but not in the boundary situations themselves. They belong to our earthly existence, but we know from our earthly existence that no final reliance can be placed in earthly existence. The world is not our being. It is where we have our being to gain or to lose. The great Puritans were right to see all earthly existence as a "vale of soul-making."

If not by escape from the boundaries, neither by mastery of nature, nor solidarity with others, can we guarantee our existence in the world? At the same time that science and technology make the world more convenient, they make it more dangerous and less controllable. Neither is banding together in community a guarantee of justice, much less of freedom. Solidarity is never absolute, for each is prone to desire his own and not his neighbor's good. How, then, is it to be done?

St. Paul summons us, as the means by which we are to be drawn into the line of justice and freedom, to "the renewing of our minds" (Romans 12:2). In more familiar language this is a summons to an ongoing repentance, which is to occupy us, as Luther well knew, for as long as life lasts.

With the summons comes also the opportunity for human beings to undertake such a renewing of the mind — an act of individual turning about in one's way, the undertaking of this ongoing reformation and radical self-dealing, which the Bible calls "repentance." As a moral and spiritual power, focusing much more on possibilities ahead than on failures behind, repentance can give hope within the boundaries and unite us with what lies transcendent beyond them.

One who does this is on the way to becoming who he is. He has no proofs that this is so. He does have what is infinitely more helpful. He has within himself the moral certitude to get on with his actual life in the actual world. He will be justified by faith. Won't we all?

This creative contention with the actual world, which unites us with the Transcendent, is an opening, not a close. The more we are realistic with ourselves, the more we are open to others.

It matters that we be open to others, that we see our neighbor.

# See Our Neighbor

I have spoken already of the reality of our personhood as including the actual and the potential. Let's start this section out by remembering once more that the person is both an individual and a corporate being. Our existence, our values, our work are good for all, else they finally are good for none.

There is truth in individualism. As already said, man is a self. He has a private life and an irreducible value. If an individual person is not worthful, it is difficult to see how a whole society of them could be. As having irreducible value, the individual is an end, at least in the one sense that no other individual or group has the right to treat him as a means. That one is "person" is the most important thing to be said about him. No modifying adjective — great, rich, smart, powerful — can ever be as important as the substantive itself: just "person." This is the meaning of a remark made here one time by Carlyle Marney: "One never weighs as much as when he's naked."

But each self finds his proper identity and range of being in a community of selves. Persons exist only in relation to other persons. Each self achieves his selfhood in a society of other selves. This is why Robinson Crusoe is possible and Tarzan is not. Robinson Crusoe carried a social inheritance onto that island that made possible an island technology and meaningful language communication with Friday. Had Tarzan from the beginning been raised by apes, he would have been much less a man and much more a hairless and speechless ape. Tarzan was an individual! People belong with people.

This is not as simple as it sounds, and utopian worlds are built less easily than some have thought. Societies emerge, held together by common traditions, languages, experiences, family ties. They give public form to these realities of their heritage, and also seek in the strength of unity and numbers to achieve security through mutual aid. People try in such societies to abolish the endless struggle of all against all. It just might work if, like the Three Musketeers, it were "all for one and one for all." But hearts are not always thus pure, nor does charity always reign over all. It is the absence of this purity and charity of heart that explains why, all around us, we know more strife than peace, more grabbing than giving. Is it not also why we see more politics than statesmanship? More learning than wisdom? And more religion than faith?

Societies, as such, do not seem to have the resources of their own perpetuity or deliverance. They rise, perhaps flourish, and fall. They are not worthy objects of faith.

What does this have to do with "things that matter"? It points up the truth, which all the great religions have stressed, and which is so distinctively a part of the teaching of Jesus. Put plainly it is this: Human societies in which people do not act humanly are self-destructive.

Any correspondence of our lives with God's, who loves and serves us all, requires sensitiveness and compassion from our side. For many of our brothers and sisters, at home and abroad, are disfranchised both of rights and opportunity. Some things must change. There are indications, increasingly difficult to ignore, that we must either reorder our priorities on this planet or number our days. These signs give warning from virtually every area of our nation's existence, both within and among the nation. Several of these may be mentioned before one is a bit more emphasized.

Presuppositions regarding limitless growth potential of the economy, long regarded as American gospel, are losing credibility. Basic economic justice, within the nation and among the nations, cannot be achieved by the mindless satisfaction of artificially created needs. In such an economy it is small comfort to an unemployed man, whose faucet has been disconnected, to be told to wait until something trickles down.

The winds of nuclear terrorism blow toward our future with increasing speed. This, along with what R. L. Heilbroner has called "wars of redistribution," is the unspeakable option, which waits like an expectant vulture around the corruption of our human indifference and moral derangement. For deterrence, we seem unable to think of anything better than improving our capacity to destroy each other. Unless it be world hunger, the nuclear arms race is the most compelling issue before us. Becoming a force in its own right, as George Kennan has observed, the nuclear race has become detached "from the political differences that inspired it, and is leading both parties inexorably to the war they no longer know how to avoid."

In our generation, for the first time, we have discovered that our very environment has boundaries — and that the environment is fragile as well as finite. As Dean Rusk put it in a speech at Furman a few years ago, "We have a foot or two of soil, a few miles of air, and two or three miles of ocean." The capacity of an industrialized society to inflict major damage on the biosphere is established fact. That such a process of damage is already traceable is ominous.

World hunger is, like death, too terrible for us to see. Our earth grows heavier each week by the weight of two million more new people. They will require food, in a world where thirty children die of starvation every sixty seconds. In the early twenty-first century there will be more living people than dead people on this planet; that is, more than half of all the people of all time who have ever lived upon this earth will still be living. This explosion of population is not always the result of ignorance or apathy. It is often related, as in Africa, to what in our setting would be called the integrity of the family and the social welfare of the aged. At stake in such exponential increase of population is not only a supply of food for hungry mouths and space in which to grow it. Also involved is the quality of life itself.

It is this latter fact that brings basic moral considerations to the fore. It is here also that the cry for a reordering of priorities on this planet is most urgent and piteous.

One morally loaded fact in earth's present demography is inescapable. It is a fact that vastly matters. As populations have exploded, the percentage of earth's produce used by the privileged nations has steadily risen. The cost of this in malnourished bodies and brains, in blighted hopes and spirits, is an intolerable affront to human life made in the image of God. We Americans, about six percent of the world's population, use thirty percent of the world's resources. This imbalance between such affluence and poverty can no longer be managed as a problem in economics or politics. It is a human, which is to say, a moral problem. It requires "repentance," both as remorse for our sin and as a change of course that will make possible a redemptive tackling of the problem.

It is in this sort of threatened world that we live. It is with this dispossessed of the earth that we will finally stand or fall. It is becoming clearer than ever before that the call to serious love-of-neighbor-for-the-sake-of-God is inseparable from our own call to self-denial, to radical philanthropy, and to the power of becoming morally superior to what we own.

Can any morally serious, spiritually sensitive person wish in such a time for a muted church? It is a time to speak. It is a time to repent. It is a time to act.

It matters everlastingly whether we see these poor neighbors who are our brothers and our sisters. The poor are just that — poor. Poor, with no clout at all, who have nothing going for them that we can turn to our own advantage. Such persons are hard to see, and sometimes a nuisance to serve. If, however, I understand correctly more than one of Jesus' parables, it is in this face of the poor that, in this world, we are to see the face of God.

You would be disappointed in your expectations of this occasion if I did not say, at last and briefly, that the seeing of God's face is the final thing that matters. For our ultimate environment is God.

## Our Ultimate Environment Is God

God is the spring of all being, in whom the private and corporate dimensions of each person are harmonized and made fruitful. God triune is the paradigm of the ideal society, in whom the diversities of the human family can be mutually enriching rather than dangerously divisive.

The Bible is essentially a book about God. The religious tradition enshrined in that Jewish and Christian Bible has put premium upon the "holiness" of God. This was originally, as Rudolf Otto stressed, not a moral but a purely religious or numinous term. It meant that the Deity was transcendent beyond us and other than us, not to be tampered with, worthy of awe for he might "break out against us" (Exodus 19:22).

This idea of holiness, in the hands of the great prophets of Israel, was moralized. God, who was indeed other and transcendent, was just and kind. A further step by the prophets embodies one of the most radical claims religion has made — that this "Holy One is in our midst." That is as great a paradox, I should say, as the Bible contains: He who is transcendent beyond us and other than us, is present for us and active on our behalf. This is the heart of the Old Testament gospel, which Christians confess as historical revelation and redemption in the Word of God made flesh.

We are taught in the Bible that God does not wait on our interest, faith, or merit before he loves us. But it does seem a sadness if, in this God-inhabited world, we miss the great Reality. He touches all that pertains to our existence and affairs.

We think of our human affairs as just that: human affairs. Sometimes, we may be convinced that we discern a divine side to these human affairs. It would be nearer the mark, I am convinced, if, with the late Abraham Joshua Heschel, we see all earthly affairs as the human side of divine affairs. The most real human fact — and factor — is God the holy who is in our midst. "Man's last end," as the Westminster Confession puts it in words less felicitous than they used to be, "Man's last end is to know God and enjoy him forever." A "last" end finally matters.

All this now must be put in ways that make it impossible to miss the meaning. I am thinking especially of student friends who do not, as I, speak in rolling periods or turgid sentences of Victorian English.

What I have said for theology is this. Our human kind is created in the image of God, and takes both its unity and its worth from that fact. Our destiny, because already it is our true being, is to be and become the family of God. The vision of God is to see that our source and our goal are one and the same, and to know that all power in heaven and on earth is on our side.

What I have said for ethics, which is the other side of the doctrinal coin, I want also to state especially for students.

First, you are not cheaters, cowards, or bums. You are not angels, saints, or gods. You are the image of God, made in the likeness of God for the glory of God. This is the truth about you. Our opportunity in this world is to make the happy discovery that when we live by this truth of God, we most fully find ourselves in that freedom and joy, which is our proper heritage.

Second, each of you is who you are, and no one of you is either only or all. There is no true ground for either isolation or pride. We are God's family, in which there is no lasting good for one who ignores or violates the good of all.

Third and last, God is our source and end. The end we both fear and long for is one and the same. A faith worth having is one of happy and patient courage in face of both the fear and longing. We are more than conquerors. "Mankind will prevail."

Our proper destiny, if we are not first decimated by "wars of redistribution" or obliterated by nuclear holocaust, is to realize for the whole race the dream of Teilhard de Chardin, "Someday, after we have mastered the winds, the waves, the tides and gravity, we shall harness for God the energies of love. Then for the second time in the history of the world, man will have discovered fire." It is better to kindle this fire in our world than to wait for the next.

## *Conclusion*

I have tried to speak truth with words. But often it takes a picture to disclose a sudden insight into a situation, an era, a lifestyle, or a known truth.

Huston Smith has written that "the Chinese word for landscape painting is composed of the radicals for mountain and water, one of which suggest vastness and solitude, the other pliability, endurance, and continuous movement. Man's part in that vastness is small, so we have to look closely for him in the paintings if we find him at all. Usually he is climbing with his bundle, or riding a buffalo, or poling a boat — man with his journey to make, his burden to carry, his hill to climb, his glimpse of beauty through the parting mist."

In such a mirror we must see ourselves: the climb, the load, the journey, enlivened and interpreted by the light from beyond.

It matters; it matters deeply; it matters everlastingly that our journey be made, how our burden is carried, and whether our hill be climbed. This can get monstrously wearisome unless we are also catching the meaning and mystery, always there, which from time to time break upon us through the parting mists. It is this meaning and this mystery, two faces of the one mirror of reality, that constitute — at once and together — the beauty of the world, the miracle of our human existence, and the glory of God.

**Editor's note:** Theron Price passed away on May 16, 1995.

# Charles A. "Tony" Arrington
## Chemistry
### *January 10, 1983*

"What really matters." I'm not sure how that phrase is to be punctuated. Does it end in a period or a question mark? What I want to do is first play a game (the question mark) and then tell you some stories (the period). You all know that I am a physical chemist, or at least you know that I am a chemist. Physical chemistry deals with the application of the methods of physics and mathematics to chemistry. One of the primary activities of physical chemistry is the development of mathematical expressions that represent physical reality. Let's play that game for a few minutes.

In the early sixties John Kenneth Galbraith, under the pseudonym Mark Epernay, published a delightful parody of politics and quantification trends in the social sciences, *The McLandress Dimension*. In this essay he describes the contribution of Dr. Hershel McLandress in the development of a significant measure of personality — the McLandress Coefficient or the McL-C for short. The McL-C is the average time between the use of any form of the first person singular pronoun in a person's conversation or public utterances. Thus, a short McL-C is characteristic of a person whose conversation and, presumably, whose thoughts are continually filled with references to himself, while a large McL-C is the trait of someone who is able to think of a great many other things for a considerable length of time before once again putting himself at the center of his thoughts. The McL-C is a value-free parameter. Would you like to know the McL-C of some important figures of the day? Here are some examples:

| | |
|---|---|
| Bob Hope | 18 minutes |
| Art Buchwald | 2 hours |
| Elizabeth Taylor | 3 minutes |
| Martin Luther King | 4 hours |
| Robert Oppenheimer | 3.5 hours |
| Billy Graham | middle range |
| Edward Teller | 3 minutes 10 seconds |
| Norman Vincent Peale | middle range |

| Nikita Kruschev | 3 minutes |
|---|---|
| John Kennedy | 29 minutes |
| Harold MacMillan | 12 minutes |
| Lyndon Johnson | low range |
| Richard Nixon | 3 seconds |
| Charles deGaulle | 7.5 hours (corrected to 1.5 minutes upon recognition that reference to "la France" was in his case a personal reference) |

With the ground having been broken by such an eminent sociometricist, I would like to apply my own professional talents to exploring the possibility of developing an even more complex measure, which I choose to call the "Mattering Parameter." If this effort is successful, what really matters can be readily determined by examination of the mattering parameter with the saving of a great deal of posturing, debating, equivocation, and wringing of hands. Ultimately, one would hope to be able to eliminate such archaic institutions as the Congress, state legislature, and local school board. We would likely then have no need of state Baptist conventions and might even be able to get by at Furman without a dean and could reduce faculty committees by half.

As I envision it, the mattering parameter, MP, is a complex function that maximizes the double integral over time and population in the "well-being" space. At this point I will have to use the blackboard to make everything clear. (A facsimile of the figure accompanying the talk is given in the attached figure and is deliberately obscure.)

$$\iint_{p \ t} [MP]\,dp\,dt$$

$$MP = \frac{\text{☺}}{\text{"smut"}} - \left[ \text{☻} + (-\text{"☻"}) \right]$$

$$+ \ \text{⚦} \ (1 - 10^{DUI})$$

$$+ \ \frac{\text{💡}(B, P, TV)}{\triangle} \ + \ \left\{ \begin{matrix} 10^{GPA} \\ 10 \times GPA \\ .1 \times GPA \end{matrix} \right\}$$

$$+ \ A_{ye} \times health \ - \ \frac{(\text{☢} + \text{🚜})}{D}$$

$$+ \ ? \ (\text{💲}, \heartsuit, \text{▥}, \text{Fu}\supset7 \ citadelo, \text{⋀⋀})$$

The integral is nothing more than a summation over all events of the contribution made to universal well-being by each event. Thus, any act or circumstance that contributes to the well-being of some set of individuals will make a positive contribution to the MP, while any factor that diminishes the collective well-being will have a negative contribution to the MP. In the process of integration, each event is automatically weighted by the number of individuals affected and the length of time over which the impact of the event is operative.

Now, what will we put into the MP that will result in the maximization of the universal well-being? How is well-being measured? What about an occurrence that produces smiles? That would make a positive contribution to the MP, while activities that produce frowns or tears should certainly appear with a negative sign since they adversely affect well-being. Any problems so far? Well, there is a problem with events producing tears of joy, which should be considered as positive terms. So we will have to distinguish two types of tearful events. Or what about the smile produced by a good dirty joke? Is the sense of well-being associated with a cold beer after a long, hot run or sparkling champagne on New Year's Eve legitimately included as a positive term in the MP? Certainly one should at least allow for the negative contribution of the misery and suffering arising from DUI events.

We must look beyond smile-inducing circumstances — or else my Chemistry 12 classes could hardly be considered to matter. I will definitely want to include a contribution *reflecting* knowledge, and at the same time put an indicator of ignorance in the denominator of the knowledge term in the MP. While we are talking about knowledge, where is the grade point average included in the MP? In this case I'm afraid we will find a difference of opinion — faculty might include the GPA with a small weighting coefficient in the numerator, and students would seem to have a significantly larger weighting factor, while parents and medical school admissions committees appear to want to include the GPA as an exponential term in the MP. Of course, we would have to develop a more complete knowledge factor that would include separately such items as books read, papers published, and programs watched on PBS.

The MP should, in addition, contain some contribution from such considerations as length of life and state of health. But does everything that contributes to a lengthening of life make a positive contribution to this function? How do we quantify the effect of billions of dollars spent for sophisticated health care in the developed countries that might relieve more suffering if they could somehow be directed effectively toward the needs of the unfortunate multitudes living in abject poverty and ignorance?

It would be easier to construct this MP if the integration were over a more limited population. Well-being cannot be measured solely in terms of length of life, but surely one must include as a negative contribution a war factor containing the life-threatening, misery-producing potential of conventional and nuclear armaments, bloated national pride, and macho genetic composition. To be fair, though, this factor should include a denominator representing the deterrence of aggressive, belligerent individuals and institutions who might, by their unchallenged force of will, bring about an overwhelming negative contribution to the MP.

How would we construct an MP to take into account those important factors associated with the economy, romance, crime and punishment, athletic success, wilderness preservation, and on and on? It is fun to play this game in an abstract, detached way, but we, of course, realize that it is not a game, but a part of the very fabric of life itself. Wouldn't it be convenient, though, if such a quantifiable, reliable function were accessible on the computer to make our individual and collective decisions for us?

I should note that as I considered the composition of this mattering parameter, I had a difficult time deciding just what to do with accumulated wealth — perhaps because I have had so little experience in dealing with such a concern — and I managed to stop before deciding where to include financial gain in the formula. Also, I have not been able to justify in any way the inclusion of an individual's denominational preference in the mattering parameter, although I can acknowledge that an individual's MP might well include a term for himself that reflects his choice of denomination, specific church, and even individual pew within that church building.

Although I enjoyed the challenge of constructing a mattering parameter to account for "what really matters," I know you realize, as I do, the irony and futility of such an exercise. The dilemma can be illustrated by a personal example — my own attitude concerning nuclear disarmament. Professor Price spoke directly concerning this issue in his lecture last fall, and his remarks reflected my own feelings as well as those of a growing number of people throughout the country.

This past December, 1982, George Kistiakowsky died in Cambridge, Massachusetts, at the age of 82. Kisty was my advisor and mentor while I was a graduate student at Harvard. The last fifteen or so years of his life were devoted with great energy and sincerity toward the goal of nuclear disarmament. He was an outspoken opponent of the attitude that seeks security behind the potential of total annihilation of one's enemies. And yet, in his earlier days, George Kistiakowsky made a major contribution to the development of the first atomic bomb and was one of two people to spend the night at the bomb test site before that first explosion, which so irrevocably pushed humanity into a new era, puzzled by the godlike power clutched hesitatingly in their hand. I never asked Kisty why he had taken part in that effort, but obviously for him at that time it really mattered that he undertake that work.

During my stay at the University of Utah I developed friendships with several people who have recently left everything — friends, relatives, possessions — to escape (their word) from the oppressive regimes they were living under in Eastern Europe. A month ago I sat at a group Christmas party there and saw the tears in the captivating blue eyes of a Czech mother who had only recently joined her husband here after a two-year separation. But next March she has to go back to join her children, who are not allowed to travel with her. Dusan and Jarka hope that some day they will be able to reunite their family in this country, but Dusan says that he will not go back. He personally destroyed two Soviet tanks with a pick-axe and flaming torch when the Russians rolled into Prague and interrupted his freshman year in college, an opportunity made possible only by the enlightenment of the Dubcek regime. For many such people it matters very much that the United States represents a military power sufficiently strong to counteract the threat of an expansion of the ideology that has so directly threatened their well-being. I can find no reliable formula that tells me how much weight to give to the legitimate claims of both sides in the issue of the laying down of arms.

I am then unable to quantify "what really matters" on an issue that really does matter. In some cases I find it difficult to discern what really matters by an objective analysis involving the intellect or to describe mattering to another person using the language of logic and reason.

It appears that I have given up hope of delineating for you a convincing analysis of what really matters. Instead, allow me to tell you a few stories — four to be exact. I could tell one or a hundred such stories, stories that will not be new to you and that many of you could tell better than I.

## Story 1: Francis of Assisi

As a young man, Francis had every reason to be content and satisfied with his lot in life. His father's prosperity as a cloth merchant provided enough money to support a lifestyle that included fine clothes, charming companions, and the arms needed for an aspiring knight and military leader to engage in an occasional battle with the neighboring Perugians. Then, Francis had a series of dreams. His mattering parameter inverted with serious consequences. Let me read to you from Johannes Jorgensen's biography.

One April day in the year 1207, Pietro di Bernardone stood behind the counter in his shop, when he heard a great noise in the street — the sound of many voices, shouting, screaming, and laughter. The noise approached nearer and nearer; now it seemed to be at the nearest corner. The old merchant signed to one of his clerks to run out and see what was going on.

"Un pazzo, Messer Pietro!" was the clerk's contemptuous report. "It is a crazy man, whom the boys are chasing!"

The clerk stood yet a moment and turned around white in the face. He had seen who the crazy man was....

And a moment after, Pietro di Bernardone stood in the doorway, and saw in the midst of the howling crowd who now were close to the house, his son, his Francis, his firstborn, for whom he had dreamt such great things, and for whom he had nourished such bright hopes.... There he came now home at last, in a disgraceful company, pale and emaciated to the eye, with disheveled hair and dark rings under his eyes, bleeding from the stones thrown at him, covered with the dirt of the street, which the boys had cast upon him.... This was his Francis, the pride of his eyes, the support of his age, the joy of his life and his comfort — it had come to this, to this had all these crazy, cursed ideas brought him.

Sorrow, shame, and anger almost overcame Pietro di Bernardone. Nearer and nearer came the shouting and howling throng — mercilessly grinning they called to him where he stood upon his steps: "See here, Pietro di Bernardone, we bring you your pretty son, your proud knight — now he is coming home from the war in Apulia, and has won the princess and half the kingdom!"

The old merchant could control himself no longer. He had to give way to rage to avoid weeping. Like a wild beast he ran down into the mob, striking and kicking to right and left, until the crowd, fairly frightened, opened and dispersed. Without a word, he seized his son and took him up into his arms. His rage gave the old man a giant's strength: raging and gritting his teeth he bore Francis through the house and finally threw him, almost exhausted and out of his senses, down upon the floor in a dark cellar, where he locked him in. With trembling hands he stuck the keys in his belt and returned to his work. Several days later Francis appeared before the Bishop in the courtroom. Francis stood up in silence with streaming eyes. "My Lord," said he, turning towards the Bishop, "I will not only give him the money cheerfully, but also the clothes I have received from him." And before anyone had time to think what he intended to do, he had disappeared into an adjoining room, back of the courtroom, a moment later to reappear, naked, except for a girdle of haircloth about his loins, and with his clothes on his arm. All involuntarily stood up — Pietro di Bernardone and his son Francis were face to face. And with a voice that trembled with emotion, the young man said, as he looked over the heads of the audience as if he saw someone or something in the distance:

"Listen, all of you, to what I have to say! Hitherto I have called Pietro di Bernardone father. Now I return to him his money and all the clothes I got from him, so that hereafter I shall not say: Father Pietro di Bernardone, but Our Father who art in heaven!"[1]

Francis shortly thereafter renounced his father and his wealth and acknowledged only his Father in heaven.

The story that follows is a familiar one even if the details are somewhat indistinct for us. Francis embraced a life of total poverty and total commitment to his understanding of the Christian gospel. His example drew to his side followers from both great and humble families — followers who shared with him the path of self-denial and service. The way he chose was not an easy one. He suffered from blindness, rejection, and disease, and had to deal with jealousy and dissension among his most devout followers. But who can doubt that Francis of Assisi knew what really mattered.

His love of nature is legendary. It is rare to see a statue or painting of Francis without the birds who were his brothers and to whom he preached with simple devotion.

He had compassion for the needs of his followers. Once, in the middle of the night, one of the brothers cried out, "I am dying. I am dying." Francis and the others got up, lit a candle, and asked who had cried out. The ailing brother identified himself, and Francis asked, "What ails thee, my brother, to make thee die?" The brother's reply — "I am dying of hunger!" So Francis got everybody up and made them all eat, recognizing that not everyone had the same capacity for self-denial and not wanting the hungry brother to feel that he was betraying his vows.

St. Francis was a poet, and I want to close this story with his "Canticle to Brother Sun," or "The Sun Song."

> Most High, omnipotent, good Lord,
> Thine are the praises, the glory, the honor, and all benedictions.
> To Thee alone, Most High, do they belong,
> And no man is worthy to mention Thee.
> Praised be Thou, my Lord, with all Thy creatures,
> Especially the honored Brother Sun,
> Who makes the day and illumines us through Thee.
> And he is beautiful and radiant with great splendor,
> Bears the signification of Thee, Most High One.
> Praised be Thou, my Lord, for Sister Moon and the stars;

---

[1]Johannes Jorgensen. *Saint Francis of Assisi, a Biography*. Trans. T. O'Conor Sloane (New York: Longmans, 1912) 43-44, 46.

Thou hast formed them in heaven clear and precious and beautiful.
Praised be Thou, my Lord, for Brother Wind,
And for the air and cloudy and clear and every weather,
By which Thou givest sustenance to Thy creatures.
Praised be Thou, my Lord, for Sister Water,
Which is very useful and humble and previous and chaste.
Praised be Thou, my Lord, for Brother Fire,
By whom Thou lightest the night,
And he is beautiful and jocund and robust and strong.
Praised be Thou, my Lord, for our sister Mother Earth,
Who sustains and governs us,
And produces various fruits with colored flowers and herbage.

Praise and bless my Lord and give Him thanks
And serve Him with great humility.[2]

Francis died lying naked on the dirt floor of a small hut in the woods of his Little Portion, longing for Sister Death to come to relieve his suffering, but singing quietly with his brothers. As his spirit left him, his brothers, the larks, sang their farewell.

For Francis, possessions did not matter, but poetry did.

## Story 2: Roger Williams

It may be difficult for you in an instant to transcend 400 years and shift your thoughts from sunny Italy to a New England January in 1636, caught in the frozen, gray, numbing grip of those Northeastern winters. Roger Williams, as he wrote years later, had "unkindly and unchristianly [been]...driven from my house and land and wife and children...in winter snow, which I feel yet." Banished from the colony of Massachusetts because of his challenge to the civil and religious authorities, he slowly made his difficult journey south into the country that was to become Rhode Island, and in this journey walked his way into a place in history where he is esteemed for his vigorous defense of the principle of religious liberty. The end of this winter's journey found him befriended by Narragansett Indians, who surely saved his life. For three months he lived with them in their "filthy smoke holes" and began an association that was to last the rest of his life. He was to publish the first book

---

[2]Quoted by Jorgensen, Ibid., 314-315.

on their language, and became one of the few English settlers who recognized and defended the Indians' rights to the land on which they lived.

But the story I want to tell of Roger Williams is not a story of adventure, peril, or deprivation, but a story of words. He was a deeply religious man, perhaps a fanatic, whose life was apparently directed by his strongly held convictions. He was contentious and seems to have been one of those people who attracted controversy and, without trying hard, generated arguments. He was admired by many, despised by many, but I suspect that he was loved by few. After his banishment he continued his fight in a number of convoluted, at times tedious writings with titles such as "The Bloody Tenant of Persecution for cause of Conscience" and "The Bloody Tenant yet More Bloody, by Mr. Cotton's effort to wash it white in the Blood of the Lamb." I think only the most dedicated scholar could read through these writings now to learn firsthand what Williams had to say. But you should hear some of what Williams did say.

In the epilogue of his book on Roger Williams, Perry Miller writes:

The American character has inevitably been molded by the fact that in the first years of colonization there arose this prophet of religious liberty. Later generations may not always have understood his thought; they may have imagined that his premises were something other than the actual ones, but they could not forget him or deny him. He exerted little or no direct influence on theorists of the Revolution and the Constitution, who drew on quite different intellectual sources, yet as a figure and a reputation he was always there to remind Americans that no other conclusion than absolute religious freedom was feasible in this society. The image of him in conflict with the righteous founders of New England could not be obliterated; all later righteous men would be tormented by it until they learned to accept his basic thesis, that virtue gives them no right to impose on others their own definitions.[3]

Wouldn't it be fun to have Roger Williams deliver the convention sermon at next year's South Carolina Baptist Convention? He was baptized by the Anabaptists, by the way, but soon became disillusioned and went his own way, maintaining his friendship with them, however.

---

[3]Perry Miller. *Roger Williams, His Contribution to the American Tradition* (New York: Bobbs-Merrill, 1953) 254.

# Story 3: Josiah Willard Gibbs

Josiah Willard Gibbs — the name sounds as if he must have been one of the staunch New England Puritans against whom Roger Williams struggled. New England at least is correct, but Gibbs lived 200 years later and was Professor of Mathematical Physics at Yale. There is no drama in the story of Gibbs. His life was so ordinary and uneventful that even now I hesitate to relate it to you. In spite of these misgivings I will tell you about J. Willard Gibbs because his contributions serve to illustrate in an effective way one more aspect of "mattering." The effectiveness of this story lies in part, I think, in the absence of drama — which in itself provides a dramatic impact in much the same way that a bare stage can convey more meaning than a lavish set.

How can anything that really matters come out of nineteenth-century New Haven? What can possibly be of significance that is not in the history books? If ninety-nine percent of the population, polled in a random sampling of educated Americans, never heard of Gibbs, surely he did nothing that really mattered. Against such questions I state that the ideas generated in the mind of this unspectacular scholar have had an impact on twentieth-century life perhaps as great as that of any other single individual. Gibbs was the father of chemical thermodynamics.

His own father was Professor of Sacred Literature at Yale — a sound scholar and good father. Gibbs' mother was a noteworthy woman of unusual intelligence and accomplishment who provided a rich and stimulating home life for her four children. Young Willard was educated at the Hopkins Grammar School and at Yale. One of his grammar school classmates wrote of him in an 1850 poem:

> Next to him Gibbs with visage grave
> Sits in the seat our Rector to him gave.
> A student he — and one who seldom looks
> With playful countenance from off his books.[4]

You see what I mean by lack of drama! In 1863 Gibbs received the Ph.D. degree from Yale — only the second Ph.D. degree to be given in science in the United States and the first in engineering. For three years he and his sisters traveled in Europe, where Gibbs studied with some of the world's most eminent physicists at Paris, Berlin, and Heidelberg. In 1869 he and his

---

[4]Lynde Phelps Wheeler. *Josiah Willard Gibbs, The History of a Great Mind* (New Haven: Yale UP, 1951) 20.

unmarried sister returned to New Haven and settled into the family house on High Street, where they lived together for the rest of their lives. Gibbs' chief pleasures were walking across the countryside and entertaining the neighborhood children on outings.

The minutes of the Yale Corporation of July 13, 1871, record that "Mr. Josiah Willard Gibbs, of New Haven, was appointed Professor of Mathematical Physics, without salary, in the Department of Philosophy and the Arts." He was to serve for ten years in this capacity, without salary, living on the small inheritance left by his father. But during this time he published three papers, which were to become the cornerstone of the application of thermodynamics to the problem of chemical equilibrium. When these papers were presented to the Connecticut Academy of Sciences, no one on the publication committee was able to understand the work, and it was necessary to take up a subscription among the Yale faculty and businessmen of New Haven to defray the costs of publication. One man was able to understand the importance of Gibbs' work — James Clerk Maxwell in England, and because he said it was good, everyone took note.

Gibbs had made it to the "big time." Honors and recognition came his way, and in 1880 Yale offered him a salary of $2,000 to counter the $3,000 offer of Johns Hopkins. Let me quote from Wheeler's biography.

> So great has been the influence of these results on our civilization that to many they would seem to comprehend the most important of Gibbs' achievements in thermodynamics. It is true that the developments outlined above are those which most affected our mode of living, and their monuments — our concrete highways, our purer and cheaper materials, and the lighter, stronger structures and tools which have resulted in so many of our "modern improvements" — are easily perceived by all. But in the final analysis the greater achievement was in the methods of thought applicable to all problems of equilibrium, which we owe to Gibbs. These are the heritage of greatest value to the race which Gibbs has left. And their results in the explanations they afford of the phenomena of phase equilibrium, of electrolytic processes, of surface tension and capillary, of solution, of catalytic action, of gaseous mixtures and diffusion as well as the insight they give into the problems of the molecular constitution of bodies, are monuments more enduring than concrete or alloy steels.[5]

Matters of the mind matter.

---

[5]Ibid., 80-81.

# Story 4: Charles Anthony Arrington

The last story I want to tell you is both easy and extremely difficult for me. It is a story that I know as well as my own and at the same time a story flawed by lack of objectivity. It is a story of my father, about whom no biography will ever be written, and yet it is a story that has in large part determined for me those things that really matter. Each of you could tell a similar story because what really matters is so often primarily determined by personal experiences.

At this point my purposes could better be accomplished if we had the opportunity to spend a long evening together in a small group, sharing our individual experiences, but unfortunately such an opportunity is not ours. So within the constraints imposed by this formal and somewhat impersonal setting, I will attempt to provide for you a portrait of a remarkable individual who pointed out for me the essence of those things that matter.

In the last weeks of his life my father recorded on cassette tape the highlights of his own history so that his children, most especially his grandchildren, and, who knows, perhaps even his great-grandchildren would come to know and understand part of their heritage. A sense of history and belonging was very important to him. It is clear from his account that a sense of place was also important to him. He devoted much of his account to his early years in Kirksey, the rural community between Greenwood and Edgefield where he was born and grew up. Throughout my childhood I heard wonderful stores of hunting, fishing, fighting, and burning down cotton gins in Kirksey. Life in that out-of-the-way place in the lost time between real history and now was rich and full of those experiences that make happy memories to be stored up for passing on to children so that they will know what really matters — memories that come flooding back as one faces the end of life and looks back to see that it was good.

There was never any question about where to go to college — he went to Clemson, lived in the barracks, ate in the mess hall, and majored in civil engineering. During the two years that he worked with the TVA he felt so strongly the call to the ministry that in the midst of the great depression he left his job and entered "the seminary." For him there was only one seminary — Louisville. During the next three years he struggled with Greek, Hebrew, hermeneutics, and loved every minute. He pastored small churches in Kentucky and courted — mainly by correspondence, but successfully — Ottie Ward, a beautiful and intelligent schoolteacher from his new hometown of Ninety-Six. They were married after he went to his first pastorate in Weeksville, North Carolina, and ten months later I was born. I felt a little guilty appearing on the scene so quickly, but I wanted to get on with living and they didn't seem to mind too much my complicating their lives — after all, there were eager grandparents waiting for someone they could spoil.

I will relate only one of the memorable events of those years among the cabbages, potatoes, and wide, ark rivers that they have told us about. Mr. Jamie was a tight-fisted, hard-hearted, covetous old sinner in the community, and Daddy thought he would benefit from hearing "A Christmas Carol." With much misgiving the young parson and his wife invited Mr. Jamie and Mrs. Molly to supper for waffles, planning afterwards to read to them Dickens' story. They realized full well that they might so offend Mr. Jamie that they would lose all hope of rehabilitating, but considered the risk worth taking in view of the gravity of his situation.

After dinner Mr. Jamie was given the best (the only) arm chair, and Mother began to read, afraid to look up from the pages of the book.

> Oh! But he was a tight-fisted hand at the grindstone. Scrooge! a squeezing, wrenching, grasping, scraping, clutching, covetous, old sinner! Hard and sharp as flint, from which no steel had ever struck out generous fire; secret. And self-contained, and solitary as an oyster! The cold within him froze his old features, nipped his pointed noise, shriveled his cheek, stiffened his gain; made his eyes red, his thin lips blue; and spoke out shrewdly in his grating voice. A frosty rime was on his head, and on his eyebrows, and his wiry chin. He carried his own low temperature always about with him, he iced his office in the dog days, and didn't thaw it one degree at Christmas.

From the corner of her eye Mother could see Mrs. Molly sitting on the edge of her seat, smiling and nodding in agreement with everything she read. In the midst of the dramatic appearance of Marley's ghost in Scrooge's darkened bedchamber, Mr. Jamie let out a loud and disruptive snore. He had not lasted beyond the first paragraph and had missed the whole story. The guests had a wonderful evening and thanked the young parson and his wife. As for Mother and Father, they learned something themselves that evening about being shepherds of a flock that contains all types of sheep.

The War ended the ministry among the farmers in Weeksville. On the day my brother was born Daddy received papers confirming his enlistment in the Army as a chaplain. Some of the first real memories I have of my father are the photoreduced, censored letters he sent home to us in Ninety-Six as we followed his progress across Normandy, France, Belgium, and Germany. He saw with his own eyes the emaciated bodies stacked like cordwood in the concentration camps and brought back pictures of these scenes, which are still in our family albums. He went illegally beyond the U. S. lines at the end of the war into Prague, where he made friends and felt their joy of freedom before the Soviet Army took control.

In later years he often spoke of the importance of the religious dimension of life for men who daily faced death in battle. He wrote many letters to folks back home telling them that a brave son or husband had been killed in battle and offering consolation for their loss. He rightly felt that the chaplaincy was one of his most important ministries. For this reason the family asked that at his funeral the casket be covered with the American flag. I think that both he and the flag were honored by this act.

Now I can speak directly from my own memory of the years we spent in Due West, where Daddy was pastor of the Baptist Church for eleven years. My own childhood in Due West was similar in many ways, I suppose, to Daddy's in Kirksey. They were certainly happy years filled with simple but significant pleasures, and my own children for some reason seem to like to hear stories about when I was a little boy and lived in Due West. There are not many towns in South Carolina where a Baptist could grow up with an inferiority complex as a member of a minority religious sect, but Due West was such a place. The ARPs and Erskine College were the dominant cultural, religious, intellectual, and social influences. This environment was one in which my father thrived and in which all four of us children grew up with an opportunity to learn what really matters. I know that such lessons are learned as well in a large city, but somehow my own prejudice lies in the direction of the small town as the best place for a child to grow up.

The people that Daddy ministered to were for the most part merchants, mill workers, schoolteachers and farmers — provincial, hard-working, usually honest. I don't recall that any of the college faculty were members of the Baptist Church, but there developed a warm, important relationship between my father and the personnel of the college. Felix Bauer, a Jewish artist and musician who had fled from Austria at the beginning of the War, was on the faculty and played the organ at our church after Daddy persuaded a few skeptics that God would still be present in the service even though non-Christian fingers produced the music.

Routine church work — organization, preaching, visiting, and living with the people — took up much of Daddy's time. He was not a great preacher, like Carlyle Marney or L. D. Johnson, but he was effective at leading his flock, and he was a good storyteller. Many of his most effective points were made during the message to the children, when he could catch the adults with their guards down. After a while it became fashionable for the Erskine students to attend the Sunday evening service in our church, and the sanctuary would be filled to capacity for that service. Daddy said it was because the Baptist Church was farther from the women's dorms and provided a chance for a longer walk home from church in the evening. But I think it was partly Daddy's sermons, the hearty singing, the cozy atmosphere of the small church, and the social hour held after church in our house next door. Sunday evening after the house was emptied by the students going back to the dorms, when I had to face my undone homework, was always a sad, empty time for me.

Of course, we always had prayer meeting on Wednesday night, and the midweek bath. The devotional thoughts at prayer meeting were simple, quiet, and direct. Daddy often worked through Paul's epistles, trying to interpret them to the faithful who came out to pray for rain or a sick relative or for the missionaries on the home and foreign fields. He introduced them to C. S. Lewis, Paul Tillich, and Reinhold Neibuhr, and they learned that God speaks in many ways and does not always use "Thee" and "Thou" and verb forms that end in "st." It mattered to him that the people become educated and that he himself continued being educated. He took courses at Erskine — I especially remember his enjoyment in the course of South Carolina history taught by Professor Lesesne, who later became President of Erskine and also became a special and longtime friend of our family.

Daddy's education continued in a year spent at Union Seminary in New York, where we lived in converted Army barracks on $90 per month provided by the GI bill. There, Daddy learned from Niebuhr, Tillich, Douglas, Steer, and others on the faculty, and broadened the cultural and intellectual horizons of his family and anyone else he could persuade to undertake the long and arduous drive from South Carolina to New York. For him, education was never confined to the library or the classroom.

Three special aspects of those years in Due West are worth mentioning — the *Due West Weekly*, the vacation trips, and the Latvian families. More than a few hours of my youth were spent turning the crank of an old mimeograph machine producing the *Due West Weekly*. Daddy felt the community needed some journalistic medium to bring the people together and help them learn about one another. The *Weekly*, delivered without charge to every resident in the town and supported by advertisements and slave labor, was for several years a vital part of the community. I wish there were time to read to you excerpts from the editorials, "Our Neighbors," the "Shirt Plant News," the school page, or Margaret Gilmore's column. A rich account of the life, loves, joys, and sorrows of a small town is stored in the bound copies of the *Due West Weekly* in the Erskine College Library. During the last Thanksgiving we spent with Daddy, my brother John went to Due West and was allowed to check out those bound copies. Reading through those old, amateurish newspapers, laughing and reminiscing, was one of the important, meaningful activities that helped us in those days.

Daddy was a nut for travel. We don't know when this compulsion developed, but I rather think it was genetic, though certainly not from his father. Many of the members of the church had never been beyond the upper state, and some had never left Abbeville County. To Daddy this was a situation worse than drinking, playing cards, or other forms of backsliding, and he took it upon himself to correct the error of their ways. The only time people could get off was during the Fourth of July vacation week when the mills closed and farming was sort of slack. He began with trips to Charleston — in those days a full day's drive away. At the end of a long day's drive in a crowded Chevrolet, Mr. Jim Fleming stood and looked at the ocean for the first time and said, "Well, it is big, but it ain't as big as I thought it was gonna be." His horizon had expanded and his life was enriched. More adventuresome were two trips to New York City. The stories that were brought back, telling of the close encounters of the third kind between three carloads of Abbeville County's staunchest and bravest citizens and the Big Apple, thrilled those of us who were left behind, left us in stitches, and provided more entertainment than a whole season of game shows and situation comedies. And for the people who went, the experience was worth more than six months of Training Union and three study courses put together, I'm sure.

Daddy was concerned about the plight of the displaced persons then living in refugee camps in Europe and decided to do something about it. He arranged for our church to sponsor a family and found a job for the husband in the Anderson hospital. First, the Freimanis family came, was greeted, showered, fussed over, and settled in. Then came a grandmother, a great-grandmother, and an aunt's family, the Puduls. I remember Juris Puduls in his short pants and knee socks marching onto the stage of the school auditorium during the shower that was given for the family, clicking his heels, bowing, and reciting, "Rain, rain go away. Come again another day. Little Johnny wants to play" — the only English words he knew when he came to his new home. They worked hard, learned our strange ways, and taught us much. One friendly neighbor took a mess of turnip greens to Mrs. Puduls, who thanked her profusely and said, "I am sorry, but we have not a cow." Eventually, they all decided to move to Canton, Ohio, where there was a community of Latvian people who could provide nurture and support for them, which all our best intentions and efforts failed to provide.

On Christmas Eve this year, a warm, sunny day in Washington, we went to the Vietnam Memorial on the Mall and found chiseled in black marble on panel 8-E the name Juris Puduls. Juris had left his pre-med studies at college after his sophomore year and volunteered to serve his adopted country as a medic. His parents told Mother and Father how proud they were of his decision, and his death was to them a devastating blow. Did it matter that he lived for a few years in freedom before dying?

The traveling urge hit Daddy again in 1953, and by 1954 he had arranged a pulpit exchange for a year with a Baptist minister in Weymouth, England. Once again, I could spend hours telling you of the experiences of that year — how my father rode the bicycle all over the town of 30,000, having tea with almost every family in the church, how he preached in a pulpit robe for the first time, but with an overcoat on underneath to ward off the cold of the English winter, how he preached a sermon broadcast by the BBC and had the entire church in a fever pitch of excitement for a month. He served and loved the people, and they came to love him so that when their own minister decided to stay in the states, they asked him to stay on with them — an offer he reluctantly declined.

When I finished high school and came to Furman, my father accepted a call to the Clemson Baptist Church. The family moved to Clemson, and Daddy served the church and people there for fifteen years in different ways from his service in Due West, but with equal effectiveness. I don't know as much about that ministry since I did not live there. I do know that Daddy loved the Tigers, and only when Clemson played Furman was his support less than anything expected of a loyal IPTAY member. He wanted Furman to play a good, close game with Clemson, just barely pulling out a victory at the end of the game. Going to Clemson for him was going home, and only his irrepressible love of adventure was able to get him to leave.

In 1971 he left the church in Clemson and began six years of service with the Foreign Mission Board as an associate missionary — serving Beirut, Athens, and Jedda, Saudi Arabia. He visited in PLO refugee camps, danced in the taverns of the Plaka, christened babies in Saudi Arabia, baptized people in the Mediterranean, and almost bargained his wife away for forty camels with a Bedouin in Yemen. The people he and Mother touched and the lives they enriched are indicated by the flood of Christmas cards that arrives from around the world every year. His ministry was his adventure, and blessing the lives of those around him was what really mattered.

I am not able to tell you the end of this story. More than one grown man wept freely by his bedside during the last weeks of his life. I cried like a child with heavy sobs when I embraced him as I was feeding him Jello one cold, lonely December evening. These were not tears of joy. Far from it — they were tears of overwhelming sorrow. And yet that moment mattered as few moments in my life ever have. I suspect you understand why it mattered although I could never describe in a rational way why an experience should matter.

The story I have told you is not unique. I said earlier that each of you could tell a similar story of someone who touched your life and made a difference. The point of all these stories is something I cannot quantify, analyze, or even describe rationally. But I hope you understand the point: Francis of Assisi mattered. Roger Williams mattered. Josiah Willard Gibbs mattered. Charles Arrington mattered. L. D. Johnson mattered. Marion Johnson matters. Ottie Arrington matters.

And, paradoxically, the most difficult and yet the easiest assertion…Tony Arrington matters.

I want to end this address by changing the title. I have talked about "who really matters" rather than "what really matters."

# James C. Edwards
## Philosophy
### January 16, 1984

The hope of any lecture is that it become an act of genuine thinking, an effort of mind that engages, in common attention to some reality, both the one who speaks and those who choose to listen. Since any such act of thinking is sheltered by texts and practices that reach far beyond that act's immediate circumstances, it is appropriate that we begin this lecture this evening by trying to acknowledge for ourselves this sheltering fabric of our thought, to acknowledge truly who and where we are, here and now, as we try to think together.[1] But that is already clear, isn't it? We are in Daniel Recital Hall on the campus of Furman University, in Greenville, South Carolina, USA; and, in one way or another, we here are all friends of this university and of its truest ambitions and ideals. These facts are so obvious that they are likely to seem silly to state. But, having now stated them anyway, don't we therefore know well enough who and where we are? In one sense, the answer is *yes*, of course. We do know our names, our Social Security numbers, our family histories, our geographical location on the planet, and so on; we even know, in some sense, what we are presently "doing" here at Furman: teaching, learning, getting a degree, doing a job. But philosophy consists in refusing consent to the obvious, at least initially. The philosopher *must return* home, if home he ever has, so let us tonight not simply take ourselves and our lives for granted. Let us push back, if we can, from our ordinary self-understandings and try to set aside that lazy self-satisfaction that tells us we are already perfectly clear about all that really matters. Let us ask what it *means* to be here, speaking and listening as we do. Do we *really* know what we are "doing" here at Furman? I am afraid that we mostly do *not* know, and that is the burden of my lecture tonight.

# I

Furman University is a liberal arts college established and supported by an evangelical Christian body, the South Carolina Baptist Convention; and that fact in itself makes Furman a queer place, full of ambivalence and divided loyalties. L. D. Johnson, the man whose life we commemorate tonight with this lecture, found in that queerness both a source of personal energy and an agenda for his own work of Christian reconciliation. Some of the rest of us, however, have found it less fruitful. If I may be permitted a personal reference here, one of the joys of my relationship with L. D. was our running argument — never settled to the satisfaction of either party, incidentally — about the possibility of a truly Christian liberal arts college.

At first glance, the very idea seems incoherent: "Christian" and "liberal arts" apparently mix no better than oil and water. How can a Christian church, an institution that by its very definition must assert that the decisive truth about reality is already known and expressed, support a place of genuinely liberal education, an education that takes nothing for granted except the mind's power to know, and takes even this for granted only in a provisional way? Doubt, the sort of doubt that refuses to assent to anything upon the mere assertion of an authority, is apparently both the enemy of revealed religion (since how can there be revelation without an unquestioned authority that reveals?) and the necessary engine of liberal education (since without doubt to clear a space, how could there ever be room for any genuine thought?). One of the defining activities of a liberal education is *inquiry*, the search for the truth for the truth's own sake, and it is always an aim of such education to develop in the student his or her *own* capacity of inquiry. Liberal education is never just *training*, not even of the most sophisticated sort. Built into the nature of such education is the recognition (or at least the deep suspicion) that the truth is not yet known, that it cannot merely be *transmitted*, but that it must, even now and ever again, be newly discovered and appropriated. From the point of view of revealed religion, however, genuine inquiry is both pointless and dangerous. Since the essential truth about reality is already assumed to be known, to continue to seek it is pointless; and to persist in such questioning is likely to injure the faithful by weakening the authority of the dogma in which the essential truth is (allegedly) revealed to men and women. But the very notion of *dogma*, a notion apparently fundamental to any developed (Western) religion, is a notion rightfully anathema to the liberally educated inquirer. For such a one, there *are* no dogmas, nor should there *ever* be; there are only beliefs provisionally accepted as true, further grist for the mills of intellect and practical reason.

# II

Thus, there seems to be a deep incoherence hidden in the notion of Christian liberal education, the sort of education we profess to offer here at Furman. Apparently we must at some point choose between Socrates and

Jesus for our paradigm; we cannot live both in Athens and in Jerusalem. Tonight, however, I do not wish to press this apparent incoherence, partly because its tensions are already so familiar to most of us, and partly because on this occasion it is more appropriate to focus upon community rather than division. While there may be profound, even irreconcilable differences between Athens and Jerusalem, between Socrates and Jesus, between liberal education and Christian evangelism, there are also, I believe, some very profound continuities; and it is the neglect of these continuities that is for me the most disturbing feature of our university today. It is our blindness to *the common* vision of Socrates and Jesus that leads me to believe that we here at Furman do not truly know anymore who and where we are. We do not know anymore what we are doing as students and teachers together.

What is the neglected common vision of Socrates and Jesus? It can be put very simply: Ordinary human life, as it is ordinarily lived, is not *worth* living. That, of course, is a very hard saying. To be told tonight that one's life is not worth living — for most of us here, myself included, certainly do live ordinary lives — is not a little unpleasant; and not a little puzzling, too, for what other sort of life is available to us? How could we *not* live ordinary lives, being the ordinary human beings that we are? And yet both Socrates and Jesus are one in calling men and women out of the world we usually know and serve. Let me remind you of their claims.

In one of his most famous remarks — you have heard it a hundred times, at least — Socrates flatly asserts that *the unexamined life is not worth living*, and the philosophical examination he requires for worthiness is very far from leaving us essentially unchanged, going on with our ordinary existence in the ordinary way. Quite the contrary: Socratic philosophy is a practice radically at odds with our life's usual structure of aim and achievement. It is not merely a sophisticated sort of mental hygiene performed to ensure that the mind's parts are working efficiently in service of our aims. Philosophy does not issue in a technique of clear thinking that allows us to fix our goals and provide solutions to the difficulties we encounter in their pursuit. Indeed, true philosophy *interferes with* such "clear thinking," as all of Socrates' interlocutors soon discover. It is the enemy of rational efficiency, discovering new mysteries rather than providing neat solutions to practical problems. Bluntly put, the wisdom of philosophy is not an aid to our ordinary life of actions and ideals; it undercuts the very *structure* of that life.

At *Phaedo* 64A Socrates says that to do philosophy is to prepare for death — or, to translate the phrase a bit differently, it is *to practice dying*. It is to practice dying to the world in which we ordinarily live, the world of aim and achievement, the world of getting and spending, the world of frantic rush after trivial satisfaction, the world of cheap sentiment and shallow sensibility. Here is Socrates on trial before his fellow citizens of Athens:

> For I spend my whole life in going about and persuading you all to give your first and greatest care to the improvement of your souls, and not till you have done that to think of your bodies or your wealth. And I tell you that wealth does not bring excellence, but that wealth, and every other good thing which men have, whether in public or in private, comes from excellence.[2]

The life here advocated, the life of excellence and the improvement of souls, was not the ordinary life of Socrates' Athens; nor, I am sorry to say, is it the ordinary life of our United States in 1984. And the Socratic criticism of that life goes deeper than mere moral distaste for the rabid consumer society. He is at odds with the very *form* of ordinary life, not just its particular moral content. Philosophy hopes for revolutionary reconstruction of our practice, not just new wine poured into the same old bottles.

Jesus, too, is a radical critic of the usual structures and ambitions of human existence; and, like Socrates, the form of life he advocates to replace them is a practice of dying to the world's ordinary standards. Here is a representative quotation from Mark's Gospel:

> And he called to him the multitude with his disciples, and said to them, "If any man would come after me, let him deny himself and take up his cross and follow me. For whoever would save his life will lose it; and whoever loses his life for my sake and the gospel's will save it. For what does it profit a man, to gain the whole world and forfeit his life? For what can a man give in return for his life? (Mark 8:34-37, Revised Standard Version)

The Sunday school familiarity of these words should not blind us to their revolutionary intention. To speak of the cross is to speak of death; it is to speak of an unwillingness to resist one's *own* death at the hands of a world committed to business as usual. To take up one's cross, as Jesus here demands, is to prepare to die; indeed, it is more than that: it is to *practice* dying, to *act out* here and now one's death to the world's usual life. The world as we know it asks us, in Jesus' idiom, to try to *save* our lives, It encourages us to try to protect ourselves, to secure ourselves against disappointment and injury, to gain control — even if only temporarily — over the vicissitudes that threaten to frustrate our defining ambitions. The world as here understood by Jesus is the realm of what Nietzsche later calls "the will to power." To live is always to will to *continue* to live; it is to will for oneself all those circumstances that promise to "save" one's life, that promise to increase one's own power and scope of action in service of one's ideal.

But Jesus insists that to "save" one's life in this way is precisely to lose it. The will to power, which defines our ordinary life in the world, is the *rejection* of the cross, not its willing acceptance. Denying oneself means much more than merely denying one's greed, or one's pettiness, or one's cowardice. Denial of self is not *just moral reform*; otherwise, the Christian would be indistinguishable from the ordinary decent person, and the cross would not be a scandal to the Jews and foolishness to the Greeks. No, to deny oneself, to take up the cross, means to die to *everything* one has heretofore been, even to die to that moral ideal which had motivated one on one's best days. It is to die to the Law: not only the psychological Law of envy and self-aggrandizement, or the social Law of status and wealth, but also the moral Law of justice and benevolence. No one who plays the world's games — even its *best* games, like moral or social reform — is denying himself as the Christian is supposed to do. No one who *resists* evil, whether or not that resistance is motivated egoistically or altruistically, has truly taken up the cross. The cross is not an event *within* life; with the cross the world does not alter, but comes to an end.[3]

So, for all their profound differences, Socrates and Jesus are one in calling us away from the ordinary life of the world, ordinarily lived. Socrates calls us to the life of virtue and improvement of soul, while Jesus calls us to the cross; and these are not the same, of course (though I suspect they are closer than either Plato or Paul, both so typically second-generation, can represent). Nevertheless, we here at Furman University, a liberal arts college where students and teachers work under a seal that proclaims *Christo et Doctrinae*, must try to exhibit a form of life that honors both philosophical wisdom and the cross.

# III

And do we? Remember, to ask this question is to ask "Do we here at this university consciously share and encourage a form of life that rejects the will to power in all its forms? Have we here found an alternative to the life of increased self-consciousness and agency, one that 'loses' such life rather than tries to 'save' it? Do we, students and teachers alike, practice dying to the world?" I am afraid that we do not. When I look at what we do here, most of the time, I see "education" in vigorous service to ordinary "life." I see an institution trying to serve its students and supporters by giving them what they want, not what — according to Socrates and Jesus — they need.

This university, like every other university I know of, seems to me a frontman of the culture for which it functions; our standards, the form of life we live here and the form of life we encourage in our students, seem largely indistinguishable from the (best parts of) the Enlightenment dream. We value knowledge, power, agency, and individual accomplishment; we do not value poverty (whether of spirit or of worldly goods), ignorance, humiliation, or uncalculating sacrifice. Here at Furman we are consciously and (so far as I can see) *happily* preparing people for a fruitful life in what we blithely call the "real world"; we are not trying to die to that world. Thus, our assumption seems to be that Socratic philosophical wisdom is a useful (or at least *classy*) adjunct to ordinary life as it is ordinarily lived, not a radical critique of the life that makes it abhorrent. Likewise, we seem to believe that the cross Jesus requires is a spiritual ornament attached to our ordinary pursuits, rather than the final death of those pursuits themselves.

Let me cite a few things about our university that convince me of what I have just claimed. Nothing I say here will be fully developed, of course, so I encourage you to follow out the arguments for yourselves. First of all, take an obvious point: our curriculum. If one sits down with the catalogue, one will find course after course the intention of which is to prepare the student for a particular niche within the society as presently constituted. And I do not refer here only to courses that seem to be patently "vocational," though they are certainly there to be found. Many courses, whose titles seem to have little to do with doing a job or earning a living, are yet basically designed to accommodate one to the life of this culture, rather than to challenge that culture at its fundamentals. Taken as a whole, our curriculum does not aim at a revolution in the student's sensibility. Rather, it aims to make of our students, in the words of our Statement of Purpose, "responsible citizens," that is, men and women equipped to become exemplars of the culture, not its radical alternative.

Intimately connected to our curricular pattern is our practice of grading. The criticism and evaluation of students' work by teachers is, of course, essential to education, but it is something of a mystery why we *grade* that work as well, since a grade as such is not an instrument of educational *evaluation* but rather an instrument of *ranking*.[4] I tell the student nothing of *educational* interest when I affix an "A" to her paper. I may, of course, *flatter* her thereby, or make her parents happy, but whatever educational benefit there is, is found in my comments on her work, in my detailed examination and critique of her facts and arguments. The grade adds nothing of educational value. So why then do we grade? I suspect the answer lies in what a student told me in my office just last week. He was complaining about the gap between the grade he had received in a particular course and the educational benefit to him of the course itself, and I was encouraging him therefore to ignore the grade. Since it doesn't represent anything important to him, pay no attention to it. He said to me, "Yeah, but the man from IBM *will* pay attention to it." And, of course, he's right. Do we grade our students for *their good as students of the truth*? Or do we grade them as a favor to the "real world," which requires them as fodder for its own continuance? I suspect the latter, and the ubiquitous and overwhelming presence of grades at our university seems to me an unmistakable indication of our bondage to the "real world," which both Socrates and Jesus despised.

To cite a final indication of that bondage, I would ask us to consider our current financial and public relations successes. We here at Furman tend to be very pleased when we raise lots of money from corporations and their puppet foundations. We tend to be very pleased when we are mentioned favorably in national magazines, right there between the advertisements for deadly cigarettes and $24,000 automobiles. We tend to think, "Hooray! We must be doing something right." Certainly that is *my* instinctive reaction, along with gratitude to those who work as hard in our behalf. But then I think, "By whose standards of 'right'? Do intelligent corporations and individuals give rewards to their radical critics? Does the 'real world' voluntarily support and honor those who are trying to die to it, and who encourage others to do the same? Did any foundations in Athens endow a professorial chair for Socrates? Did the religious establishment in Jerusalem open up its Cooperative Program to support Jesus' ministry?" In Matthew's Gospel Jesus says:

> Blessed are you when men revile you and persecute you and utter all kinds of evil against you falsely on my account. Rejoice and be glad, for your reward is great in heaven, for so men persecuted the prophets which were before you." (Matthew 5:11-12, Revised Standard Version)

If curses and persecutions by the "real world" are the usual and proper reward of the prophet, what should we say of our growing acceptance by that world? Has the preserving salt lost its savor? Has the philosophical gadfly lost its bite?

If so, and I myself cannot deny it, then we have sold our dual birthright for a mess of pottage. We are being true to neither the Socratic nor the Christian gospel, and liberal education has become nothing more (or *little* more) than the process by which the "real world" replicates itself in every new generation. Oh, to be sure, we may do a bit in a few courses here and there to challenge our ruling assumptions, but by and large it's business as usual here, with the "real world" of Enlightenment/American culture calling the shots.

# IV

Let me close this lecture by trying to forestall certain objections. First, and perhaps most obviously, one might object to what I have said tonight by defending the Enlightenment dream, and thus defending the intelligent and morally sensitive form of the will to power which it encourages. In such a spirit, one might ask, "What is wrong with a university that is a spokesman for high culture and practical reason? Why should we *not* try to increase our self-consciousness and our power of agency, and thereby try to increase the quotient of satisfaction available to each individual? What is so wrong with the ordinary life we lead — or try to lead — as thoughtful and productive citizens of this enlightened republic?" These are good questions, and since the criticisms of Socrates and Jesus go very deep, I cannot give full answers to them here. Indeed, I will not try to answer them at all, but will instead cite a *fact* for us to consider as the beginning of such an answer.

Right now, the United States of America and the Union of Soviet Socialist Republics have in their possession more than 60,000 nuclear warheads — I repeat, more than *60,000* of these weapons of horrible mass destruction, poised and ready to fire.[5] These weapons, along with their delivery systems and the contingency plans for their use hatched in Washington and in Moscow, place us right now, even as we calmly speak and listen, one step away from an abyss that will swallow up our lives and the lives of our children and friends. More, that abyss, as near to us as a tyrant's whisper or a computer's malfunction, threatens to swallow human civilization as a whole. It even threatens to swallow the planet itself, considered as a habitat for plant and animal life. I ask us tonight, especially those of us tempted to defend our latter-day Enlightenment culture against the animadversions of Socrates and Jesus, "Is our present peril just an *error* in the cunning of reason, an error reason itself will soon put right? Are those missiles so painstakingly buried in Kansas and in the Urals an *aberration* of our enlightened idealism? Have we not been 'enlightened' enough, not been 'rational' enough, not been 'good' enough? Will we find the grace to draw back from the abyss by application of even more of the same techniques that caused the abyss to open before us in the first place? Or, on the contrary, was it not *our very idealism itself*, our very pursuit of the good for ourselves and others, that put those missiles in the ground? Was it not the Enlightenment notions of rational self-interest and intelligent resistance to evil that led us so unerringly to our obscene strategy of Mutually Assured Destruction?"

I do not say that truthful answers to these questions are obvious. Perhaps those 60,000 warheads *are* a freak accident, a temporary deviation in the steady progress of reason toward Utopia; perhaps they *don't* tell us a profound but ugly truth about the consequences of our highest ideals. Or perhaps, on the other hand, they represent the end of the Enlightenment dream, the haunting Shadow of our defining will to power. But this much is clear: If one inclines toward the latter view (as I do), one will *not* be likely to want this university (or any other) to carry on educational "business as usual." One will *not* want it to prepare its students for the "real world" of ordinary life, ordinarily lived. On the contrary, one will want the university to explore the common ground of Athens and Jerusalem — ground that both promises and requires a radically different way of dwelling on the earth.

Finally, let me acknowledge two related *ad hominem* protests. I can easily imagine someone saying to me, "For all your rhetoric, you yourself are essentially no different from what you criticize. You are yourself, as we all are, a part of Enlightenment culture in its contemporary American expression; you are neither Socrates nor Jesus, neither philosophical martyr nor Christian saint, dying to the world." This is certainly true, and my lecture tonight is an attempt to remind you *and* myself of the inadequacy of where we all stand. If one waited until one was pure to begin to think or speak, one would never think or say anything at all. And how then, locked into the purity of our silence, could we ever learn anything of one another?

In the same vein, someone might object to me: "You are an ungrateful child, biting the hand that feeds you. How can you presume to question an institution that once educated you and now pays your bills for books and groceries? Common gratitude, if not institutional loyalty, should incline you to praise, not to criticism." But such an objection rests upon a misunderstanding. As a graduate of Furman University, and as a member of her faculty for thirteen years, I do have special reason for gratitude, a gratitude that indeed I feel. But not every act of homage must take the object of admiration on its own terms. All of us know, in fact, that it is one of the chief graces of love that it often refuses assent to the favorite self-image of the beloved.

# V

It will not have escaped you that this lecture has its fair share — perhaps more than its fair share — of confusion, anger, and despair. Let me conclude, then, on a different note. Here is Thoreau, writing in *Walden*, giving us a word for this winter's night, and for tomorrow morning: "Be it life or death, we crave only reality. If we are really dying, let us hear the rattle in our throats and feel cold in the extremities; if we are alive, let us go about our business."[6]

# Notes

[1] The L. D. Johnson Memorial Lecture, delivered at Furman University on 16 January 1984. I have made no effort to eliminate the lecture style. I would like to acknowledge my pleasure and gratitude at being asked to contribute to this series.

[2] I am indebted to R. F. Holland for suggesting this translation of the Socratic phrase. See his essay, "Suicide," in G. N. A. Vesey, ed., *Talk of God* (London: Macmillan, 1969) 74.

[3] This last sentence is a paraphrase of Ludwig Wittgenstein, *Tractatus Logico-Philosophicus* (London: Routledge and Kegan Paul, 1961), sec. 6.4311.

[4] I ignore here, for reasons of space, the role of grades as an aid to motivation.

[5] It is understandably difficult to get hard data about the size of our nuclear arsenal. The figure I use is due to Terry Eagleton; see his *Literary Theory: An Introduction* (Minneapolis: U Minn. P, 1983) 194. More circumstantial, and more horrifying, detail can be found in Jonathan Schell, *The Fate of the Earth* (New York: Knopf, 1982), *passim*.

[6] Henry D. Thoreau, *The Illustrated Walden* (Princeton: Princeton UP, 1973) 98.

# Duncan McArthur
## English
### January 28, 1985

One day, seven or eight or nine years ago, I was sitting at a table in the faculty dining room alone, minding my own business, when the chaplain of the university and the assistant chaplain of the university came into the room and, of all the empty seats available, took the ones opposite mine. And the assistant chaplain, one James Pitts, leaned across the table and said to me, "Do you know what the three greatest threats to the Christian faith are?" I did not know, but I had a feeling that Chaplain Pitts would tell me. He said that a learned Baptist divine, speaking somewhere in northern Greenville County, had identified the three greatest threats to the Christian faith as "the Pope, Rudolph Bultmann, and L. D. Johnson." I was impressed. I had always had a high opinion of L. D., but if he could generate that reaction from that quarter, I realized he must really be doing good work.

I am a Baptist. Does that surprise you? It surprises me! When I consider that people called Baptists have said some remarkably stupid and uncharitable things in the name of God, and when I consider that attacks on free inquiry, which is important to me, are not uncommon in Baptist history, and when I consider where the Southern Baptist Convention seems to be heading now, I'm surprised that I haven't gone to Nashville or Dallas or Greer and burned my card. That I haven't is partly because of laziness and inertia. It is also partly because of L. D. Johnson, whom we commemorate tonight, and some other Baptists I have met at Furman, who are indeed a "threat" to a narrow and uncharitable conception of the Christian faith.

But there's also a third reason why I remain a Baptist. I teach here at a college that particularly serves Southern Baptists, a group that, because of its size, wealth, power, and its tendency at times to be narrow and intolerant, deeply needs what liberal education offers. What is done here matters more than it would at church-related colleges whose denominations have stronger traditions of liberal education than the Southern Baptist denomination does. So I keep my card as a sign that I haven't yet despaired of our work.

In thinking about this talk during the last year, whenever an idea or an observation came into my head, I jotted it down on a scrap of paper and stuffed it into a paper sack that I kept in my briefcase. When I finally dumped them all out and sorted through them, I discovered a lot of peevish complaints and intemperate statements about what I thought did *not* matter, rather than wise sayings about what did. Maybe this is what happens to an English teacher who has been criticizing essays day and night for sixteen years. So, if you find my tone cranky and splenetic, not sufficiently optimistic at this beginning of a new year and a new quadrennium, I trust you'll forgive me and attribute it to a job-related disability.

I trust you will also believe me when I say that I do not mean to suggest that I believe I live up to the ideals I shall mention or imply tonight.

I have found something, though, that I think matters. It was in the sack all along, in fact, and was related to most of the other ideas. It is ambiguity. Ambiguity matters. Rather, what we do when we're faced with ambiguity matters.

Before going any further, I should tell you how I'll be using the term *ambiguity*. I'm taking it broadly to mean uncertainty, but that sort of uncertainty that exists not so much when we lack information as when we have information that can be interpreted in more than one way. It's not that we lack meaning. It's that we have more than we want. The meanings may clash or may peacefully coexist, but we are uncertain of which to choose.

There's one sort of ambiguity that is of particular interest to students of literature. In that sort, a word or statement will bear two or several meanings. The meanings will be different, and that difference is usually intentional. The author intends a combination or interplay of meanings. The meanings may be of equal importance, or one may dominate and the other be counterpoint to it. The result, though, is a richer meaning. This variety of ambiguity — not essentially defined as uncertainty — I shall return to near the end of my talk, but it is not the sort of ambiguity I am principally concerned with tonight.

I'm concerned with the ambiguity that causes uncertainty. A word or statement can be ambiguous in that sense, too. A statement can mean more than one thing, and one of those meanings will not fit the context. My composition students know all about this type of ambiguity. They know that if they write something that can be read in two ways, I will — out of perversity and mean-spiritedness — choose the wrong one and then write in the margin very irritating questions based on that unintended meaning. Ambiguity in an expository essay usually clouds the truth, and I enjoy pointing that out.

But sometimes it reveals the truth, unintentionally. Two weeks ago I received a fancy document from the U. S. Navy supposedly honoring me on my retirement from the Naval Reserve — my transfer from the Ready

Reserve to the Retired Reserve. It read: "This is to certify that CDR William D. McArthur, Jr., USNR, in recognition of honorable service and continued interest in the defense of our nation was transferred to the Retired Reserve." Now some of you, rather baldly, have told me that my being a bastion of defense did not make you feel especially secure. And I'll have to confess that despite the success of my efforts over the last fourteen years or so to keep the Russian Navy out of the Reedy River, probably my most effective contribution to the national defense during the last several years was to retire from it. And, of course, it is good, they say, to face the truth. But it is hard.

A statement, then, can be ambiguous.

An action or an event can also be ambiguous. It can have different meanings for different people. It can have different effects on different people — even different effects on the same people. Consider winning, for example. Consider the utterly human, all-American desire to win. It is supposed to bring out our best efforts, the expression of our God-given talents, and I believe it does. Nearly always, of course, winning requires that we make someone else lose. Usually it means exercising our power over someone else. Harmless enough in a game, vital in a war. But winning has its dark side for the loser and also, I think, for the winner. Events or actions, then, can be ambiguous.

A situation or state of being can also be ambiguous. Anyone who has held a position of authority or influence and thought about it knows it offers contradictory possibilities of good and ill, knows it puffs you up and makes you feel small, all on the same day and perhaps for the same reason. But you don't have to be boss to experience ambiguity. All you have to be is alive — and thinking. I don't know if other creatures perceive ambiguity, but to be a human being — a rational and imaginative being — is to be face to face with it. It is to be aware, at least from time to time, of our contradictory natures, generous and greedy, foolish and wise. It is to wonder what it means to be halfway up the great chain of being and halfway down. It is to wonder about the meaning of life. It is to wonder whether there is a God, and if so, what kind. It is to wonder what we should do. It is to wonder what really matters. It is to be uneasy. It is a mixed blessing.

Several years ago, when I was asked to give a talk at one of the values dinners at the student center, I spent some time trying to figure out what seemed to matter to me, and one of the things that clearly did was order. Now, I didn't then and don't now think that order is an ultimate value. It just mattered to me. A lot. Probably too much. I like poetry to rhyme. But I believe it is a fairly general inclination in human beings to try to find order in — or to impose order on — what doesn't seem to make sense. It gives us security and perhaps a sense of power or pleasure. It's natural. The first thing

Adam did was to name the animals, and we've been putting our labels and interpretations on other people's work and the world around us ever since.

Of course, a taste for order is at odds with the way things are, with the ambiguities I've been talking about. But here we are, with a taste for order, yet faced with ambiguities and full of ambiguities. How we respond to this tension matters, makes a difference, and not merely to ourselves.

How do we respond? It seems to me that we — the American people of the 1980s — respond to ambiguity in essentially four different ways. The first way is to avoid it. After recognizing the ambiguity and being unsettled by it, we find a way to ignore it or forget it or repress it. For example, faced with the ambiguous issue of a need for national defense and the fact that it may destroy us, some of us are so unsettled that we will not think about it. We get ourselves sufficiently busy with our jobs or a hobby or some other very worthwhile cause so that we don't have time to think about it. We crowd it out of our minds or into a dark corner.

A second response to a profoundly unsettling ambiguity is to acknowledge that we're not going to be able to figure it out, but still to evaluate it — with increasing pessimism and perhaps with narrowing focus — according to what may be inadequate criteria and, as we find no clear answer, to reject the possibility of meaning and to give up hope and effort. This is, of course, the path to cynicism or to despair, and it tempts us all at times.

The third response to ambiguity is the one that, in my opinion, is ascendant at this time in America. It is to respond to ambiguity with certainty. It is to meet ambiguity with an answer, with *the* answer.

Over 100 years ago, at a time just as ambiguous as ours, Matthew Arnold wrote his poem "Dover Beach." It was, as you know, a time when the Industrial and Agricultural Revolutions were replacing the hereditary bond of lord and tenant with the purely economic relationship of employer and employee. Political revolutions were driving out kings and, with them, the security of a predictable succession and of God-given ruling powers. Scientific discoveries were raising questions about the creation, man's special place in it, and the Bible. From these changes and questions, modern man emerged with more freedom but with less certainty and, in some cases, with a shaken religious faith. Arnold expressed the anguish of a human being at his loss of a comfortable order, a familiar meaning, and an easy faith. You are, I expect, familiar with Arnold's lines, which still address us:

The Sea of Faith
Was once, too, at the full, and round earth's shore
Lay like the folds of a bright girdle furled.
But now I only hear

Its melancholy, long, withdrawing roar,
Retreating, to the breath
Of the night wind, down the vast edges drear
And naked shingles of the world.

Ah, love, let us be true
To one another! for the world, which seems
To lie before us like a land of dreams,
So various, so beautiful, so new,
Hath really neither joy, nor love, nor light,
Nor certitude, nor peace, nor help for pain;
And we are here as on a darkling plain
Swept with confused alarms of struggle and flight,
Where ignorant armies clash by night.[1]

The terrifying image of the conclusion of "Dover Beach" seems all the more immediate today. But while Arnold's speaker offers faithful human love as the solace of people whose vision of the world and whose religious faith have been shaken, the voices one most often hears today, the loudest voices, offer instead — no, insist on — a return to certainty. I'm referring to the representatives of a newly militant and aggressive fundamentalism. The certainty they offer, I would argue, requires ignoring an awful lot. This should not in itself bother us, but inasmuch as it is having political and social effects, perhaps it should.

I have no statistics on the recent growth of fundamentalism, but newspapers and television offer strong evidence that it must appeal to many. As ignorant and prejudiced as some of the preachers are about the churches, theologians, and beliefs that they attack, believers support them well. The preachers ask, and the people pay. I have already alluded to the Southern Baptist Convention's having been virtually taken over recently by people who not only read the Bible literally, but would (to begin with) insist that all seminary professors do so, too.

Being associated with a Baptist college, I am naturally concerned about absolutism in religious belief. But I'm also struck by what appears to me a parallel desire for simple answers and certainty in dealing with political and social problems. Of these problems facing us in the 1980s, the gravest is surely the possibility of nuclear war. It is a complex problem, related as it is to our ambiguously protective and threatening national defense. As I mentioned earlier, this is an issue so unsettling to some of us that we won't think about it. Others do, though, and there is a growing belief worldwide that we need to do something significant, creative, and soon. Despite this, our

President seems serenely confident that the real key to peace is simply in building a bigger weapon over the next decade or so. Such a reading of — or ignoring of — Soviet concerns and reactions strikes me as wishful thinking, a form of escapism. It avoids the fact that the old way won't work anymore, that that form of certainty, if it ever existed, has not been possible for the last twenty-five years.

I believe that the second most serious problem facing us in the 1980s is poverty and its corollary, hunger. It is made all the more difficult a problem because one theorist's solution is to another theorist part of the problem. Any action becomes ambiguous. One of the chief difficulties in dealing with poverty will again be our desire for simple certainty.

Last November the bishops of the Roman Catholic Church in America issued a draft of a *Pastoral Letter on Catholic Social Teaching and the U.S. Economy*. Even before the letter was published, economists, politicians, and ideologues were attacking it, as it turned out, for some things it did not say. Since its publication, the attacks have continued, the letter being characterized as naive, dishonest, and irrelevant or immoral.[2] The intensity of such attacks suggests the disquiet and vulnerability that we wealthy people, proud of our accomplishments and our country, feel, and ought to feel, when we look around us and see such poverty and hunger — and begin to think.

But what did the bishops really say? I'd like to repeat a few details from the letter:

- The dignity of work is available to a smaller percentage of the American population than it used to be. Levels of unemployment in good economic times have been rising during the last three decades, and during the last few years of this period a higher level of unemployment has been deemed "acceptable" than was before.

- Poverty, which had been declining between 1966 and 1979, climbed from 11.7 percent of the population to 15.2 percent between 1979 and the end of 1983.

- The richest twenty percent of Americans received in 1982 nearly as much income as the other eighty percent combined, and the disparity in incomes has been increasing.

- The wealthiest five percent of American families own nearly forty-three percent of the net wealth in this country, while the bottom fifty percent of American families own only four percent.

• Americans stigmatize as lazy the poor who receive welfare benefits, and they exaggerate the amount of those benefits while the middle classes actually get more from the government than do the poor.

• The growing gap between rich and poor in this nation is paralleled by a widening gap between rich and poor nations. The poverty in some other nations is abject.[3]

The bishops do not argue that inequalities in wealth and income are wrong, or even undesirable, but they argue that "gross inequalities are morally unjustifiable, particularly when millions lack even the basic necessities of life." They argue that such inequalities, violating a "minimum standard of distributive justice," exist in the United States today. They say we should do something about them and that decisions, policies, and institutions should be evaluated "primarily in light of their impact on the poor." They remind us that "the justice of a community is measured by its treatment of the powerless in society, most often described as the widow, the orphan, the poor and the stranger...in the land."[4]

The letter is a radical statement, but apparently not radical in the way people expected it to be. It doesn't insist on particular methods. It doesn't advocate socialism over capitalism; it's not so easy to dismiss. Rather, it advocates Christian action; but that, we perhaps need to be reminded, is radical.

How will we respond in the 1980s to the problem described in the letter? Probably in many ways, some of which will be constructive, but I am afraid that the most popular response now will be a rejection of this call to action since it is not simple, does not promise unambiguous results, and seems to question what we have thought was the answer for so long. Strict disciples of Adam Smith point out that determining all the effects of economic decisions is impossible and argue that, therefore, self-interest remains the best guide and the freest possible market the best vehicle. They point out that a decision based on the most moral intentions can ultimately undermine its goal or have other bad effects. Clearly, many of our institutional and governmental efforts to relieve poverty have not worked well or have had bad effects. Even more clearly, though, countless people for generations have gone hungry waiting for "the invisible hand" to bring them something to eat. I like paradoxes; I'm comfortable with them. But I'm suspicious of the one that tells us that the best way to feed and help the poor is to have another helping ourselves.

But enough of poverty. What about ourselves? In three words: We're just fine. Last year we took our national temperature and discovered it to be 98.6. We feel good. We went to the spa. Our tummies are flat. We won the

Olympics: we got 999 medals, and the Russians didn't get any. We invited the world to our party in Hollywood, and we sang patriotic American songs so that everybody would feel at home. We carried the flag. Having conquered the dickens out of Grenada, we sent the Cubans back where they belong; we went to Nicaragua. We declared ourselves off-limits to the World Court; we put Iran behind us. By a terrific landslide, we elected a man president who — better than any other world leader of the twentieth century — can sleep. We completed the Vietnam War Memorial in Washington; we added a statue to that black gash in the ground, having already added a flag. We began to redefine that ambiguous war. We shall put it behind us.

We shall put other things behind us, too. We have heard that values have changed since the Vietnam years, that then college students included among their chief goals "developing a meaningful philosophy of life," that now they would rather be "very well off financially."[5] We've realized that as demanding and relentless as numbers can be, there's a certain comfort in knowing that when you have the right answer, that's it. We've realized it is simpler if values are figures on price tags rather than moral choices. We've realized it's easier if the "bottom line" really is in dollars and cents.

We thought we had lost our innocence forever in Vietnam, but it seems we're getting it back. People were afraid something Orwellian might happen in 1984 — and I think it did: We found "the memory hole." It's natural to prefer things to be simple and certain and clear and as they were in our childhood, when we were not yet responsible. It's natural to yearn for our innocence. But there's something unnatural — and grotesque — about returning to it at our age.

I said earlier that there were four main responses to ambiguity. I've been talking most of this time about what I believe is the most popular and the most dangerous response. But let me turn now to the fourth, which is not often easier than the others, but offers worthier results.

The fourth response to ambiguity is toleration of it, a willingness to entertain it, to live with it, to get to know it, to try to understand it, and, yes, to seek to resolve it, but with no false hopes that that task will be quick or easy or final. During the effort one may find unexpected benefits, even delights, in ambiguity.

We may be perfectly comfortable living with ignorance. As important as an issue may be, if we don't know anything about it, we may not be impelled to find out. An issue, however, that has forced its way into our awareness with not one but two or three competing meanings creates a tension that is hard to ignore. We are impelled either to hide from it, to surrender to it, to deny it, or to think about it. If we choose the positive course, we may think through to a resolution of the ambiguity that will settle the matter for a time, or for good. We may come to believe that there is no resolution of it but, in doing so, develop a deeper understanding of why there is none and thereby be better composed to carry on. We may discover some things we weren't even looking for.

For example, faith remains difficult; the degree of evil and suffering in the world leads most of us to some hard thinking at one time or another. Some people may find an explanation for innocent suffering that they can reconcile with their conception of God. Some cannot. But searching for a satisfying answer and testing the solutions of others — Milton, the Pope, the author of Job, the people around us — is a humanizing experience. It may lead to patience and sympathy.

Poverty has been around all along, but this year the starvation in Ethiopia has made it harder than usual for us to ignore other people's need in the face of our wealth. We wonder what we, in the land of plenty, should do about poverty and hunger, and we hear conflicting answers based on Adam Smith and Keynes and the Supply-Siders. There is no denying, however, that the most cost-effective way to deal with a surplus of starving children is to eat them — and to do that is kinder than to do nothing at all. The horror of Jonathan Swift's observations should not hide the fact that it is correct.[6] If we read Swift or Amos or the Gospels or other humane writings as we ponder our response to this great contemporary problem, it is less likely that we will be paralyzed by indecision or will take refuge behind any theory that absolves us of a personal responsibility to act.

Many people today believe America has an historical, even a divine mission; some would say Americans are the new "chosen people." One could easily infer that belief from the actions and attitude of America in 1984. Certainly we have had blessings. We should realize, though, that the title *The Chosen People* remains no less ambiguous for us than it was for the Hebrews. If we as a nation and we as individuals truly are to fulfill the role and be a blessing to the world, we would do well to reflect on the various meanings of the title. We would do well to consider the interpretation of Second Isaiah, that to be the chosen people is to be the suffering servant.

Each of us approaches issues with his own resources. Mine is literature, so you are not surprised to hear me suggesting literature as an aid to living with ambiguity. It is, of course, just one of many aids. Each of us has his own. Some are common to us all. I shall mention this one and two more that are common to us all, but there are others.

I think it is the case that literary figures, particularly poets, explore ambiguity, also paradox and mystery, more fruitfully than most other thinkers. Just as the tension of a string permits the violinist to make music, so the tension of meanings seems to serve a poet. When reason tells us the situation is intractable or absurd, imagination (the writer's and ours) can take us to where we see the essential elements more clearly or to where things make a different kind of sense, a place where two meanings can become more than their sum, a place where we can, perhaps, glimpse something beautiful and true. The poet Yeats, for one, offers us such experiences.

Another help in dealing with ambiguity is one's sense of humor, the ability to laugh. What makes us laugh when we do is incongruity; incongruity is the stuff of all comedy. And incongruity is usually present in ambiguity. At the beginning of my talk I told you how I ungraciously mistreat my students for writing ambiguous sentences, which then give me delight as I read them perversely. It is recognizing the incongruity between what my students mean to mean and what their sentences can mean that strikes me as funny and keeps me going. Recognizing an incongruity of meanings is also what makes us laugh at a pun, at a *double entendre* — or at ourselves.

Many of us would be embarrassed to admit how many of our favorite jokes are based on sex or on human plumbing. But it may not be quite as bad a sign as we fear. Such jokes confront us with our physicality and irrationality. They remind us of our dual nature, our ambiguity; and they counteract our prideful tendency to consider ourselves more reasonable, more spiritual, and more dignified than we are. So, in a sense, your dirty jokes have socially and spiritually redeeming value. On the other hand, maybe they're just funny.

One of my heroes is the eighteenth-century novelist Laurence Sterne. Although Sterne was in debt, was incompatible with his wife, was for long periods separated from his beloved daughter, and was dying of tuberculosis, he wrote during his last years two of the funniest novels in English. They depend mainly on ambiguity. *The Life and Opinions of Tristram Shandy* is actually about Tristram's Uncle Toby, who, unluckily, at the Battle of Namur — "in the attack of the counterscarp before the gate of *St. Nicolas*...in one of the traverses, about thirty toises from the returning angle of the trench, opposite to the salient angle of the demi-bastion of *St. Roch*" — received a wound upon his groin. O unhappy wound! Now, Uncle Toby, a bachelor — and a man of propriety and virtue — was the subject of some interest to his neighbor, the Widow Wadman. The widow was extremely concerned about Uncle Toby's wound, out of Christian charity. After years of genteel and roundabout and dissatisfying inquiries, the widow is finally direct: "And whereabouts, dear Sir, quoth Mrs. *Wadman*, a little categorically, did you receive this sad blow?" "You shall see the very place, Madam; said my uncle *Toby*.... You shall lay your finger upon the place" — whereupon Uncle Toby drew forth and displayed, for Mrs. Wadman's particular inspection, his map of the battlefield.[7]

Sterne was not only a novelist. He was a priest. He had the honor of preaching his sermons at York Minster, but then published them under this title: *The Sermons of Mr. Yorick.* What did a priest mean by assuming the name of a fool? In *A Sentimental Journey*, Sterne's final novel, Yorick appears again as a character whose actions and words can almost always be interpreted in two ways. Moreover, the novel ends, stops, in the middle of a sentence, one that allows the reader to supply any number of ludicrous conclusions.

In the chaos of Sterne's novels there is order, not the sort that I could diagram and not the sort that would comfort a tidy mind. In the ambiguity and interplay of meanings, we find that sort of complex literary ambiguity I mentioned at the beginning of my talk. Two meanings of a word or statement or action set the reader to thinking along two different lines, each of which makes sense and each of which has its own suggestions and overtones. From the combination and interplay of the two lines of meaning comes a third, the most important.

But Sterne goes beyond even this. He mingles with his characters and hauls us into his novels, too. Sterne can be seen in not one, but two or three of the figures in *Tristram Shandy*. His narrator addresses us directly and chides us for our inclination to bawdy misreadings. The hero of *A Sentimental Journey*, the second novel, is a character from the first; he is also, we are to believe, the author of Sterne's own sermons. In this crazy interplay of identities and meanings, the author's intention is achieved. He creates laughter and, by so doing, drives out the bad humor of depression and irritability that can get in the way of affection for others or pleasure in life. His is a wise foolishness. Tristram called his method Shandeism. "*True Shandeism*," he says, "think what you will against it, opens the heart and lungs, and like all those affections which partake of its nature…makes the wheel of life run long and cheerfully round."[8]

Ambiguity exists. When we genuinely collide with that fact, we can react in different ways: We can escape; we can despair; we can become certain; or we can live with it. Escape is not a worthy response. Despair, though it may come, is to be resisted. Certainty has a strong appeal; there's no denying it is more comfortable than the uncertainty and doubt of living with ambiguity. But is it truly better?

Doubt is the civilizing worm.[9] It inclines us toward humility, tolerance, and sympathy. Certainty is absolutist, abstract; it tends toward pride, complacency, and isolation. It seems to me that faith and hope lose something of their meaning in certainty and that the qualities associated with certainty are antagonistic to love. In "Dover Beach" Matthew Arnold saw love as his best refuge in an uncertain world, and I think he was right. That irrational, inexplicable feeling that exists in friendships, in families, and in the best part of religion somehow makes sense when nothing else can.

Yes, I think ambiguity matters. I think the way we respond to it really matters.

## Notes

[1]Matthew Arnold, "Dover Beach," *The Norton Anthology of English Literature*, ed. M. H. Abrams et al., 4th ed., 2 vols. (New York: Norton, 1979) 2:1378-79.

[2]See, for example, Robert J. Samuelson, "The Bishops and Adam Smith," *Newsweek* 3 (Dec 1984): 75.

[3]*U.S. Bishops' Pastoral Letter on Catholic Social Teaching and the U. S. Economy*, First Draft, 11 Nov 1984, *Catholic Herald* (22 Nov 1984). The six points are from, respectively, pages 17A, 20A, 21A, 21A, 23A, 26A-30A.

[4]*Letter* 21A, 12A, 8A.

[5]Alexander W. Astin, address, College Students in the 1990s: Duke Endowment Sixtieth Anniversary Colloquium, Furman University, Greenville, SC, 4 May 1984.

[6]In *A Modest Proposal.*

[7]Laurence Sterne, *The Life and Opinions of Tristram Shandy, Gentleman*, ed. James Aiken Work (Indianapolis: Odyssey, 1940) 82-84, 638, 623-24.

[8]Sterne 337-38.

[9]Adapted from a line in Trevor Griffiths' play *The Party* (London: Faber, 1974) 60.

# Thomas Cloer, Jr.
## Education
*October 14, 1985*

## *Introduction*

So, what really matters? As I sit in my office with enough Apple software to manage the NASA space program, and as I talk with our students and faculty colleagues of the eighties, it becomes increasingly apparent to me that success in the United States is associated with material wealth. Regardless of the camouflage we wear, the bottom line in this decade has involved electric gates, circular driveways, and Gucci accessories. I tell my friends that expensive athletic spas and fancy gyms are fine for sweaty socializing, but it's so much cheaper to run in the fields and lift heavy furniture. They seem totally unimpressed. Have you noticed these days that one must never casually mention an interest in buying a home to a friend who works in real estate? Nor can one sit down in a car dealership to drink a Coke on Saturday mornings and look at the pamphlets unless one has decided to buy.

The focus on materialism is incredible. It has infected all of us to some degree. As I sat in my office, I tried to think of what one would say if one actually believed that material wealth was that which really mattered, or more to the point, what I would say if I believed such. Knowing that some in attendance probably feel the tug of materialism and would appreciate any insights I might have gained about material well-being, I thought I might share the only important things I have learned. Politically, I would like to try to please everyone with this lecture. You must remember, however, that these tips come from one who has always looked up to see the bottom rung of the socioeconomic ladder, but should prove helpful regardless of your value system and socioeconomic status. So, if I were giving a speech that was based on the assumption that materialism really matters, I would give the sum total of my experiences in eight succinct points. I learned these from my readings in *Modern Maturity*.

1. Find a friend who is a plumber. Ingratiate yourself.

2. Anything-of-the-month club is the mail-order version of chronic lower back pain.

3. Never shop for groceries on an empty stomach. That has taken more of my Furman paycheck than anything I can remember.

4. In the South, car payments are the financial equivalent of the boll weevil. They will literally eat away your profit.

5. No one ever sells a used car because it runs too well. After ten used cars, I have stumbled upon that insight.

6. The chief beneficiary of life insurance policies for young, single, and newly married people is the life insurance agent.

7. The only thing worse than asking people how much money they make is telling how much you make.

8. It is no disgrace to use coupons in public. (Smith, 1985, p. 35)

Good students and colleagues, one of the real problems with our focus on material wealth as a measure of success is that the majority of us will never be successful if that's the standard. We will never succeed in that which really matters if material wealth is the criterion. Ricardo Montalban and Tatoo will never greet us to complete our fantasy. I like Waitley's (1983) definition of total success. I think L. D. would have liked it as well. "Total success is the continuing involvement in the pursuit of a worthy ideal, which is being realized for the benefit of others — rather than at their expense" (p. 26). I concur with Purkey and Novak's (1984) view of what our worthy ideal as educators should be. Purkey and Novak suggest that our ideal is to help others: to join in the real progress of civilization, to realize their human potential, and to join in the celebration of their existence. If we accept these views as being at least related to something that really matters, then we might look more closely at the implications for a place such as Furman University.

# Self-concept and Success

Being a product of Stinking Creek, Tennessee, and having received my undergraduate degree from a school where ninety-five percent of the students received financial aid are factors responsible for my early interest in the relationship between self-concept and school achievement, between self-esteem and accomplishments. If we at Furman University are to help students realize their human potential, to join in the genuine progress of civilization, and to join in the celebration of their existence, we might consider what Combs et al. (1978) said about human behavior.

> Human behavior is always a product of how people see themselves and [how they see] the situations in which they are involved. Although this fact seems obvious, the failure of people everywhere to comprehend it is responsible for much of human misunderstanding, maladjustment, conflict and loneliness. Our perceptions of ourselves and the world are so real to us that we seldom pause to doubt them. (Combs, Avila, and Purkey, 1978, p. 15)

One thing that really matters to me, Furman family, is that Furman's educational activities be affected somewhat by an understanding of and respect for students' perceptual worlds. These perceptual worlds provide the basis for their behavior. These perceptions change through numerous encounters with professors and peers. It is through these fundamental perceptions serving as organizing filters that people try to make sense of their world. Of all the perceptions learned, none seems to affect identity and our search for personal significance more than our self-perception (Purkey and Novak, 1984). Alice in Wonderland said,

> Dear, dear! How queer everything is today. And yesterday things went on just as usual. I wonder if I've been changed in the night? Let me think: Was I the same when I got up this morning? I almost think I can remember feeling a little different. But if I'm not the same, the next question is "Who in the World am I?" Ah, that's the puzzle. (Carroll, 1971, pp. 15-16)

Alexandre Dumas in *The Three Musketeers* (1962) said it so well. He said that a person who doubts himself is like a man who would enlist in the ranks of his enemies and bear arms against himself. He makes his failure certain by himself being the first person to be convinced of it.

If what really matters is helping generations of students to fully join in the progress of civilization and to realize their total academic, social, and spiritual potential, then we might look more closely at how important self-esteem is and how we promote and nurture positive self-image in an academic institution.

There was hardly a moment in my childhood when several coon hounds were not leashed to saplings next to our mountain home. I remember one such hound much more clearly than the rest. His name was Ready, a rather discreet testimony of his eagerness to reproduce. My dad gave me Ready when he was just a pup because he was the tiny runt of the litter and needed much pampering to survive. Ready grew very little, except his ears, and was never able to stay even close to the other hunting dogs when a coon race occurred. As the months passed, his ears grew disproportionately large in relation to his small body. He was so full of energy and spirit, however, that he couldn't keep his nose out of anything. He would investigate the bank of the creek, inevitably fall in, and come to the porch to furiously shake dry and roll in my mom's washbasket of dried clothes. When mom would take a switch to him, he would bark and snap at the stick, thinking it was all a game.

Ready would always greet my friends and me when we arrived from school. I would turn the curve that brought our little mountain home into view, and call, "Where's my hunting dog?" Ready, usually lying on the porch and facing toward the curve, would whine and bark as he came frantically down the steps, and would anxiously make his way to my pants leg. I often told my friends that Ready could run incredibly fast; he just ran too long in the same place. When the little hound reached us, he would bark and charge valiantly at my pant leg, growling and tugging to show how furious and full of spirit he really was. I would usually walk the last stretch stiff-legged with Ready hanging on tenaciously to his quarry.

One Autumn afternoon, I was sitting on the porch with Ready when I discovered something quite fascinating. Because Ready's ears were so huge, I could tie them into different bow knots without apparently causing him any pain. I had just tied them up in a manner that resembled an old lady with a head rag when two of my buddies came by to go squirrel hunting. When they saw Ready, they cracked up, laughed raucously, and made fun of him. They said that he looked like a "granny woman". They touched his ears and continued to laugh at him. This treatment was not what Ready had expected, and he reacted by running and hiding under the porch.

The next day when I came home from school, I called, "Where's that coon dog?" Ready quickly cowered out of sight, ears still tied. When he had to eat, he would slip out and do it furtively, after I was gone. He mostly hid under the porch, and would even growl when anyone came near. When we finally got a chance to pet him, the entire family had to love him, hold him, and convince him that he was fully acceptable.

I tell this story, good Furman family, because it taught me one of the most important lessons of my life. How important this lesson is if we are going to help people realize their academic and spiritual potential! When Ready heard the derisive laughter and felt the degrading touches, he felt he didn't belong. He felt afraid, alone, and rejected. His self-esteem plummeted. I suggest to you that his reaction is not significantly different from the reaction of thousands of people hiding under the porch because of rejection. Ready's reaction reminds me of the inner voice that hides in each of us, whispering about our vulnerability, a voice that Elkins relates in the book *Glad to Be Me* (1976).

> Don't be fooled by me. Don't be fooled by the face I wear. I wear a mask. I wear a thousand masks — masks that I am afraid to take off; and none of them are me.
>
> Pretending is an art that is second nature to me, but don't be fooled. For my sake, don't be fooled. I give the impression that I am secure, that all is sunny and unruffled within me as well as without; that confidence is my name and coolness my game, that the water is calm, and I am in command; and that I need no one. But don't believe me, please, My surface may be smooth, but my surface is my mask, my ever varying and ever concealing mask.
>
> Beneath lies no smugness, no complacence. Beneath dwells the real me in confusion, in fear, in aloneness. But I hide that, I don't want anybody to know it. I panic at the thought of my weakness, and fear being exposed. That's why I frantically create a mask to hide behind — a nonchalant, sophisticated facade — to help me pretend, to shield me from the glance that knows. But such a glance is precisely my salvation, my only salvation, and I know it. That is if [the glance that knows is] followed by acceptance; if it's followed by love.
>
> It's the only thing that can liberate me from myself, from my own self-built prison wall, from the barriers I so painstakingly erect. It's the only thing that will assure me of what I can't assure myself — that I am really something. (Elkins, D. P., 1976, pp. 22-29)

If our ideal is to invite others to fully realize their potential, then we must understand more about the nature of invitations.

## Invitational Education

An invitation is nothing more than a formal or informal, verbal or nonverbal way of saying to other people that they are valuable, capable, and responsible. Purkey and Novak (1984) use the term "disinvite" in referring to formal, informal, verbal, or nonverbal ways of saying to others that they are not very valuable, capable, or responsible. Students at Furman are asking daily that ancient biblical question: "Who do you say that I am?" Our answers to those questions have powerful implications in relation to our ideals. People need invitations as badly as the Furman flowers need the fresh sunshine.

There are two paradigms of education that have emerged in the past two decades and purportedly guide us in helping people realize their human potential (Purkey and Novak, 1984). One model is the factory model. Words such as accountability, behavioral objectives, and exit skills are associated with this model. We are feeling the pinch of this model in our self-study at Furman. Everybody has to demonstrate exit skills. Soon, exit skills will be required on wedding nights. Minimum competency is sought after with a mechanistic frenzy. People "being developed" according to this model have little control of their work-a-day world. This model requires obedience, conformity, and most of all, bustle. There must be agitated, excited movement; people must remain busy. There is immediate identification, labeling, and rerouting of deviants into modified programs.

The other model is the family model. This is the model of education I personally endorse. Lots of invitations are offered in this model. People are told in numerous ways that they are valuable, capable, and responsible. Uniqueness is valued rather than scorned. Allowances are made as in the family when someone blows it, or as my two teenagers say, when someone becomes a "spaz." And there is a prevailing attitude that anything worth doing is worth doing poorly when we can't do any better. If art, music, physical activity, philosophy, or any other human activity is really worth doing, then it's worth doing poorly when we can't do any better. For years my mother drove thirty miles (one way) on a narrow, winding, dangerous mountain road to a music lesson because of her unyielding belief in this principle. Today, I can't play a recognizable tune on any musical instrument, but I love music. I'll do my own singing. Don't let the Osmond Family do your singing for your. Don't let the dance companies do all your dancing. Do your own dancing. Come to Pickens and we'll dance, because anything worth doing is worth doing poorly when we can't do any better.

One aspect of my work at Furman that I enjoy the most is working with small children. I'm constantly amazed at how uninhibited, natural, creative, and honest these little ones are in relation to adults. I often ask them, "How many can sing? How many of you can dance?" Arms will wave high in the air in expectation of an opportunity to do just that. "How many of you can do art? How many can read Latin?" Arms will invariably wave high in the air with fingers quivering. Vice-president Crabtree was visiting and talking with the children in one of my classes this summer when a first-grader just catching the magic of reading asked if he could sing a song for the Dean that he had just composed — and sing he did. Well, where have all the waving arms gone among the rest of us? How many of you do your own dancing? Our society has a way of saying to people that unless they are scientifically rare specimens, they should not desire to participate. I'll do my own art, thank you. I'll bike race with any of you even though my old bike is taped together with only one gear left, and I know that I am slow as a sick snail.

As I analyze myself in an attempt to determine how I was educated, or more importantly how I was validated, confirmed, and began the celebration of my existence, I think of certain people. I would wager that you do the same. I always remember and always revere Ms. McGhee, not so much for what she taught, but for the kind of person she was. I'm going back by Strinking Creek next week to an alumni awards dinner. I am going to find Ms. McGhee and tell her how much I appreciate her. She was a huge lady with very short hair and hands like Hulk Hogan. Ms. McGhee was a bundle of invitations. She had a penetrating smile followed by a muscular hand shake; she was always shaking hands. She would return my paper on Robert Frost, give me that penetrating smile, and crunch bones with her handshake. "May I sharpen the pencil, Ms. McGhee?" I would work my hand nervously after the handshake in order to rotate the pencil sharpener.

Ms. McGhee would be walking around the room and whisper, "Happy birthday, Tom Cloer." Or she would sometimes say to me in the hall while standing as huge as the Jefferson Memorial in Washington, "You're such a capable boy. I value your presence in the class." I would think, "This woman has me confused with another set of Cloers." Ms. McGhee was the first teacher that I can remember to miss me when I was absent and tell me so when I returned. Have you ever been absent from school for a week with the flu, and upon returning discover that the teacher hadn't missed you? What a disinvitation that is! Ms. McGhee knew the secret of teaching, of validation, and confirmation. She knew what really mattered.

## Education That Disinvites

I would warn each of you that as you attempt to realize your human potential, there will be those that disinvite. Pay no attention to people who tell you lies about yourself. It's part of the demolition derby that we call education. I remember so many lies that were told to me in my own life. I remember being on the missile range. Purkey's (1969) characters in "Miracle at Herbert Hoover High" reminded me of the power of disinvitations.

I remember Principal Snappington who was so unaccustomed to humor. He was the Edsel of American education. When Mr. Snappington laughed, little dust puffs came out of his mouth. He didn't understand the need for validation and confirmation. He was too busy counting milk money, working on the assembly bells, and completing state department forms. He had no ideas about that which really mattered.

There was also Mrs. Sullenby, queen of the teacher's lounge mafia. Mrs. Sullenby had a perpetual sour look on her face, as if she had been weaned on one of Granny Cloer's Appalachian dill pickles. No one took coffee in the lounge before Mrs. Sullenby was served. Mrs. Sullenby found it very difficult to tolerate a mountain boy's lack of understanding.

Mrs. Puresen was so easily horrified, especially at common humanity. She spent her life dressing for the coroner. "You never know when you might get run over." Mrs. Puresen was so proper that when she burped, all one heard were chimes, like those from Furman's bell tower. When her husband got up during the night, Mrs. Puresen made the bed. She was not the kind of person to make allowances.

I think I remember Mr. Conceitman the most vividly. Oh how he loved teaching! It was ignorant Appalachian students that he couldn't stand. His philosophy held that if these hillbillies needed a friend, let them get a good coon dog. He was being paid by the school district to teach history.

Our guidance counselor, Ms. Sternwell, was the only one in the state of Tennessee to hold a first-degree black belt (Shodan) in counseling. Her husband got in trouble with the Internal Revenue Service by writing off her trips to the beauty parlor as a total loss. Ms. Sternwell enjoyed more than anything in life the time of year when SAT scores returned. She would close her door, take out a Las Vegas visor and little bands to hold up her shirt sleeves, and play with those cards like a Mississippi riverboat gambler. Her favorite game was "Just as I Thought!"

I could wager that all of you have encountered either these types or other genres of disinviting circumstances. I agree with what Maslow (1970) says in his book *Motivation and Personality*.

> Let people realize clearly that every time they threaten someone or humiliate or hurt unnecessarily or dominate or reject another human being, they become forces for the creation of psychopathology, even if these be small forces. Let them recognize that every person who is kind, helpful, decent, psychologically democratic, affectionate, and warm, is a psychotherapeutic force even though a small one. (p. 254)

# Examples of Invitations

Purkey and Novak (1984) provide an array of examples of classic invitations. Over two decades ago, I sat in a small playhouse in the mountains of Kentucky watching a rough, but for me, mesmerizing rendition of George Bernard Shaw's classic, *Pygmalion*. I think Eliza Doolittle's words to Colonel Pickering are incredibly important to those of us who attempt to invite others.

> You see, really and truly, apart from the things anyone can pick up (the dressing and the proper way of speaking, and so on), the difference between a lady and a flower girl is not how she behaves, but how she's treated. I shall always be a flower girl to Professor Higgins, because he treats me as a flower girl, and always will; but I know I can be a lady to you, because you always treat me as a lady, and always will. (Shaw, 1940, p. 80)

People need invitations, as Furman's rose garden needs the soft spring rains. Life need not be a demolition derby. Education need not be a missile range.

R. V. McMurphy, in Ken Kesey's novel *One Flew Over the Cuckoo's Nest* (1962), knew something about inviting. His antagonist, Nurse Ratched, is a good example of a disinviting personality. She would tell the inmates that they were in an institution for the criminally insane and it was important for them to adjust to their conditions. But old R. V. McMurphy, while not the epitome of moral strength, knew how to invite. He would say, "You're not a bunch of crazies. You're not a bunch of rabbits. You're men! Now act like men. Let's go! Let's hit it! Let's watch the world series. Then we'll go fishing!" If McMurphy could have survived the turpitude clause of a teacher's contract, he could have been shaped into a fine educator.

Purkey and Novak (1984) point to *The Wizard of Oz* as one of the most profound works dealing with human behavior. In that classic, there were four important characters: a scarecrow who thought he had no brain, a tin woodsman who thought he had no heart, a lion who believed he lacked courage, and Dorothy, who thought she lacked the power to make changes in her life. They were all under the grand delusion that if they could meet the great and terrible Wizard of Oz, he would grant them all the things that they lacked. Little did they realize that they already possessed the very things that they sought. The Wizard sent them invitations to see things in themselves that they had overlooked. He invited them to use what they already possessed. The people to whom one can look for help are those people who see positive things that others overlook. Ms. McGhee saw things in people that others had overlooked. She believed that IQ was not as important as "I can," and that "I can" was not as important as "I will." People need invitations the way Furman lawns apparently need tons (and tons) of fertilizer.

I think most of us realize that what really matters is not material wealth. I think most of us as faculty also realize that teaching knowledge to others isn't enough. I had a speech instructor that believed knowledge was enough, and he focused on technique. For years after his class I'd tremble while leading silent prayer. If knowledge were enough, medical doctors would be the healthiest people in our society. Psychiatrists would be the best-adjusted people in our land, and Mr. Conceitman would have had a more positive impact on my life.

In summary, I believe that what really matters is that something matters. That something can be the pursuit of a worthy ideal that is being realized for the benefit of others — rather than at their expense. Our worthy ideal as an educational institution should be affected by an awareness of the importance of the spirit of people; I think the answers to life's greatest problems lie not in a silicon chip, or will never be found on more complicated software. The answers lie in the spirit of the people. What really matters to me as an educator on the back side of forty is that I help those I encounter to realize their human potential, to join in the progress of civilization, and to join in the celebration of life. I think L. D. Johnson's life was totally invitational and that he was perpetually celebrating.

In keeping with his tradition, I ask each of you now to validate yourself. When we validate ourselves, we begin to take risks. As we risk, we succeed, and as we succeed, we become. As the Wizard of Stinking Creek, I now validate you one and all and invite you to join in the celebration of your existence. I leave you with a quote of Waitley (1983).

> People who live with fear grow up standing at the end of every line. People who live with praise learn to stand alone and lead their parade, even if it's raining. People who are spoiled with indulgence and permissiveness grow up full of compromise and greed. People who are given challenges and responsibilities grow up with values and goals. People who live with depression will need a drink, a puff, a pill to get them high. People who live with optimism will grow up thinking they were born to fly.
>
> People who live with hate grow up blind to beauty and love. People who live with love live to give their love away and are blind to hate. If our people are reminded of all the bad we see in them, they'll become exactly what we hope they'd never be! But if we tell our people, "We're so glad you're in the game," they'll be glad to be alive, right now, and glad they wear their names. (pp. 41-42)

To me, L. D. Johnson, you blessed old rascal, this really matters.

# References

Carroll, L. (1971). *Alice in Wonderland.* New York: W. W. Norton.

Combs, A. W., Avila, D., & Purkey, W. W. (1978). *Helping Relationships: Basic Concepts for the Helping Professions* (2nd ed.). Boston: Allyn & Bacon.

Dumas, A. (1962). *The Three Musketeers.* New York: Macmillan. (Originally published 1844.)

Elkins, D. P. (1976). *Glad to Be Me.* New York: Prentice-Hall.

Kesey, K. (1962). *One Flew Over the Cuckoo's Nest.* New York: Viking Press.

Maslow, A. H. (1970). *Motivation and Personality* (2nd ed.). New York: Harper & Row.

Purkey, W. W. & Novak, J. (1984). *Inviting School Success* (2nd ed.). Belmont: Wadsworth.

Purkey, W. W. (1969). *Miracle at Herbert Hoover High.* Paper presented at the Clemson Reading Conference, Clemson, SC.

Shaw, G. B. (1940). *Pygmalion.* New York: Dodd, Mead.

Smith, W. (1985, June-July). Welcome to the Real World. *Modern Maturity,* pp. 34-36.

Waitley, Denis (1983). *The Winner's Edge: The Critical Attitude of Success.* New York: Times Books.

# Bingham Vick, Jr.
## Music
*January 27, 1986*

Good evening! As a conductor, I am accustomed to being in front of an audience, yet not looking at the audience while I "perform." Tonight will be somewhat of a new experience for me in this regard, and you will get to see, for better or worse, a different side of me. I thank Betty Alverson and her staff for inviting me to speak, and for encouraging you to be here. I thank each of you for your interest in what I have to say.

The story is told that the great British conductor Sir Thomas Beecham once said this to his orchestra:

> There are only two things to remember — you begin together — and you end together. What you do in between doesn't matter. The audience won't know, anyway. That is the Golden Rule. If you are satisfied that what you are doing at the moment is right — even if it is wrong — that is all that matters. Whether you are singing or conducting or misconducting — do it with conviction. And remember the English may not like the music — but they absolutely love the noise it makes.[1]

Tonight, I hope you like both the "noise" and the "music."

I am honored to be asked to be a part of this lecture series honoring L. D. Johnson. My seven predecessors have plowed deeply and thoroughly into the field of what really matters. For the opportunity to share my thoughts with you I am grateful. Even more so, I am grateful for the necessity of life I have faced over the past year to think about and develop concrete words to express what really matters to me. I was privileged to know and work with L. D. from 1970, when Judy and I arrived at Furman as new kids on the block, until his death in December, 1981. Judy and I enjoyed the hospitality of the Johnsons' home; we shared an enthusiasm for gardening with L. D.; we worshiped and prayed with him at Thanksgiving and Christmas services at Furman; and, not least important, he and I shared the same name — his first initial and my second initial representing the same "Lafayette." (We both preferred the initial!) His influence continues to be felt and experienced. He was a great man! Thanks to those who make this lecture possible, he will be remembered for a long time.

This is an awesome podium from which to speak. I am wondering what you are expecting to hear. In this series, you have already heard from one of the religious giants of our day, Theron Price; from the faculty president and leader of the local chemists, Tony Arrington, from business-economist, Charles Alford; from a Furman-bred philosopher, Jim Edwards; from an historian and sports analyst, John Block; from an English professor and proud Baptist, Duncan McArthur; and from Furman's resident "Mark Twain" and beekeeper, "the Wizard of Stinking Creek," Tom Cloer. And now, a representative of the music world steps forward.

Borrowing a preparation technique from Duncan McArthur, I have kept a file over the past year of thoughts, musings, insightful quotes, and other bits of information that I thought would be helpful in preparing my lecture for tonight. I have found myself looking actively for inspiring "words of wisdom" to add credence to my talk. On the back of the door to my studio, there is a sign for my students to read as they leave. It says, "All things cometh to him who waiteth, if he worketh like hell while he waiteth." I assure you, I have been both waiting and working for tonight to come.

So, what is expected of me tonight? I understand that this lectureship is planned to gradually move through the various departments of Furman University. That being the case, and since I am somewhat representing the Music Department, I guess I should talk about what really matters to a musician: intonation, tone quality, rhythm, being on time for rehearsals, dressing appropriately for concerts, understanding the composers and what they mean when they try to express their musical desires through a system of notation that can never really put on paper what they wish, or a thousand other details of successful musical performance.

I could use musical analogies: What matters to life and to music is form, or the use of correct materials in building a composition or building a life; or playing the right notes with the right rhythms — saying and doing the right things in life. Or perhaps there is a great composer whose life and contributions could be a model for us all, or a great conductor who has done and said exemplary things.

What really matters to a musician? Do those things really matter to non-musicians? There are a lot of pithy sayings about music and life: "Music is love in search of a word" (Sidney Lanier). "Music expresses that which cannot be said and on which it is impossible to be silent" (Victor Hugo). Martin Luther said, "Next to theology, I give to music the highest place and honor.... It is one of the most magnificent and delightful presents God has given us,..." [and] "I am strongly persuaded that after theology there is no art that can be placed on a level with music, for besides theology, music is the only art capable of affording Peace and Joy to the heart." Certainly, music matters to us all in one way or another. However, music is not *all* that matters.

If I don't speak about music, then just what approach shall I take? Who am I tonight and what can I say that is worthy of this lectureship? I am my parents' son — that causes me to think of those good things that have been important to me because of my parents and family. I am Judy's husband — certainly what matters to me is related to Judy and our wonderful life together. I teach at Furman — part of what matters includes salary, benefits, health coverage, and periodic memos to let me know when Christmas and Easter will be observed. I conduct the Furman Singers — I must have inherited from DuPre Rhame a tenacity and dedication to that very special Furman tradition, and *that* matters. (Little did I realize what power the director of the Singers has until this fall when the *Paladin* reminded everyone that the scheduling of our *Messiah* concert determines the academic calendar.) I am a church choir director — what matters is bringing to God the best efforts of our church musicians, and enhancing the worship experience of the congregation. I am a gardener — Judy and I have enjoyed our garden plot, especially when L. D. was there to share our joys of good crops, and our agony of no rain, or too much rain, or too cold, or too hot, or crow invasions, or cutworms! What has become very important to me has been the total experience of that crop-growing activity!

So, which hat shall I wear? Are there "things that matter" that include all my activities and relationships? What really matters to Bing Vick? I begin by saying "Amen" to what my colleagues have discussed — God and our personal beliefs, family and friends, Furman and our work, what to do when ambiguity strikes, the economy and where it is heading, what do we do with our educational opportunities — these things do matter. Also, these things matter: love, great ideas, friendship, ideals, creative risk, artistic communication, faith.

In March, 1982, the final concert of the Furman Singers' tour was at First Baptist Church, Spartanburg. The program was impressive — early motets, Handel, Haydn, Bruckner, a very difficult and exciting setting of "Lamentations of Jeremiah" by Alberto Ginastera, some lovely spirituals, and contemporary anthems. At the end of the concert, Dr. Alister Walker, Minister of the church, remarked that three things came to his mind as the Singers performed: discipline, perfection, and beauty. The more I have contemplated this lecture, the more those three words have come to mind. As Reverend Walker complimented the Singers that night, it became clear in my mind that what he said was exactly what I strive for with the Furman

Singers. And now, after a year or so of thinking about what really matters, I can reaffirm that discipline, perfection, and beauty are essential ingredients.

## Discipline Really Matters

Discipline is important for individuals, for marriages, for organizations, for the art of living. We speak of the successful athletic team as being "well disciplined." We refer to admirable children as well disciplined. We teach various subjects at Furman and call them disciplines. It takes self-discipline to maintain a regular regimen of physical exercise. It takes enormous discipline to refrain from excessive eating and drinking when we would like to have more. Scott Peck in *The Road Less Traveled* refers to discipline as "the basic set of tools we require to solve life's problems." The "four tools" he describes as:

1. *Delaying gratification.* A process of scheduling the pain and pleasure of life in such a way as to enhance the pleasure by meeting and experiencing the pain first and getting it over with. It is the only decent way to live.

2. *Acceptance of responsibility.* We cannot solve life's problems except by solving them. We must accept responsibility for a problem before we can solve it. A saying from the sixties (attributed to Eldridge Cleaver): "If you are not part of the solution, then you are part of the problem."

3. *Dedication to truth.* For truth is reality. That which is false is unreal. The more clearly we see the reality of the world, the better equipped we are to deal with the world. A life of total dedication to the truth also means a life of willingness to be personally challenged.

4. *Balancing.* The discipline that gives us flexibility. It is required for successful living in all spheres of activity.[2] According to Peck, "An essential part of discipline is the development of an awareness of our responsibility and power of choice."[3]

Vince Lombardi, the legendary coach of the Green Bay Packers, listed as the key to success in football, "Know the fundamentals, have discipline to work as a team, and love each other. The difference in mediocrity and greatness is team spirit — feeling for each other." Furman's football success this year can certainly attest to the value of team spirit, executing the fundamentals well, unity of purpose, love for each other, and discipline.

Discipline is important to the musical and personal accomplishments and achievement of the Furman Singers. The Singers must discipline themselves in rehearsals: to respond to my conducting gestures, to listen, to produce the best and most appropriate sounds, to work together and as individuals to produce their best efforts. In performance, the Singers must display discipline: appropriate decorum before, during, and after the concert; guide the audience visually and aurally toward sympathetic understanding of our music. The Singers must adhere to organizational discipline: have faith in my leadership and judgment, understanding the purpose of Furman Singers as a part of this college; be willing to fulfill our responsibilities in a variety of settings. Each Singer invests about 128 hours in rehearsal each year. A disciplined approach to that experience will produce an enjoyable and productive investment of time, and a valuable long-term benefit.

Discipline is important, I have learned, in gardening, whether it be "veggies" or orchids. (I grow veggies; my wife Judy grows orchids; we both enjoy the discipline of the process!) In order for things to grow successfully (including personalities and people) there must be enlightened nourishment — the right amount of water and fertilizer is very important. There must be regular removal of unwanted growth; we must prune raspberries back drastically each year for the strong new growth to come forth (cutting out those branches is not always easy to do). We must keep the weeds out. If not checked, that unwanted intrusion of energy-snapping growth will quickly stifle and kill the wanted crop. There must be regular removal of the ripened fruit. For me, it takes great discipline to cut zucchini when it is small — I always want to wait and let it get bigger! Harvesting is necessary to encourage new growth for the future. Achieving goals as a person, understanding and accepting the new responsibilities that come as we grow through life, being a mature member of society — all demand great discipline.

Dietrich Bonhoeffer, one of the great, martyred Christian theologians of the twentieth century, wrote a prose poem, "Stations on the Road to Freedom," from his concentration camp cell during the closing years of World War II. The four "stations" he calls self-discipline, action, suffering, and death. As one who was a German Christian, a member of the political resistance toward the Nazi regime, imprisoned and executed as an "enemy of the State," and whose writings on religion and theology have had significant influence on contemporary thought, Bonhoeffer wrote: "If you would have freedom, learn above all to discipline your senses and your soul." Discipline matters.

# Perfection Really Matters

More accurately stated, *striving for perfection* matters. One of the big frustrations of life is knowing that some people never taste "the thrill of victory." They never learn to stretch and reach for the best they can do. Many people are more afraid of their best efforts than of their poorer efforts. The security of mediocrity means risk in reaching is avoided. Terry Cole-Whittaker, in her book *What You Think of Me Is None of My Business*, has this to say about risk:

> We avoid risk for four reasons. First, we fear that we will get what we think we want, only to discover that we didn't want it at all. Second, we fear failure and believe failure so painful we won't even try. Third, we fear we will lose what we already have. People spend a lot of energy trying to keep what they have and avoid what they fear. And fourth, we fear we will be successful and that we will not be able to handle our success.... When you realize that God is constant and that you are an individualized expression of God, you can create what you want regardless of what's going on around you. You are free to risk, to give up what's comfortable and familiar in favor of that which is satisfying, fulfilling, and exciting.[4]

As a conductor, I am always working toward that perfect performance: absolute fine intonation, exactly appropriate tone quality, musical phrasing according to the composer's directions, excitement and expressive emotion that comes from reading between the lines of music. (As Gustav Mahler said, "The most important part of music is not written in the score.") At the same time, I know (deep in my mind) that the perfect performance will never happen. Yet we keep trying, and *that* matters.

Joe Paterno, the head football coach at Penn State, had his pick of the bowl game invitations. He asked his players what kind of demands they wanted to make of themselves for the national championship. They chose the most difficult challenge, Oklahoma in the Orange Bowl. Said Paterno, "If you back away from a challenge, you diminish yourself. Sometimes you may not be able to handle the challenge, but you're bigger for trying even if you fail."

Striving for perfection matters. Stated differently, striving for self-actualization matters. Psychologist Abraham Maslow describes "self-actualization" (the ongoing life process in an individual) as "experiencing fully, vividly, selflessly, with full concentration and total absorption."[5]

Harriet Simons, a college choral conductor in New York, has written that a good conductor is one who works diligently toward "self-actualization of ensemble musicians." For the performer, self actualization means reaching for the peak experience — "the sense of totality, of emotional involvement, of wonder, ecstasy, immediacy."[6] Furman Singers is not the perfect ensemble. Yet we strive for perfection.

Wouldn't life be exciting if every person could understand the importance and enjoyment that come when one seeks and finds those "peak experiences" in the living experience.

Striving for perfection means using our full and best efforts in whatever we do. In a musical performance, perfection is elusive. However, putting forth one's best effort is possible for everyone. The key is attitude and willingness to produce the effort. The Furman Singers are not perfect. Yet they are willing to strive for perfection. Rehearsals are at times tedious, but they know the performance that will result will make the work worthwhile. After an exciting concert, there is always a certain sense of let-down. "Getting there" was maybe *more* than "half the fun." Individually and corporately, the joy and thrill come in the process as well as the accomplishment. As we push ourselves, we grow; as we grow, we come to know self-fulfillment; as we become our best, we realize our true purpose — to be, as a part of God's creation, a part of God. Paul, writing to Timothy, said, "Stir up the gift of God which is in thee.... For God hath not given us the spirit of fear; but of power, and of love, and of a sound mind" (2 Timothy 1:6-7).

Tom Cloer said last fall that "anything worth doing is worth doing poorly, if we can't do any better." Doing our best really matters.

Striving for perfection means knowing that change is constant. "There is nothing in life that is constant except change." Giving our best efforts, accomplishing our goals, reaching levels of achievement — all result in new perspectives and new goals to be met. When we travel with the Furman Singers abroad, our primary guideline and advice to the students is…adjust, adapt, and accept. Regardless of the careful planning and attention to the details, there will be times that the expected does not happen, and the unexpected is suddenly at hand. Enjoying the trip, accomplishing the goals and plans made beforehand, can only happen if we adjust, adapt, and accept what really comes our way. The well-balanced offense on a football gameplan will "take what the defense gives us." The so-called "quarterback option" is difficult to defend because the quarterback is in the position to take advantage of the weak spot in the defense at the moment. A well-balanced person is able to deal with life when the adjust-adapt-accept policy is in place. Coping, growing, maturing, enjoying, learning — all mean dealing appropriately with change.

I am currently involved in my first marriage (and, I hope, my only marriage). With humility and brazen courage, I would call it a "perfect marriage." Our relationship is based on love, respect, acceptance of change, and a common faith. Now, we don't always agree. We don't always want the same thing for supper. We don't like the same movies all the time. We even, on occasion, have different religious and political opinions. But we agree to occasionally disagree without being too disagreeable. We share each other's interests (I have sure learned a lot about orchids in the last few years!). We tolerate each other's shortcomings (my pipe smoking tends to produce a less-than-tasty goodnight kiss). We give each other support in times of stress and discomfort. We have grown together over the years by encouraging the best in each other, by accepting and dealing with change in our lives, and mostly, by giving our best efforts to our marriage. We have learned to adjust, adapt, and accept each other, and we are better for it.

Do you remember when you first came to Furman University? Is your position or relationship to Furman what you first expected it would be? For me, Furman has turned out to be exactly what I had hoped for — that is, for the most part!

I arrived in 1970 to join the faculty in the music department. Over the past sixteen years, a lot of interesting things have happened! Most of my highest musical expectations have been and continue to be met. I did not realize then that recruiting talented musicians would become as necessary as recruiting talented athletes. I have felt great frustration from the increase in student cost to attend Furman and our limited music scholarship funds. When I first arrived, I knew nothing about the joys of "self-study" projects. Over the years, I have learned about the importance of SWOTs analysis, defining Strengths, Weaknesses, Opportunities, and Threats. Working toward excellence in performance and never seeming to have enough tenors have been concerns. Yet there have been many unexpected and satisfying, pleasure-filled moments as well: graduation, 1984, when Dr. Johns called me to the platform to receive a Meritorious Teaching Award — numerous musical experiences that brought intense emotion to my soul. I have been very proud of my students who have gone on to great musical and professional achievement. Being able to visit and perform in many of the great cathedrals of Europe has been wonderful!

In 1970 Judy and I were excited about coming to Furman, but we had no idea about what would *really* happen to us here. Indeed, adjusting, adapting, and accepting have meant a most enjoyable and productive career thus far.

A book on the best-seller list for some months now is *In Search of Excellence: Lessons from America's Best-run Companies,* by Thomas Peters and Robert Waterman, Jr. It was interesting to me to notice how many of the principles of successful business operation could be renamed "successful striving for perfection" for an individual. Discussing the values and success of IBM, one of the most successful corporations, an IBM executive said, "We seek a reputation for doing little things well…. Any organization, in order to survive and achieve success, must have a sound set of beliefs on which it premises all its policies and actions. The most important single factor in corporate success is faithful adherence to those beliefs."[7]

From observing successful companies, the authors arrived at what were called basic values found in all these companies. These basic values are important in striving for perfection as well as in search of excellence:

1. *A belief in being the "best."* Doing the best we can with what we have.

2. *A belief in the importance of the details of execution, the nuts and bolts of doing the job well.* Taking pride in accepting the responsibility for doing the "little things" of life well.

3. *A belief in the importance of people as individuals who need each other.* Our humanness is best observed in personal relationships.

4. *A belief in superior quality and service.* Whatever we do, we cannot be complacent with mediocrity.

5. *A belief that most members of the organization should be innovators, and its corollary, the willingness to support failure.* We can accept the fact that someone else might prefer a different solution to a problem.

6. *A belief in the importance of informality to enhance communication.* Our actions often communicate more strongly than our words.

7. *Explicit belief in and recognition of the importance of economic growth and profits.* Personal growth, openness to new ideas, being willing to reach, and being humble in achievements. As a movie actor turned President once advertised for General Electric: "Progress is our most important product."[8]

In a successful business, in a successful marriage, in a fulfilling teaching career, in a successful athletic competition, in a meaningful musical performance, in our day-to-day journey in life, being "in search of excellence," striving for perfection matters.

# Beauty Really Matters

For beauty, three things are required: in the first place, integrity or perfection, for whatever is imperfect is *eo ipso* ugly; in the second, proportion or harmony; in the third, clarity; for there is a splendor in all objects that are called beautiful.[9]

Beauty really matters. Beauty can be seen in nature — in art, in people. Beauty can be heard — in the music of men and the sounds of life. Beauty can be experienced — in love and friendship. Beauty can be shared — in acts of concern and kindness. Beauty cannot be defined, only described: "a quality…that pleases and gratifies."

Consider some examples of Beauty: (1) a Bobby Lamb to Charles Fox pass for a touchdown (indeed, Furman's football program under the leadership of Dick Sheridan); (2) Durufle's motet "Ubi caritas" sung by the Furman Singers in the beautiful Stephansdom in Vienna; (3) the chorus "Dona nobis pacem" (Give Us Peace) with full orchestra and chorus at the conclusion of Bach's monumental B Minor Mass; (4) an orchid in bloom; (5) full, perfect gleaming in sunlight; (6) a caring friend at your side in a moment of concern; (7) the Furman campus in the spring; (8) blue sky, blossoming trees and shrubs, the swans gliding *molto legato* over the lake; (9) students who want to learn and grow, giving us the opportunity to share what we know. Each of these are "beauti-ful" — full of beauty.

Good teaching is a thing of beauty. Everyone is a teacher. Some of us devote our lives and livelihood to the teaching profession, but all of us are teachers. We are constantly teaching those with whom we interact every day. We pass on knowledge to others in everything we do. We signal what responses we expect. We create and display our personal attitudes and understanding in our speech and actions. Sometimes we know we are teaching; sometimes we don't realize we are teaching; sometimes we are trying but it doesn't seem to be working! When it does work, it is a thing of true beauty! Tom Bradbury, an associate editor of the *Charlotte Observer* wrote recently:

> Teaching's magic. There is, I know, method and science to teaching. But there is also something magical about the way good teachers strike sparks that catch and glow in thousands of minds and hearts over the years. It is a thing rare in itself, yet pervasive in its impact. That is, the moments of insight and excitement fill but a fraction of school's long hours. But like moments of religious inspiration, they light the darkness and give purpose to school's workaday tasks, that education might result.

The dictionary says that beauty is "that quality or aggregate of qualities in a thing, which gives pleasure to the senses or pleasurably exalts the mind or spirit; physical, moral, or spiritual loveliness."

Beauty results when discipline is applied to the striving for perfection. Beauty really matters.

L. D. Johnson, wrote in his Sunday article, "What makes life satisfying? Being yourself, reaching out":

> An important ingredient in the satisfying life is realizing that I only need to be who I am, and that I am not responsible to be anybody else. This is not to say that I need to make no changes in my life. What it does mean is that I don't have to depend upon excelling according to other people's standards in order to be somebody.... God does not ask if you are bright or witty or rich or famous or powerful or good looking. He only wants you to be in the family picture because you are his and you belong with your brothers.[10]

We can all make the most of what we have and what we are! The bumblebee is too big for his wing size to fly. Yet he does! Furman's football team this past season was too small to compete; they were struck by injuries to many key players — players important to winning; they played against more talented teams from much larger schools with much greater football budgets; yet they won, and won big!

Erich Leinsdorf, in his book *The Composer's Advocate*, closes with what he calls "The Conductor's Task."[11] I would like to paraphrase some of his "admonitions" to conductors in light of what really matters — what discipline and giving our best efforts and seeking and appreciating beauty mean.

1. *Be prepared.* A conductor must be prepared for the rehearsal — know the music, be secure in his understanding of the composer's intentions, knowing what should be heard and diagnosing the problem if it is not heard. What matters is being prepared for whatever happens. No one promised us that life would be easy. We all have problems and need to learn how to best deal with them. It serves no purpose to always blame others. We *must* be prepared to adjust-adapt-accept.

2. *Plan rehearsal time.* Some works require more rehearsal time than others — knowing the abilities of our ensemble members, their strengths and weaknesses, should allow the conductor to move efficiently through the learning and working-out processes in preparation for the concert. Every minute of life is important — it will never come again. Being organized and efficient will help bring fulfillment to our activities.

Lee Iacocca, in his autobiography, said, "The ability to concentrate and to use your time well is everything if you want to succeed in business — or almost anywhere else, for that matter.... If you want to make good use of your time, you've got to know what's most important and give it all you've got."[12]

3. *Understand players and their parts.* Understanding the psychology of communicating with the various musicians as well as the instruments the players work with, players must be helped to see their individual notes as a part of a greater whole. The conductor's task is to bring continuity, understanding, meaning to the ensemble's corporate performance by guiding the individual to do his best with his part. Every instrument in the orchestra plays an important part — whether it be with a lot of notes or with a few notes. What matters is understanding that all people and each person are important. What I do affects others, and what others do affects me. Marriage or friendship or business association or community, all demand our understanding of each other — our needs, desires, hopes. We need each other, and we should try to understand each other.

What really matters is discipline, striving for perfection, and beauty. With these as foundation stones, life can be fulfilling; we can meet and deal with life's problems and responsibilities; our witness to others will be strong and meaningful, and God will be served — as a part of his creation, we will have found our full and perfect purpose.

Have you ever considered what matters in a pickup truck? Before I close, I would like to share with you a few thoughts. I call this the Parable of the Pickup Truck. Judy and I bought a pickup truck last summer. This was our first pickup truck. We enjoyed the process of deciding which truck to buy, and we have enjoyed our Mazda B-2000 shortbed very much. When you look at a pickup truck, what do you see? Is the pickup what you see, or is it something different? What difference does it make what kind of pickup truck a person has? Let's imagine a pickup truck: What do we see? On the outside is it old or new; clean, dirty, perhaps shiny metallic paint or faded old paint; is it dented/scratched; are there fancy mirrors, racing stripes, a roll bar, oversized tires, chrome bumper; is it a longbed or shortbed? What about the interior: used upholstery; worn mats; dusty dash or fancy; pile carpet; velour seats; airplane cockpit instruments; gauges to measure everything; AM-FM cassette with multiple speakers; gun rack, tilt steering wheel; cruise control; air-conditioning; dangling fuzzy dice? Under the hood: standard, basic engine; or souped up with chrome parts, fuel injection, multiple carburetors? When you look at that pickup truck, do you know what that truck is like? How does it handle? Is it automatic or "5 in the floor"? What really matters in a pickup truck is: adequate inside comfort and convenience for the driver; adequate size bed for intended use (what is going to be hauled); adequate engine for the tasks ahead; regular maintenance attention, use of appropriate fuel and oil. If appearance is important, then a clean and repaired exterior is needed.

What that pickup truck *is* depends on the intended use. The purpose determines what really matters — whether heavy hauling, off-road work, farming chores, or a fancy toy, a nice compliment to the family fleet, useful for moving music stands and timpani to church. Each of us is like a pickup truck — our purpose will determine our physical appearance, personal priorities, and internal makeup. The core of our being, our basic purpose will dictate what really matters to us.

Our purpose is, in the words of the US Army commercial, "to be all that we can be." Each of us should strive to reach our full potential in life. What really matters is discovering, determining, deciding what that purpose is — what really matters to *me!* Our purpose determines how we keep our bodies and minds in good working order; we need preventative maintenance — a continual influx of knowledge and nourishment; we need regular exercise to keep the equipment in good working condition; we need continual updating, refining, reevaluation, renewal of our attitudes and goals. Just as over a period of time the pickup truck might change its purpose, so over a period of time we must understand the changes that happen to us in life.

L. D., in his article "Making the Living Worthwhile," referred to Paul writing to Timothy (2 Timothy 1:6-7):

> There is plenty of common sense in what Paul wrote to Timothy. If you are drifting along without much purpose and with no sense of accomplishment in your life, then what you are doing isn't very worthwhile to you. It probably wouldn't help to change your address or spouse or job, but a change of attitude would do wonders. Reach down within yourself to the bedrock of conviction about the meaning of your life. Is God trying to do something with you and for you, and by you.[13]

## Coda

That is a musical term meaning the end is in sight!

What really matters is deciding what really matters! The process is important for everyone. L. D. knew because he decided — he thought, he cared, he hoped, he tried to do something when he could to help.

Too many students are stuck in that wonderful major — "undecided." Too many people, with blind eyes and deaf ears, accept whatever seems to have the most attractive package, and they ignore the content! Too many people live life aimlessly — few risks, much comfort and ease. They do; they are; that's it! (They spend life treading water.)

Too often, we "do what we know we should not do, and we do not do what we know we should do." Why? Because it is easier to let someone else, or something else, decide for us. In L. D.'s words, "to reach down within yourself" may require effort, and work, and prayer, and hard thinking. Yet we must!

Again I quote Erich Leinsdorf: "To discover the composer's grand design for each work is both the conductor's mission and his reward." To discover in life our "grand design," to decide what really matters, is our mission and our reward when we then do something about it in an effective way. What really matters is *deciding* what really matters!

I encourage each of you to consider yourself anointed as the next L. D. Johnson lecturer. What really matters to you? Thank you.

## Notes

[1] Charles Neilson Gattey, *Peacocks on the Podium* (London: Hutchinson and Co., 1982) 139.

[2] M. Scott Peck, *The Road Less Traveled* (New York: Simon and Schuster, 1978) 18-69.

[3] Ibid., 280.

[4] Terry Cole-Whittaker, *What You Think of Me Is None of My Business* (Lajolla, California: Oak Tree Publications, Inc.) 47-49.

[5] Abraham Maslow, *The Farther Reaches of Human Nature* (New York: The Viking Press, 1971) 45.

[6] Arthur Warmouth, "The Peak Experience and the Life History," *Journal of Humanistic Psychology* 3 (1963) 86.

[7] Thomas Peters and Robert Waterman, Jr., *In Search of Excellence* (New York: Harper and Row, 1982) 260-261.

[8] Ibid., 285.

[9] J. Maritain, *Art and Scholasticism* (Sheed and Ward, 1939) 24.

[10] L. D. Johnson "What Makes Life Satisfying? Being Yourself, Reaching Out" *Greenville News-Piedmont* (July 20, 1980).

[11] Eric Leinsdorf, *The Composers Advocate* (New Haven: Yale University Press, 1981) 175-178.

[12] Lee A. Iacocca, *Iacocca: An Autobiography* (New York: Bantan Books, 1984) 20.

[13] L. D. Johnson and Marion Johnson, *Images of Eternity* (Nashville: Broadman Press, 1984) 34-35.

# David Turner
## Physics
### October 12, 1987

In trying to prepare for this talk I spent a long time thinking about things that have been of value in my life.

One of my earliest memories, from about age two, was a trip to the Coca-Cola vending machine near my parents house. I had been promised a treat. I hesitate to mention this story because of the now evident truth about sugar and caffeine. And I also hesitate to mention this because of the generosity of a man named Hartness. Well, anyway, I remember the machine — this large red and white thing with a handle that you turned after the money went in. Alas, the machine was empty.

What do I find of value in this story? I might say that it prepared me for the troubles of life, but I don't remember sadness and frustration in that experience. I remember that it was fun despite the emptiness of the machine, that I was with my family, and that I was safe and happy.

I believe that our society puts far too little value on our children. Their tiny bodies carry the genetic future of humankind. Their minds will have to deal with problems like overpopulation, shortages of food and shelter, and shortages of raw materials and energy. We must see them for what they are — the future. So I believe that the education provided to our children should be one of the very highest budget priorities of our governments — and one of the priorities for our own time. Indeed, legislation that supports the children in our society should be considered urgent.

I say this because of my own personal experience. As a cub scout I came to be interested in constructing a small electric motor from wire, nails, wood, and tape. My project was completed with more than a little help from my father. With my "arrow point" earned, I set off to my fourth grade class with my motor and train transformer to perform my first electricity and magnetism demonstration. I still perform this kind of demonstration.

At school the teacher was so entertained that she said I should show it to the fifth grade class across the hall. Suddenly I didn't feel well. This kind of sinking, nervous feeling came over me. I later learned that it was called stage fright. The same feeling came over me often in thinking about giving this talk.

Sadly, our problems are far more difficult to deal with than stage fright, frightening though they are. I came to know this greater fear in the fifth grade as I practiced ducking under my desk to be "safe" if a nuclear attack should occur. This was during the Cuban Missile Crisis. We are an entire species living under the shadowy specter of a mushroom cloud, facing tribulations and even extinction at our own hands. Jonathan Schell points out the in *The Abolition* that we live surrounded by doom, like people in a town at the foot of a rumbling volcano, and that we have the peculiar distinction not to have built our town next to Vesuvius but to have built Vesuvius next to our town.

Despite the relative newness of nuclear weapons, this is not a new situation. The story of Adam and Eve, found in Genesis, is really quite similar. Listen to these words from the second chapter of Genesis:

> The LORD God took the man and put him in the garden of Eden to till it and keep it. And the LORD commanded the man, "You may freely eat of every tree of the garden; but of the tree of knowledge of good and evil you shall not eat, for in the day that you eat of it you shall die." (Genesis 2:15-17)

Well, as you know, the story goes on:

> But the serpent said to the woman, "You will not die; for God knows that when you eat of it your eyes will be opened, and you will be like God, knowing good and evil." So when the woman saw that the tree was good for food, and that it was a delight to the eyes, and that the tree was to be desired to make one wise, she took of its fruit and ate; and she also gave some to her husband, who was with her, and he ate. Then the eyes of both were opened, and they knew that they were naked. (Genesis 3:4-7a, New Revised Standard Version)

The story does not find Adam and Eve punished by immediate death; instead, another fare awaits. Listen to a few words God speaks to Adam: "Cursed is the ground because of you" (Genesis 3:17).

In this story, Adam and Eve change roles. In the garden they were under God's care; they did not need the protection of clothes, and their food was found easily. In the end they are cast out and Adam is forced to till the ground and have it bring forth thorns and thistles, and Eve would bring forth children in painful labor. They are naked in a new and frightening world.

To me, their story is about our coming of age. Upon leaving the garden, Adam and Eve, representatives of all humankind, are more in charge of their destiny than ever before. And, like them, all future generations will face difficulties not known before. From that day on we had the knowledge of good and evil.

What happens next? What do they (or we) do with this knowledge? Many of you already know. It is in the next chapter of Genesis that we read that Cain kills Abel. That is not the only thing that happens and we hope not the only possibility. We shall look at a less noticed outcome of this story shortly.

The narrative has come to be known as the fall, although I find that a misnomer. This story has many interpreters. Many see the myth of Adam and Eve as pointing out how women should not be trusted. The most common interpretation of this myth, in Western Christianity at least, is that it shows that humankind is inherently sinful.

I don't see either of these in this myth. Rather, I see a story that describes the history of each of us in some way, because at some point each of our lives change — we change from children to adults. As adults we are responsible for our behavior because we should know good and evil. Our lives move from the world of the make-believe, parental protection, and forced naps to a world with problems that no child deserves and responsibilities that often appear to be beyond our abilities.

I also see this as a story about our species and our discovery of nuclear energy. The tragedy of the nuclear age is reflected in the life of J. Robert Oppenheimer, the father of the atomic bomb.

Oppie, as he was often called, attended Harvard as a young man. He mastered the curriculum in three years, graduating summa cum laude. He spoke six languages and had particular interest in theoretical physics and sixteenth-century French poetry. He read *Das Capital* in German in an effort to understand the politics of his day.

This wonderful man embodied all that we can hope for in the liberal arts tradition here at Furman. As chairman of the admissions committee, I say that if you know of some high school students with this kind of talent and ambition, please suggest that they apply to Furman.

Oppie also loved nature. He and his brother took many long horseback rides through the mountains in New Mexico. Oppie always wanted to take the longer and more scenic route — even if it was midnight and raining.

Oppie also loved people. He was the life of any party he attended. His friends, particularly the ladies, always found his company stimulating.

In spite of his love of people, Oppie found himself in a key role in World War II. In 1945 the United States was ready to test an atomic bomb. This test was made possible because of Oppie's genius. Only he had mastered every aspect of the bomb.

In July of that year, an unmarked Pontiac sedan arrived at a remote location in New Mexico. The Spanish name of the place translates as "the journey of death." The sedan delivered a ten-pound, perpetually warm, hollow sphere of plutonium that cost about one billion dollars to produce. Even though the driver had no idea of what he was delivering, he asked for a written receipt.

This was the first time the species *homo sapiens* had produced something that cost a billion dollars in the name of science. The design and construction of this hollow sphere of plutonium and the triggering mechanism were incredible achievements to have been completed in just a few years. This first atomic bomb was perhaps the most remarkable feat in human history.

This was not, however, the achievement of just one man. It was, in truth, a remarkable collaboration involving thousands of highly talented and motivated people. Indeed, humankind had entered a new age: Science, with the backing of unlimited resources from the government, could do something that had never been possible before. It is sad that the first such achievement would be used to destroy two cities — each in the blink of an eye. By contrast, I will always find it remarkable that the Chinese invented gunpowder, rockets, and fireworks without inventing guns and bombs.

While Oppie was viewing the fireball of the first atomic bomb, a passage from the *Bagavad Gita*, which he had read in the original Sanskrit, came to his mind: "Now I have become death — the Destroyer of worlds." In a later press interview, Oppie was asked to reflect on the project. He said, "We physicists have known sin — and this is a knowledge we cannot lose."

Oppenheimer's qualms about the production of a bomb 1000 times more powerful, the hydrogen bomb, eventually led to the removal of his security clearance. Once ostracized from this beloved nuclear physics, he became a sad and broken man. Indeed, Oppie had been drawn irresistibly to the ripe and glistening apple of scientific and technological elegance that was the atomic bomb. He had been cast from his garden by his own conscience. Uncle Sam removed him from responsibility once he had lost his innocence.

In fact, it seems that none of the voices expressing concern about limiting nuclear weapon production has been heeded. The nuclear arsenals of the United States and the USSR are larger than any reason can justify. We are confident that use of only ten percent of the arsenals would drastically, if not fatally, damage the planet. If we were to divide up the current arsenals into Hiroshima-sized chunks and drop these at the rate of one per minute, the rain would last for more than forty days and forty nights.

Humankind, it seems, has been cast headlong from the garden. We have tasted of the fruit. We feel naked. We have built fallout shelters. Some movies about the present state of the nuclear arms race have titles that reflect this concern, titles like *No Place to Hide* and *The Last Epidemic.*

What can we do? Must we follow the path of Cain and Abel? Many of us feel paralyzed and impotent. But we must not. We must learn from the less noticed outcome of this story. As outcasts, Adam and Eve did not simply die; instead, they continued, despite some failings, to seek life. Surely this is what all that begetting that the Hebrew Bible is famous for is all about.

Perhaps some of this same symbolism is seen in the suggestion made by Helen Caldicot, medical doctor and outspoken critic of the arms race. She suggests that when the Senate begins debating the next nuclear weapons appropriation that 100 toddlers should be released onto the Senate floor.

I like her plan very much, although it would probably not work. A two-year-old can change from charming and disarming to intimidating — when it becomes evident that their diapers are carrying a full load. And besides, the solution to this great predicament will demand serious and level-headed thinking.

Her point is very well taken. One cannot look into the face of a two-year-old and contemplate spending billions on implements of mass destruction. The money spent on nuclear arms could instead be used to pay our public school teachers a salary consistent with the value of their role in the future of our country or to provide quality daycare for the many infants and children who are now left without adequate care and stimulation.

On the other side of the issue we must accept the fact that the serious proponents of nuclear armament do have a legitimate concern. The safety of these children is important, and their safety depends on the political future of democracy and freedom. We must not make decisions about defense matters that will leave the United States vulnerable.

Having said that, I must also say that I very strongly believe that our decisions about defense needs are often based on emotions or false principles, rather than realistic needs.

The emotion I find the most detrimental is one we know well. "We're number one." We often chant it at our games when our team is winning. Most games we play are so-called "zero-sum" games. One player wins while the other player loses. We often see this "number one-ism" take rabid forms — like cheating in recruiting, or honestly believing that someone else is inferior in some way because he or she is not "number one." If we are not careful at Furman, we could play this same game with our academic rating as well.

Proponents of new weapon systems often cite the need to "stay ahead of the Soviets" or catch up to the Soviets in any area where their strength is perceived to be greater. As a country we feel compelled to be number one.

But life is simply not a zero-sum game. I am always offended by church sermons or other such talks based on the lessons of athletic contents. Athletic competition is a valuable human enterprise — but not so valuable as to offer many lessons for the leading of one's life or for making moral decisions in the reality of national and international politics. To let nuclear policy be dictated by athletic sentiment is, to say the least, shortsighted.

Helen Caldicot puts it well when she says that there are not capitalist and communist children. Children are simply children. My sister, now the mother of a two year old, says that only mothers should be asked when decisions about nuclear issues are made. Having had the experience of interacting with this child myself, I can see her point. To sees this child fall and get hurt is far worse than having the injury yourself. The thought of this child suffering in nuclear war is torture.

This is Jonathan Shell's point as well. We have reached the time when we could destroy the futures of all the individuals in our species — both born and unborn. The fact that the complete destruction of our species and even the entire planet as a home for living creatures of many kinds exists as a possibility, however remote, is of pivotal significance. Even if it could be proven that this possibility is remote, the possibility, no matter how small, when weighed against the infinite damage of the destruction of our species and planet, is still unacceptable.

As I've said, we must not surrender. We must do something, but what should we do? I may have already spent far too long describing the bleakness of the present state of affairs. But I have suggestions.

I think that the greatest hope for improvement in the present state of nuclear armament lies in the adoption of a freeze on the testing of all nuclear weapons. Present technology guarantees that this can be done and that any cheating could be detected. This agreement alone would stop much of the evolution of weapons systems. New and untested warhead designs would not be attractive.

Oppenheimer's advice is also very helpful. He said, "The only hope for our future safety must lie on a collaboration based on confidence and good faith with the other peoples of the world." When asked when arms control talks should have been started his comment was, "the day after trinity" — the day after the first atomic bomb test.

Admiral Noel Gayler also has a suggestion. The United States and the USSR should bring their old warheads to a neutral place to be turned into nuclear power reactor fuel. He wants to paint them up with stars and stripes and hammers and sickles. This way, the emotion of the entire world might give disarmament the same kind of "life of its own" that the arms race has shown. He wants to beat swords into plowshares.

The arms race has consumed far too much of our previous human spirit already. There are far better uses for our God-given creative talents. The efforts of many gifted and well-intentioned people lie poised in silos and submarines. These are grand feats of human accomplishment that, at best, will go unused.

In spite of all the knowledge that we have of the dangers and the many warnings, our nation is embarking on a great folly. The "star wars" weapon system proposed by our President promises to cost so much money that it threatens the stability of our society. Many critics estimate that the cost would be a trillion dollars or more.

Sadly, the system cannot, because of the very nature of the arms race, offer us anything other than greater risk. The Soviets simply cannot tolerate our making seventy percent of their weapons — that is, their ICBM force — obsolete, while all of our weapons remain credible. The Soviets will construct weapons to defeat or circumvent the system. I have absolute confidence that this would be a far easier task than designing the star wars system, and I am also absolutely confident that the Soviets would succeed if the need exists.

Such a system, if set up by the Soviets, would threaten only about nineteen percent of our strategic weapons. We have no reason to lead or even compete with the Soviets in this field.

There is one thing that the star wars weapon system will guarantee — more Soviet subs off the Eastern coasts of the United States — subs ready to launch cruise missiles, immune to the star wars defense. These are submarines that could suffer an accident at any time and pollute the Eastern seaboard.

The "star wars" project promises to consume the talent of tens of thousands of our best engineers for decades — all to produce something that will be undone by the talents of their best engineers. The talents of these scientists and engineers are vitally needed to help our country find the technology to survive in the near future.

It is time for us to realize that humankind has come of age. We have the abilities to accomplish things beyond the imagination. Problems of shortages could be overcome by building colonies in space to mine asteroids. Metals could be purified in space with solar energy — conserving previous fossil fuels and reducing acid rain.

We will have to work hard to survive now that we have left the garden. And for our work to be effective we must learn to cooperate. Cooperation is a very hard concept for children — and is little easier for most adults. We have to give up the idea of "being number one" in favor of the idea of being fellow citizens in the same ecosystem. We must rethink our priorities in the arms race.

We as a society must devote serious attention to building the kind of strength that really matters. If we fear the Soviets, we can best overcome this fear by hiding strength of mind and character in our next generation — and the generations to follow. This kind of strength can do more to shape the world and its government in this nuclear age than military strength.

We must demand that the education given to our children be truly excellent. Our children need to know science and engineering, languages — our own as well as that of other nations. They need to know history, culture, and the arts. They need to study philosophy to learn to deal with ideas and to have ideas of their own. They need to understand that something other than a six-figure income really matters.

Important steps in this direction can be made now by the Furman community. A new survey instrument, to be used in the evaluation of potential teachers for our public schools, is all but in place. This instrument asks for only one comment about the potential teachers' knowledge of subject — did they make any blatant mistakes, that is a quotation, so noticeable that someone out of the field would detect this as a mistake? The evaluation instrument states that it is not intended to assess proficiency — only *minimal* competence.

How can we find the best teachers if true knowledge of their subject and their ability to present it do not even enter into the evaluation process? We should never be satisfied with an elaborate evaluation process that admits at the outset that it is testing for minimal teaching skills, and not the teacher's ability to accurately teach appropriate materials. Further complications with a new set of guidelines have produced much talk among departments of simply withdrawing from the teacher certification process.

I believe that Furman should not withdraw, but insist on changes and improvements. It is our responsibility as a regional university to contribute to the standards of our public educational system.

Many young people today feel a sense of inevitable doom. The future seems so bleak for so many reasons. This may be the reason that so many of us lose ourselves in materialist concerns. The middle class, the strongest element in American society, is failing to reproduce itself. This feeling of doom is a major factor in the lives of many today.

There is a way to come out of the shadow of the mushroom cloud. We must get on with the work of "begetting" — not just children, although that is important, but with the work of creating new life out of the seeds of description. We must spend our lives and our money working to build our strength as a society — and ensure its future strength by providing for the education of our children.

We must stop the arms race and prepare for the future. Even outside the garden we must live to life and not death. This is what I believe really matters.

# Richard W. Riley
## Former US Secretary of Education
### January 25, 1988

After serving eight exciting years as Governor of South Carolina, I have pondered seriously about how I could best use my remaining years on this earth. Tunky and I have talked long hours about freeing ourselves up from the "bureaucracies of life" — spiritual, economic, governmental, professional, and social. Not that these systemic structures are unimportant. They are very important and very necessary in our orderly and democratic society. But we both had been so "scheduled" for the past eight years that we craved some unstructured experiences: thinking in the abstract instead of in preparation of a "State of the State Address"; working with people instead of with committees and task forces — substance instead of structure — what we *should do* instead of what we are able to do. My opportunity to return to Furman and spend some time with the students and faculty has been most rewarding by partially filling this need.

And now, to discuss with this thinking audience my view of "what really matters" makes me desire to seek the security and comfort, once again, of bureaucratic decision-making — a study committee on spiritual growth in the "me" generation; or a task force on integrity in government; or a staff research "working paper" on survival in a destruction-oriented world. But, as you know, I have no such crutch to rely on this evening. You see, just as those who have given this lecture before, the "former Governor has no clothes" — no "Hail to the Chief" power with the state plane and SLED protection — and, unfortunately, no original ideas. But, as uncomfortable as this experience is, it does carry with it the excitement of forcing myself to think out my own personal answer to the query — because I would seriously like to know what really matters, and so would each of you. But it is difficult to write these thoughts. As was said by Antoine de Saint Exupery in his book *The Little Prince*, "It is only with the heart that one sees rightly. What is essential is invisible to the eye."

The setting for this discussion is important to me. When asked to give this lecture, my first reaction was that I was far too busy and that I had more productive ways to spend these hours of preparation. But my deep love and respect for the messenger, Betty Alverson, and for the message, the life of L. D. Johnson, required me to accept the challenge.

During the Christmas season, I took the occasion to inquire of many of my friends, my family, my partners the simple but weighty question "What really matters?" The first answer I received was an interesting one — "The Citrus Bowl." This, needless to say, was a Clemson man. People are usually caught off guard, and are somewhat embarrassed by not having a quick and easy answer. I fear that one of the shortcomings of our times is the simple answer for the complex question. We tend to decide important issues from the news flash on TV, the headlines in the paper, or the thirty-second ad, usually negative, in the political campaign. Just as there is no "free lunch," there are no simple answers to the complex issues of our day. And there is no simple, fit-every-situation answer for every single person as to "what really matters" in their life.

So the starting place in my view is to look at the individual — his or her culture and condition of life and the historical setting in which he or she lives. This examination calls for an inward look at ourselves — our character, our vision, our faith. People really matter more than things and it is clear that quality really matters more than quantity. This examination further calls for a realistic understanding of our strengths and weaknesses and where we find ourselves on the ladder of life. For example, a very bright child comes from a different vantage point than a child who is slightly mentally retarded. The former may have a strength of knowledge while the latter may have a strength of love and of sharing. Their views of what really matters would be different for certain things. And, finally, this examination calls for an awareness of our history and of "the times" in which we live. I would classify this part of my discussion as "relevance." "What really matters," you see, must be relevant to an individual's special qualities, and each individual's values must be relevant to their place in life and their time in history.

## Relevance Really Matters

Tonight in Ethiopia the drought and political upheaval are causing thousands to starve to death and thousands more to suffer from serious malnutrition. To be relevant, one would have to say that food is what really matters to them.

In Iran and Iraq, Israel, Afghanistan, and Nicaragua, peace at home is what really matters. With the superpowers of the world, nuclear arms disarmament has to be the most important and relevant issue for a lasting world peace. We see signs of real progress with the signing of the INF Treaty by President Reagan and General Secretary Gorbachev.

In Brazil, where their inflation rate has reached an unprecedented 340 percent, inflation would have to be the key relevant issue. And on our economic front, our great and powerful and wealthy country is weakened by unprecedented debt and deficit spending and unbearable trade deficits. In human terms, our people are confused by moralistic rhetoric on the one hand and examples of public dishonor by officials in government and Wall Street greed on the other hand. Mental discipline of our young seems relevant, while moral and fiscal discipline appears to be the relevant issues for our leaders.

When we look at relevance, we must weigh heavily the issue of an individual's health. A young AIDS victim or a person with terminal cancer certainly would say their fatal conditions are most relevant and really matter to them. An elderly person suffering with painful and chronic arthritis or struggling with the tragedy of mental illness knows what really matters to them. A young and viable man or woman who is out of control due to addiction to alcohol and drugs has to know that any progress in their lives must mean freedom from their condition of slavery. Until that is done, very little else really matters to them.

In our highly industrialized economy, balancing economic development with a quality environment is a very relevant issue. The Japanese speak of "harmony" between growth and environment. I think they *express it* better than they *do it*. But nuclear waste, hazardous waste, clean air and water — all are relevant issues for our times. As Governor, preserving the Mountain Bridge area was important to me, and we substantially got it done. This, in the future, will be important to the beautiful setting for Furman University here in the foothills of the permanently preserved natural crest of the Blue Ridge Mountains.

Much of my public life has been spent on attempting to improve the access and the quality of education for the children of South Carolina. To me, this has a clear relevance to our people, their past, and their future. But in order to participate in a school system of higher standards and higher expectations, a child who is entering the system must have a fair start. This means that the child's health and early development are relevant to improving our schools and their effectiveness. It means that a low birth weight infant born without decent medical care for its immature teenage mother doesn't have a fair start. Such an infant, if it lives at all, probably won't make it in the competitive life they face in our knowledge-based information economy. These are issues of relevance. We must ask ourselves, "What is most important to our children this evening — now, for today's jobs, in today's society, today's world?"

It really matters in 1988 for America that each individual child has a fair chance to "make it" — has a true opportunity to reach their personal goals in this "land of opportunity."

The needs for education have changed over the centuries; also, the requirements of an education have changed. Today, knowledge by itself is not enough. Our competitive requirements call for creativity and flexibility in addition to basic knowledge. However, education has always been important to individuals who think about what really matters. The late Dr. Benjamin Mayes was a close friend of mine, and he was a human being of the same mold as Dr. L. D. Johnson. However, Dr. Mayes was black, the grandson of a slave, who grew up in poverty and the struggle of a tenant farm family in rural Greenwood County, South Carolina. As a child, he was taught by society to have low expectations, to work hard, and to keep his mind closed and his mouth shut. But young Benjamin Mayes was no "sunshine soldier." One evening in Columbia, he told me that as a young boy of ten or twelve, he would work in the blazing hot cotton fields from sun-up to sun-down. When his work was finished, he would walk down to the creek where there was a patch of cane and it was cool and fall on his knees and pray to God for one or sometimes two hours. He told me, with a sparkle in his eye, that he prayed hard for only one thing — "an education." He didn't pray for a big house or farm, not for power and prestige, not for security and health. He prayed for "an education." For most people in Dr. Mayes' time and place in history, this prayer would have sounded ridiculous. But this young man had a handle on what really mattered. His priority was absolutely relevant, but painfully difficult. With his purpose and his commitment, Benjamin Mayes got an education at a time when it was virtually impossible. He went on to be a great educator and mentor for such leaders as Martin Luther King and many others.

Dr. Mayes, in his book *Disturbed About Man*, had this to say to young people who had no hope — no goals in life — because of their time and place. "It must be born in mind," he says, "that the tragedy in life doesn't lie in not reaching your goal — the tragedy lies on having no goal to reach." Goals, to Dr. Mayes, were what really mattered and he urged young black students at Morehouse College, where he was President, to be willing to take the risk of setting goals relevant to the times, and "go for it."

When I speak of relevance, I do not in any way mean to infer that an individual should be satisfied with their status quo, but they should understand who they are, what is important to them, and where they are in time and place. And then they should set goals that are relevant to our world — relevant to our times.

So in thinking out what really matters, one must, it appears, analyze their own individualistic uniqueness and determine how they might improve the quality of their own life — as it is and as they would like for it to be. And their personal goals must be relevant to the conditions of life and the times in which they live. But to keep their self-study all within oneself would make one's life very limited in value to the world. What really matters is taking one's value system and goals and using them to impact others. To effectively move from an individual's own personal domain to impact others depends upon their capacity to understand and respect others, to have meaningful relationships with God, with their family and friends, and their job and fellow employees, with their neighbors, and with those whom they do not know and who may be very different in many ways.

## Relationships Really Matter

Now, let us please turn our interests outward and examine our relationships with others. In a global sense, we see that our great need in the world is probably more sociology than technology. We have been far better in the development of science than in the development of political science. We all understand that favorable treaties will result only through negotiations from strength. But, in my belief, we have a clear opening in the window of opportunity for further reducing nuclear and other arms — and for obtaining better understanding through trade and dialogue. We all share a concern for the many little trouble spots of the world, but the big things seem to be moving in a better direction. Things are hopefully better than they seem. Mark Twain loved Wagner's music, and when asked about it, his reply was that "Wagner's music isn't as bad as it sounds." I hope we can say that about our relationships in the world, because they really do matter.

For our relationships to improve, however, we must start with our own personal feelings about people. We must respect the dignity of all men and al women. For that is the way each of us can help reach world peace. The beautiful children's song says it all: "Let there be peace on earth — and let it begin with me."

Senator Harris Page Smith from Pickens County was a grand human being and a trusted colleague of mine in the state senate. He died at an early age from a heart condition and, as you know, his wife, Nell Smith, was elected to take his seat in the Senate. Harris had a delightful sense of humor and he would often make points in debate through storytelling and often using his personal warmth in an effective way. I was honored to be requested by his family to deliver the eulogy at his funeral, and it was a very difficult task for me to perform. After his death, Senator Nell Smith brought to me a framed copy of a handwritten note that was found in Harris Smith's wallet. The note read as follows: "A hundred years from now it will not matter what my bank account was, the sort of house I lived in, or the kind of car I drove. But the world may be a little different because I was important in the life of someone!"

It is my feeling that this clear statement of philosophy says that relationships are what really matters — that what one does on this earth should impact others in a good and positive way.

## A Future and a Hope

When I was elected Governor in 1978, my attention was immediately directed to the question: In this era of South Carolina's history, what really matters to her people? After hours of deliberation during the campaign and afterwards, I and many of my friends and colleagues systematically studied our state and our needs and attempted to determine what was the most important thing that we could be about during this period. I felt that preparation of our young people, their health and education, was of utmost importance; that preparation of our state for sound economic development would take a certain discipline, jobs for our people were important; that our environment needed attention, particularly in the area of toxic materials, since we were clearly the "dumping ground" for America's nuclear waste; that government institutions needed to be more accountable and that government action needed to be more ethical. I decided that for our people to move into this era with proper leadership, they would have to recognize that they had a duty to their state and to each other — a duty to make some significant long-term commitments for the future. This word "duty" then became one of my key subjects as I approached my first inauguration. Also, I felt that a call for "involvement" on the part of all people working together was a clear need for this particular time and place. I went to my beloved friend, Dr. L. D. Johnson, to help me place this theme in its proper perspective. I asked him to deliver my Inaugural Prayer Service sermon and to think out the best way for me to approach the heavy responsibilities that I faced. Dr. Johnson was of tremendous help to me personally, and through his words he helped our people understand that love and respect were very important but that duty and personal involvement were mandatory for any real long-term progress. He used as his text Jeremiah 29:4-14, which contains Jeremiah's letter to the Israelites being held captive in Babylon. The nation of Judah and its capital, Jerusalem, had fallen to the Babylonians with her leading citizens being taken captive and being hauled off to Babylon. The people found themselves without hope and without leadership, without direction and without the will to move forward. Some of the prophets (false prophets) went to Babylon. There, they made shallow pronouncements about their situation, telling the displaced exiles, "Don't worry; it will be over soon, and we will be home in two years, and this will seem only like a bad dream. Just hold on…. Just pray, and God will eventually take care of us."

But Jeremiah was no "peace of mind" preacher, and while he too had confidence in God's ultimate purpose, he in plain language told them to make the best of things, to build houses, to plant gardens, to settle down, to marry, and to go on with normal processes of human existence. He urged them not to drift — don't just wait for a better time. Be involved — don't forfeit the present or imperil the future. Be good citizens — have faith — and God will give you a "future and a hope". This was the challenging message that Dr. Johnson delivered to our people…and you could tell that he really meant it.

Yes, his charge, just as Jeremiah had charged in another time and place, was to live in the present; to decide what is important for the times, what is relevant; to become actively involved in serving others and working or meaningful progress; and South Carolina and her people would indeed have a great future and a hope.

So as I close my remarks this evening, I would like to express my thanks to our friend and loved one, Dr. L. D. Johnson, for the spiritual and human leadership that he provided our people. He was a person who was relevant and who provided relevant counsel and advice to all who dealt with him. He was a person who indeed understood that the relationships we have with God and with each other and with our environment are of utmost importance. He did me the personal favor of setting the tone for my service as Governor of this great state. For all of these acts of love and service, I express my appreciation to this leader. And I express my appreciation to each of you for allowing me to think with you this evening on the subject of "What really matters?"

And, as L. D. Johnson would say and as Willie Nelson says in one of his songs, "The preaching is over and now the lesson begins."

# Marguerite Chiles
## Vice-president for Student Services
### October 9, 1989

When Betty extended the invitation for me to be your speaker tonight, my spontaneous reaction was the same as that expressed by Elaine Nocks: "Why would anyone attempt this?" My second reaction was that Betty surely is running out of people who knew L. D. (For those here who may not have known him, I say "L. D." as did others before me, because that is what all of his friends, young and old, called him. Seldom was he addressed as Dr. Johnson.)

I think I know how I got this assignment. The Johnson family is well known to the Furman community, and the relationship is one of devotion. There is a Carole Johnson Scholarship awarded each spring to a freshman woman at Furman, given in memory of Carole's outstanding, though short, life. After a committee selects five applicants from a pool of seventy or so, a second committee holds interviews with these five outstanding women in order to choose one. I am on this second committee. The intent of the committee is to evaluate each candidate's potential for growth and service. The candidate's answers to our questions are always important. On that day last April when the committee was in session, I was pleased with my first question for a candidate I considered to be especially promising. I had explained to her what the L. D. Johnson Lecture Series is about before asking, "If you were invited to lecture on the subject 'What Really Matters?' what would your focus be?" I quickly realized that my question was unfair. This brilliant, confident, young student could not suddenly respond. I withdrew the question, and now it has come back to haunt me!

I am the fifteenth speaker in the series. Many of you have been here to listen to the other fourteen, as I have. Some lecturers were more intellectual in style than others; some were more or less humorous. All have been inspirational. Each speaker has provided some food for thought fitting to honor the life of our friend and colleague. Theron Price began the series by telling us that it matters "what we become, who we are." Tony Arrington talked about people along life's way who mattered. Jim Edwards challenged us to question whether we really know and understand the direction in which the

Furman community, this university, is headed. Duncan McArthur talked about how ambiguity matters; and through telling of her personal life in a war-torn country, Lore Johnson helped us to reinforce our belief that peace indeed matters.

One would think that the subject had been thoroughly exhausted. I have learned from this study that there is no way to exhaust such a subject as "What Really Matters?" We have a tendency, perhaps, to think mostly in terms of the good things that matter, but there is a negative element in life that also matters. It matters that certain things not happen if we are to make a difference. There must be thousands of ways to further develop the topic. It touches every aspect of life. But I am convinced that we would do well to separate those things that matter from those that *really* matter. It may surprise us how much time we waste each day on things that matter a bit, but do not really matter.

My life has not been quite the same since Betty called me about the lecture. My mind has seldom been free from a feeling of responsibility in preparation for this event. I have awakened in the night, as if from a troublesome dream, with the question of "What really matters?" filling the night air. The thought of my lecturing following fourteen scholars from this community has been hard to deal with, especially so when it fell my lot to be placed on the schedule between Schaefer Kendrick and John Crabtree. While I am no threat to John Crabtree, following Schaefer is an awesome task. I was in his office the other day to sign a legal form he had prepared for me. It took only about two minutes, but Schaefer insisted that I sit and talk a while, "Because," he said, "the longer you are in here, the more I can charge you." So I did stay long enough for Schaefer to help me to come to terms with the fact that it does matter that I do this lecture, and that it really matters that I do it in my style. So with that in mind, you will not necessarily hear a scholarly approach prepared with humor. You will hear a forthright dealing with some things, both simple and complex, that I think really matter in our daily living, and how my philosophy on the subject may have been supported by L. D. Johnson, who was indeed an intellectual and a scholar wise enough to put ordinary people at ease.

I have survived the preparation. Now let us see if you can survive the delivery. It is my belief that anything that really matters in our world of self-development and growth, and especially in our interpersonal relationships, can be placed broadly under one or more of these three headings: "The God We Worship," "The Choices We Make," "Our Response to Life Situations."

# The Choices We Make

My first draft put "The God We Worship" first in my presentation simply because I consider that to be a first priority. But when I began my study, and my notes began to take shape, I had so much trouble with that section that I put it aside in favor of beginning with "The Choices We Make" — a much easier approach. Among Betty's many fine student programs stemming from Watkins Center, one is called simply "Choices." This is a concerted effort to offer students, while they are still young, some help in learning how to make choices that will lead to living responsible and more stable lives as older adults. The leadership is guided by the philosophy of Dr. William Glasser as found in two of his books, *Reality Therapy* and *Control Therapy*. He has written another good book, *Positive Addiction*. These books and Betty's program help in making a conscious choice to become and remain a responsible human being. Of course, students have a choice concerning signing up for the program!

Choices we make on a day-by-day basis within families matter. Consider if you will, the earlier Johnson family. Most of you have read L. D.'s writings, so you probably know that his parents died when he was small. His aging grandparents chose to raise the Johnson boys. It mattered that they didn't say, "We are too old. Somebody else should take on this responsibility." It also mattered that they gave him more than food, clothing, and shelter. They nurtured him with loving care, and taught him a sense of responsibility.

And L. D. often mentioned an older brother who chose to remain a worker on the family farm, whether or not that was his preference, so that L. D. could get a different and more suitable education. The brother's choice made a difference.

If I may make one more observation here, I would like to point out that L. D. made a good choice in Marion for his partner and the mother of their children. The parental combination in family life matters. These personal references reflect wise choices on the part of the Johnson family. These examples can be repeated with regard to many families we all know and appreciate. It is good to reflect upon such examples, because today I fear we see and hear more of the unhealthy aspects of family life, relationships, and choices. If we can believe what we read in the local paper, many domestic disputes ending with the blast of a gun began with an incident that didn't really matter!

The choices made today by our elected leaders matter to us and often affect the entire world. Harry Truman suddenly became President on April 12, 1945, at the death of President Franklin Roosevelt. Soon thereafter, he was informed for the first time about the development of the atomic bomb, which according to scientists would be completed within four months. Consider the choice President Truman had to make. Would he authorize dropping the bomb on cities in Japan, or would he permit World War II between Japan and the United States to continue its traditional course? I searched the pages of his memoirs for a description of the hours I thought he would have spent in agonizing over the choice he would make, but I found none. President Truman appeared not to suffer over this extremely important decision as much as President Nixon agonized each day over what choices he would make as Watergate unfolded. Certainly, Mr. Truman's decision was one of the gravest a President ever had to deal with up to that point in history. He seemed confident from the earliest moment that his choice to drop the bomb would save more lives in the long run than the alternative.

A South Carolinian named Richard (Dick) Riley went into politics. His choice was to perform his duties as a statesman. The means to an end matter to Dick Riley. His procedure is always based upon integrity. Another South Carolinian went into politics — his name is Lee Atwater. With a "no holds barred" philosophy in achieving any desired goal, he has chosen to be a politician rather than a statesman. The means to an end don't seem to matter to Lee.

Let us turn for a moment to choices in the uses of wealth. Certainly it matters how we make our money with regard to integrity and abuse of other people. I think it matters also how we choose to use our money, even those of us who are not wealthy. Those among us who profess to try to follow the teachings of Jesus probably have considerable trouble with his advising his followers to sell what they own and share with those less fortunate. Do you happen to know anyone who has come close to practicing such a choice?

A man named Millard Fuller was a very rich fellow a few years ago. He was a successful lawyer, but a most unhappy man. He decided to sell his property and close his law office. He made a choice that took him in another direction. He became a happy and fulfilled man. Millard Fuller founded an organization called Habitat for Humanity. Many of you know of it and support it. Through careful and responsible planning, and money and labor from thousands upon thousands of volunteers worldwide, this organization provides low cost but adequate housing for those who cannot otherwise achieve this goal. The choice made by Millard Fuller mattered not only in his own personal development, but to thousands of people around the world. Compare this kind of a choice-making to the James Watt and Sam Pierce choices in favor of greed related to the Office of Housing and Urban Development in Washington — an office whose concern is also supposed to be for the less than affluent.

It matters that we put our priorities in correct order. Some things matter more than others at different periods during a lifetime. I have known families who would not sacrifice even a little, or temporarily lower their standard of living in order to assist their children in earning college degrees. I have also known just the opposite.

During my tenure at Furman, over a thirty-eight year span I was fortunate in having been invited to visit in the homes of students from time to time. One such visit is implanted in my mind. This visit was with a farm family in North Carolina's tobacco country, but because the parents thought the use of tobacco was not a good or healthy habit, they worked hard to earn a living by other means. I arrived with one of their four daughters on a Saturday for our weekend visit. I noticed that the house had never been painted. It was an old house, in good condition, simple in style. Inside were good books, many of which were classics; a piano, sheet music and song books; some quality craft objects and more. There was an absence of expensive furnishings. The food was simple but very good: fresh eggs, milk, and vegetables — all home produced. The parents had a plan for their children's higher education. They managed to save enough money to send each child to college for two years with assistance through on-campus jobs and scholarships. Each child would then be responsible for her last two years, and upon graduation was expected to assist the next child with college expenses. The daughter whom I knew best from her Furman years now has an earned Ph.D. in counseling and is recognized as one of the outstanding family counselors in the Southeast. All the children grew up to be successful adults in terms of what really matters.

I would be amiss if, as I end this section of choices, I leave the impression that the responsibility for making choices is always simple and easy. It is not, and for some to choose at all is almost impossible. It is a sad observation that choices made today by many adults, especially some parents, result in extreme suffering for children: such as abuse, separation, abduction, and being born with an addiction. Consider a twelve-year-old who for years has been sexually, physically, and emotionally abused by a parent. The child considers telling the other parent who may not believe the story. The child considers running away from home to become a street person. What good choices are available to this child?

## Our Response to Life Situations

I have stated that I believe it matters how we respond to life situations. Responses of individuals matter in a personal way and in relationships. Responses by institutions, including churches, schools, businesses, and governments, matter. Few of us in a lifetime are spared tragic experiences: grief, heartbreak, extreme illness (including physical and mental pain), the shattering of dreams, despair, and more. We are sometimes victims of situations over which we may have no control, but each of us has to respond in some way. Although we cannot always control what happens to us, we can control, to some degree, our response.

\* \* \* \* \* \* \* \* \*

Freddie has just completed her freshman year at Furman — a year marked with joy of living, success in academics and in relationships, and a proven talent for music. Then Freddie suddenly became very ill. The diagnosis: a severe case of polio. Freddie's treatment at Warm Springs, Georgia, took about a year. Her progress from the first day amazed her doctors. They credited her attitude. Her reaction to pain and loss inspired other patients, families, and doctors. The Warm Springs papers began to publish articles about this unusual young girl of nineteen years.

Freddie returned to Furman, ready to begin a new life from a wheelchair, having no use of her legs and limited strength in the muscles of her body. She was graduated and worked after graduation as a member of the Dean's staff. Freddie married Frank, whom she had met at Warm Springs.

Frank contracted polio while serving in the US Navy. They designed a house to accommodate wheelchairs and crutches, and had it built in the warm Florida climate. Frank, although classified by the Navy as totally disabled, has been a highly successful businessman. He and Freddie are parents of two daughters. They are involved in many worthwhile activities within their church and community. Their response to the debilitating effects of polio has been so healthy that to know them is an inspiration. To visit them is pure fun!

\* \* \* \* \* \* \* \* \*

It was late afternoon in the spring. I had a phone call for which I was not prepared. The message was that my close friend of more than half a century had been seriously hurt in an automobile accident. I rushed to the hospital emergency room to join family and friends for the long wait for the medical report. When it did come, the report included broken ribs, damaged heart, collapsed lungs, dislodged teeth, and a broken neck, among other injuries.

We all waited quietly, encouraging each other, until midnight when we learned that Ruby would live. She never lost consciousness. She never lost control. She never lost her faith. Her first concern, even in those hours filled with pain and wonder, was for her family, whom she urged to go home and get some sleep, and for the other occupants in the cars. During the hot summer months, she had to lie on her back in a heavy brace, looking only at the ceiling. Visitors came away from the bedside feeling better for the visit because the accident victim always showed more concern for family and friends than for her own discomfort. There was no self-pity. Visitors were inspired and doctors amazed at her steady recovery and healthy attitude.

* * * * * * * * *

Mr. and Mrs. Sofey live near Atlanta. Mr. Sofey is gainfully employed, and Mrs. Sofey is a homemaker. They are citizens who have contributed much to the cultural and religious climate of their community. They have one daughter, Priscilla, who at the end of her first year at Furman received the Carole Johnson award. Why am I telling you this? Because Mr. and Mrs. Sofey are totally deaf. Their response to an unfortunate situation in their lives was to accept what could not be changed, to learn to communicate in a different way, and to live responsibly. Priscilla at age five was using sign language. Today, she communicates beautifully in two ways.

* * * * * * * * *

There are so many examples of what a difference our attitude toward hardship can make. Among the publicized ones is Ted Kennedy, Jr., who at age twelve lost a leg to cancer. His response as a youth was to learn to ski and then as an adult to devote much of his time to working with the handicapped. Franklin Roosevelt did not let polio prevent him from serving as President of the United States longer than any other president. Stevie Wonder's response to blindness resulted in his becoming a successful musician.

And there are other kinds of responses. Those of you who are about my age will recall the hard times we experienced during the Great Depression of the late 1920s and early 1930s. My sister, brother, and I were teenagers living on a small farm. There was good country food for everyone, we even had meat on Sunday — but never enough cash to buy the necessities. Forgive me for remembering many responses to those hard times, only one of which I will share. Farmers often bought flour and other supplies in large cloth sacks. If enough handmade starch was added, the cloth looked from a distance almost like linen. My mother carefully made two-piece suits for my sister and me from the cloth saved from flour sacks. My parents were able to impress upon us the idea that beautiful handmade suits from cloth that had been used to hold flour, were very special and that other teens would be envious of us. I remember thinking how very creative my mother was, and I was indeed proud of my suit. Many values for living came out of that period, if only we could recognize them. For the past two weeks we have seen remarkably healthy responses to our state's visit by Hugo — responses by those who suffer and those who helped the suffering.

* * * * * * * * *

I had just retired from my work at Furman in the summer of 1980. That fall, a local church sponsored a two-day workshop to assist retirees in choosing ways to be of service as volunteers in the community. I shall never forget an experience related to the workshop. In the afternoon I joined the group discussing hunger, housing, street people, etc. Early in the discussion a man rose to ask how we intended to find out just who might be truly hungry; what kind of screening system could the churches work out so a person would not receive soup twice during any one day? (That seemed to matter to him.) When this man mentioned listing names and addresses of those seeking help, I realized how little he knew about street people whose only address in Greenville might be under one of the bridges crossing Reedy River.

With all this on my mind, an interesting thing occurred that evening during the worship service. I was seated at the end of a row near the center of the chapel. I faintly heard what sounded like a man sobbing. The sound continued, and so did the service. I turned my head toward the aisle as a man carrying some belongings in a pillow case walked toward the pulpit. He was elderly, dressed in dirty, raggedy clothing, and his sobs reflected his hurting. One of the ministers came down from the pulpit, put his arm around the man, and walked out with him. For a moment my mind went back in history as I thought of Jesus in the Holy Land, as suffering people tried to reach him. Our afternoon dialogue about the street people raced through my mind. No explanation was given to those in attendance, and we went home pondering what we had experienced. At our first session the next morning, the minister told us that the street person, having been turned away by his family, was known to the church. A month earlier he had been taken to a local hospital by church volunteers for help with a heart problem. Out of fear, he had disappeared from the lobby and had not been found until this night. Church members responded again by putting him up for the night, feeding him well, providing loving care, and transporting him to the veterans' hospital.

* * * * * * * * *

After living in Furman's residence halls for many years, I moved into a house of my own in 1962. I chose a street in one of the city's modest sections near old downtown. I enjoyed my new privacy from the start, and my neighbors seemed to accept me. I liked them, too.

A few years passed, and the house to the left of mine was listed for sale. I was somewhat aware of a bit of rumbling when a black family came to look at the house. Up to this time Randall Street had had only white residents. One day, when I arrived home from work, an elderly neighbor, who lived in the house to the right of mine, was waiting for me. She was crying. She told me of the concern she and her husband had about the possibility of black people buying a house in the neighborhood. Her exact words were, "I am praying every day to God that he will not let black people buy the house." This was my first opportunity to discuss the matter. I knew immediately what my personal response to the situation was, But I had to think quickly how I would share it with my neighbor, whose concern I also understood. I took her hand in mine and said softly, "My good neighbor, I do believe we are praying to the same God, but we are not praying the same prayer. I am praying that God will help me to be a good neighbor to whomever moves next door." She stopped crying...perhaps in shock at my response. She then asked if I was not concerned that the value of my house would depreciate. I replied (honestly) that the thought had not crossed my mind, but since I had paid only $7,500 for the house, it wasn't worth much. I heard no more from my friends on Randall Street. My black neighbors are good neighbors to this day.

\* \* \* \* \* \* \* \* \*

The response of government to those being governed matters. Some things matter because they are wrong and should never have happened. Some things matter because they are right and can bring about change. It matters that the man in government known as "Silent Sam" closed his eyes and ears when greed took charge at the Office of Housing and Urban Development. It also matters that Jack Kemp appears to be responding in a positive way. It has been a while since the episode we call Watergate happened, but the characters played by Chuck Colson and Jeb Magruder come to mind. Their personal responses to the tragic situations they got themselves into are interesting. In due time one has become dedicated to prison ministry; the other is a respected minister in a well-established church.

I am sure all of us are grateful to live in a country where we are free to choose our leaders, and free to respond to that leadership in a number of ways. We continually ask ourselves what is the correct response our government should exhibit toward the cruelty in South Africa, the hunger in Bangledesh, the plight of the Palestinians in Israel, the extreme repression of the Students for Democracy in China, and the rapidly growing gap between the very rich and the very poor in America. We are indeed in the process of becoming one world. In a free country such as ours, we have responsibility to respond in our own way to what we see that motivates our elected and appointed leaders.

\* \* \* \* \* \* \* \* \* \*

In the late thirties I was a sophomore at the Woman's College of Furman University. The beloved Virginia Thomas was Dean of the college. Times were hard, and she had no full-time secretary. Because I had studied short-hand and typing, I became her secretary for the hours I was not in class. I adored Miss T., as she was lovingly called. She was my mentor. Probably without realizing it, by the time I reached my senior year, she and others like her had inspired me to choose college administration as my professional goal.

It is important, as I continue my story, to ask you to recall (if you are old enough) what life in the segregated South was like in 1938. One day I answered the office phone. A voice said, "This is Hattie Duckett at Phillis Wheatley Center. I know you are sponsoring Erskine Caldwell as a lecturer tonight. He is a favorite of mine, and I am wondering if I might attend by sitting in the balcony." Mrs. Duckett was the outstanding black community leader in Greenville at that time. The lecture was to be held in Ramsay Auditorium, and only a few seats would be occupied, and the entire balcony would be unused. My spontaneous response was, "Of course, Mrs. Duckett, the college will be so happy to have you." When Dean Thomas came to the office in late afternoon, I gave her the messages, including my joy that Mrs. Duckett wanted to hear Erskine Caldwell. I was naive. I was not prepared for Miss Thomas's reaction, which was that I had made a mistake. It just would-n't do for a black woman, regardless of her standing in the community, to be in attendance. I knew Dean Thomas as a person, and I understood where her heart was, but I was young and inexperienced. I was too shy and unsure of what was the right thing to do, in terms of institutions like the college, to dis-cuss this matter further with her. I was so confused. I had grown up in a community where balconies were reserved for black people. But I was unable to put myself in the place of Dean Thomas and to understand the decision she thought she had to make in response to what was happening at that point in history. I was unable to understand the fear that overcame her in response to the situation. I knew Dean Thomas from 1936 until her death in the early sixties. This is the only time I was ever disturbed by any action on her part.

Hindsight is always easier than foresight, but were Miss T. here today, she would probably agree that her response to *this* life situation was in error.

## The God We Worship

We who are here tonight to honor the life of a man of God can almost assume that the God most of us worship is the God we came to know as a child: the God as revealed in the Holy Bible, and as known to billions of people around the world. Perhaps if I had been born into a Buddhist, Hindu, or Muslim family, my religion today might be a different one. The God we worship does matter. But when I ask myself "Why?", I have difficulty putting the answer into understandable words. I just know that it matters.

As a child, my first memorized Bible verse consisted of three words: *God is love*. I accepted that philosophy at an early age. It was easy to say and to believe. The hard part, as I grew older, has been to understand the meaning of love in that context.

I hinted at the beginning of the lecture that this section has been problematic for me. You can sense my struggle, but that struggle has been good for me. I was tempted to change the wording of my topic from "The God That I Worship Matters" to "It Matters That I Worship God." Marion Johnson has put together in a small paperback some of L. D.'s best editorials not included in other publications. In view of the subject of the lectures, a title of one of his columns in this collection caught my eye. The title was "Does Religion Really Matter?"

I have lifted a little story from his writing. It goes like this:

> During half-time at a football game last fall, my wife and I noticed several young women pinning flowers to the coat lapels of college boys and collecting dollars, occasionally as much as five dollars…or whatever the young man would give. The girls represented a notorious cult which owns hundreds of millions of dollars in real estate in this country, and which gets its money by such deceptive methods. Marion went up to the young man who had just handed over five dollars and asked him if he knew what he had contributed to. He said he didn't know but was sure it was for a good cause! That is what comes from living in an environment where all religions are considered equally true.… No, not all religions are the same any more than all families are the same. Jesus said: "By their fruits you shall know them." Test the religion that knocks at your door in terms of what it has done to bring man to God and to unite him with his fellow man.

Most of us do not confess our weaknesses in public, especially if we fear that our thinking may not coincide with the thinking of those around us. I am confessing, first of all, that I am not a good student of the Bible. I am confessing also that I have had some difficult understanding the nature of God from my reading, and slightly studying, the Old Testament. My God of love has been, at one time or another in my faith journey, a mystery to me…jealous, harsh, demanding. Being a lover of all animals, childlike, I have never wanted to read about sacrificing the most perfect of lambs as burnt offerings on the altar, as described in the Old Testament Scriptures.

As I pondered these thoughts I discovered a small, rather controversial book with the title *For Christ's Sake*, authored by a minister named Tom Harper. Mr. Harper supports my observations concerning some of the Old Testament portrayal of God. However, he concludes his remarks on this topic by writing,

> It is to the prophets and the Psalmist that we owe the concept of God as a living, forgiving and peace-seeking Lord who longs for his children to return and find pardon and wholeness (salvation). It is to the prophets that we are indebted for the stirring vision of God's desire for justice and mercy for the oppressed and needy of the earth. It is the former herdsman Amos who cries that God cares nothing for burnt offerings and the "noise of solemn assemblies" while injustice flourishes. (Amos 5:21-24)

In my continued search to find a way to answer my own question, "Why does the God we worship matter so much?", I accidentally found some help in Harold Kushner's book *When All You Have Ever Wanted Is Not Enough*, with a subtitle, "The Search for a Life That Matters." He is the rabbi whose first book was *Why Bad Things Happen to Good People*. In his latest book, Kushner devoted a chapter to analyzing the Old Testament book of Ecclesiastes, which some biblical scholars consider to be "a difficult book which displays the dark philosophy of one who sought to find peace apart from God, but in the end realized that only futility is to be found there" (introduction to Ecclesiastes in the book). According to Kushner,

> Ecclesiastes asked, "What makes my life matter?" What makes it more than a passing phenomenon, not worth noticing while I am alive, and destined to be forgotten as soon as I am dead? God is the answer to the question: Why should I be a good and honest person when I see people around me getting away with murder? God is the answer, not because he will intervene to reward the righteous and punish the wicked, but because he has made the human soul in such a way that only a life of goodness and honesty leaves us feeling spiritually healthy and human.

So...the answer is that we cannot deal with the ultimate meaning of life without understanding the difference that God can make in our lives.

The July 31 issue of *Time* magazine included a colorful four-page advertisement prepared by the Royal Embassy of Saudi Arabia, Washington, DC, with this heading: "For Over Fifty Years, Saudi Arabia and the United States Have Shared a Dream for Their People." Following the two-page description of the economic relationship between our two countries, the last page was devoted to the subject "New Dreams to Share." Under this title, the writer has this to say:

> Saudi Arabia's concern for the day-to-day welfare of people is conditioned by two enduring traditions: our religion, and the commitment to the family. Islam is the vital force that guides and sustains all Muslims in every aspect of their daily lives. The religion of Islam preaches equality and the rights of the individual. It is a religion of peace and tolerance. Our faith in God is a way of life.

Most of that statement sounds as though an American of the Christian faith might have spoken. We Christians look at Islam and we sometimes see needless suffering, lack of tolerance, and absence of respect for some of their people. Islam looks at Christians and they sometimes see needless suffering, injustices, cruelty, etc. The God of Islam is Allah, a faith established by the prophet Mohammed.

Many religions have the same goals, and, to some degree, each fails in reaching them. Isaiah warned the people of his time against the worship of idols and false gods. Perhaps today we should be cautious about the possibility of our spiritual God being gradually replaced by gods of pleasure, wealth, popularity, or power. There are many ways to interpret God's love to his many followers: some healthy, some strange. Two illustrations come to mind. Give your own evaluation to each.

The third day of each month is the magic day to millions of Americans...the day the Social Security check arrives! On this magic day I always go to an address of a drab street where a person with severe arthritis remains in bed. I take her check to the bank, and return to her the cash. Last week a part of my conversation with Lizzy went like this:

"I ain't gonna be here when you come next time."
"Where are you going to be, Lizzy?" (She named a street not familiar to me.)
"Where is that street, Lizzy?"
"I don't know."
"Well, are you happy about this? Do you think you will be OK there?"
"I don't know and it ain't none of my business. I leave these things to God."

\* \* \* \* \* \* \* \* \*

Chuck was a student who had lost control of his life, which deteriorated steadily with each new day. He never made an appointment to see me, but always seemed to be waiting when the office door was opened. I pleaded with Chuck to voluntarily remove himself from the student body to avoid what would surely be dismissal for academic and social failure. He resisted, using the same denial so many of us use regarding our bad choices. Chuck finally did disappear from our midst. Several years after I retired, and some ten years since I had seen Chuck or heard from him, he contacted me with this message: "I just want to thank you for loving me into the kingdom of God," and he told me of his experiences since Furman. In my sessions with Chuck I did not mention God, or love, nor did we have prayer in the office! God does work in mysterious ways!

\* \* \* \* \* \* \* \* \*

The God I worship matters because he has been revealed to me through Jesus, his divine son who lived as a human on earth for some thirty years, setting standards for later Christians to follow. The God I worship matters also because the Holy Spirit, which completes the Trinity in the Christian faith, reminds me that *God is love*. And all of this is recorded in the Holy Bible, which has endured through the ages.

As I come to the end of this presentation, it occurs to me that a simpler approach might have been to reduce my headings simply to "The Choices We Make." Certainly we are free to choose the God we will worship, and consciously or unwittingly, we choose how we will respond to life situations. In the search for what really matters, by way of making the right choices and exercising wise responses to life situations and by worshiping God, I know of no better way than to practice a little prayer written by Reinhold Niebuhr. It goes like this: God, grant me the serenity to accept the things I cannot change, the courage to change the things I can, and the wisdom to know the difference.

# John Henry Crabtree
## Former English and Vice-president for Academic Affairs and Dean
### January 15, 1990

On November 20, 1989, the day on which I finally faced up to the fact that I had to stop thinking about this lecture and put some words together on a piece of paper, our fifth grandchild was born. Rebecca Arlyn Crabtree came into the world in St. Petersburg, Florida, at about 9:30 that morning, after more than thirty hours of strenuous effort on the part of her mother and the assistance of a team of surgeons. Having been emphatically described three months earlier by her mother's doctor as a robust boy, Arlyn confronted both incredulous parents and smug grandparents. The latter had never completely trusted the technology anyway and derived some satisfaction from its failure.

Given this event in the family, the proximity of Thanksgiving, and the essence of the task that this lecture imposes upon whomever Betty Alverson has managed to persuade to give it, I approached it in a strongly reflective state of mind. For me, the question "What really matters?" began to involve other probing inquiries: Who am I? Where am I? Why am I here? Does it really matter that I am who I am where I am? Do I know what matters? Does what I think really matter? Elaine Nocks was right to the point when she described the process of responding to the challenge of this lecture's imposed topic as "an exceedingly difficult task that truly invades and occupies the mental and emotional capacities from the moment of acquiescence to the moment of final presentation." The process of discovering, analyzing, and evaluating one's values can be a disturbing journey into one's intellectual, moral, and spiritual self. Sharing the results with one's family, friends, and associates becomes a personal testimonial — a situation with which I have always found myself thoroughly uncomfortable. But, so be it. That is the nature of the responsibility which I took upon me when I accepted Betty's invitation.

Before I go any further, however, let me say something about my association with L. D. Johnson. L. D. became Furman's Chaplain to the University in 1967. As a member of the Furman community, I admired his eloquent and forceful preaching, and I was pleased that we had a scholar of national reputation in a highly conspicuous position. In 1968, I became

Dean of Students, and in this job I discovered the L. D. Johnson who gave himself tirelessly to creating and sustaining on our campus the person-centered environment, which he described in his powerful essay "The Character and Values of Furman University." It may seem a bit odd to some of you, but it was through his and my love of gardening that I got to know L. D. as a person. Those of you who have arrived here in the last five to ten years are perhaps unaware of the fact that fifteen (or more) years ago many of us on the faculty spent some hours of each summer day raising vegetables in carefully defined plots just outside the back gate over beyond the railroad track. Only a few stalwarts continue in that character-building activity, notably Bingham and Judy Vick and Bill Pielou. But in those days there were many of us. My garden plot and L. D.'s several garden plots shared a common boundary. While working there late on hot summer afternoons, I came to know L. D. as a powerfully strong, amazingly energetic man who wanted passionately to feed all the hungry people in the world. And if physical strength, energy, and hard work could have accomplished such an extraordinary goal, he would have rung from that red clay the food necessary to do it.

What really matters? What *really* matters? I confess to you that I lack any real confidence that I *really* know the answer to this question. On one of the many occasions when I confronted both the philosophical and practical problems in which Betty Alverson has entangled me, I have played a little fill-in-the-blanks game. I asked, "What really matters to _____?" After all, how one answers this question depends upon who one is, what one is doing, and what one aspires to be doing — whether one is young or old, strong or infirm, rich or poor, married or single, etc., etc. So for a few moments I played with the kaleidoscopic quality of the question. What really matters to a college professor — good students? rank? salary? laboratory equipment? computers? academic freedom? social freedom? Do not black American youths have answers to this question that differ radically from the responses of white American youths? What really matters to the Polish, East German, Czechoslovakian, and Romanian workers? What really matters to the children and the mothers of the children in Ethiopia? What really matters to Ted Turner or Frank Lorenzo? What really matters to Leona Helmsley right now? Or Ronald Reagan? Or George Bush? Or Manuel Noriega? As these questions and the answers they inspired tumbled through my mind, I was tempted again and again to admit the futility of my effort to make it worthwhile for us to gather here this evening. At one point I fantasized that I would simply give the question back to Betty, explaining that my answer to the question is, "Well, that depends." But at that moment, I knew she had me (and that indeed L. D. Johnson would have had me); for Betty's answer would be, "That exactly the point, John. The answer depends upon who you are, etc., and that's why I've asked you to do the lecture. I'm not asking you to do anything more than tell me [us] what *you* think really matters."

From that perspective, then, I will try to answer the question.

To me, self-knowledge really matters. It matters to me that I try to understand how the circumstances of my childhood and my adolescence, my experiences as a student, husband, father, and, indeed, the ups and downs that have characterized my professional life have helped to form the person I am, or think I am. It is important to me to be able to identify the people who were influential in molding or shaping or refining whatever character or personality I have or am. It is necessary to my psychological and moral health that I be (or least try to be) honest with myself when I take pride in my strengths or seek someone to blame for my weaknesses. It is essential to my sense of personal integrity that I attempt to understand why I believe what I believe, say what I say, and do what I do.

I came to Furman University to teach English about thirty-two years ago this past September. Prior to joining this faculty, I had spent eight years at a university preparing to become a college professor; and I had taught during a three-year interim between receiving my MA and beginning my PhD, in order to test the wisdom of my decision to be a teacher. Because, on a brilliantly sunny afternoon sometime in 1945 I had sat alone on a catwalk leading from the hangar deck to the flight deck of a small aircraft carrier on duty in the Pacific Ocean, and I had made a decision to be a college English teacher. I had confronted my aspirations for a career that could have brought fame and fortune, and I had found myself lacking the personal resources that such a career would require, so I set a goal for myself, and I began the long process of trying to achieve it. Along the way I met Francis Bonner, who offered me a position at Furman University. After a short visit on a blustery day to a new campus consisting mainly of four completed buildings, several others in the construction process, a few trees, and a great deal of red mud, I returned to Chapel Hill and told my wife that I felt I had to take the job. The Furman University envisioned by the men and women with whom I had talked was "just the kind of college we have always said we wanted to find." It was a college where I could be a teacher, where I could commit myself fully to being as good a teacher as my talents, my skills, my education, and my personal limitations would allow me to be. That I also became an administrator is probably the great accident in my life. That I continue to teach, however, derives from my need to be who and what I am. Most of the famous lines in Shakespeare's *Hamlet* are spoken by the Danish prince. A major exception, however, is found in the words with which the sententious Polonius concludes his counsel to his son, Laertes:

This above all: to thine own self be true,
And it must follow, as the night the day,
Thou canst now then be false to any man.

It matters; it *really* matters to me that I try to know myself, that I try to be honest with myself about myself.

Education really matters, I believe. As far back into my life as I have been able to travel through memory, I can hear my father telling me that I must get an education, that I must honor my teachers and do what they told me to do, that I must try to learn everything they tried to teach me, and that I must never be satisfied with anything less than the best possible results. Usually that meant no grade below an "A." My father's parents had died when he was just a boy, and while he was in the third grade, he had been taken from school and put to work in a mill. Denied what his brain and his soul hungered for, he demanded that his sons "get an education." I shall never forget the night I received my PhD. Even in those days, the graduating classes at Chapel Hill were so large that only the candidates for the PhD were accorded the privilege of walking across the platform and receiving their diplomas from the hands of the president. So, for the first time, my father actually saw me get a degree. As we talked casually at a family gathering following the ceremony, he suddenly looked at me with deep seriousness and said, "Tonight, I saw my dreams come true. Everything important that I ever wanted to do has happened." What had happened was that I had finally got an education.

But what did my father think would happen to me as I became educated? Well, to be quite honest, he did indeed think that getting an education would prepare me for a good job in this world, and by a good job he meant one that paid a good salary and provided financial security along with the good things available in the world. I can recall even now how he could not hide his disappointment when I told him that I was going to become a teacher, a college English professor. He understood much more easily my brother's decision to be a civil engineer. My father thought that education really mattered because it provided an entry to a vocation or a profession in which, by virtue of ability, knowledge, and hard work, one could rise to success. But in our many conversations on the subject, he revealed to me that he also understood that education has deeper values. He felt fettered, indeed imprisoned, by his lack of education. One of the most intelligent men I have ever known, he felt limited in what he could read and what he could write; he felt stifled in his efforts to say what he was thinking; he felt crippled by his inability to use algebra. So I believe that he did indeed understand (perhaps *feel* would be a more appropriate word) that education really matters not for what it gets for us, but for what it does to us. It really matters because it has the power to set us free — free indeed from poverty and economic subservience — and this is what *really* matters, free from ignorance, free from the intellectual limitations often imposed by one's heritage, free from prejudice, bigotry, pride, emotional subservience to unworthy or false loyalties. Educational institutions deeply committed to these ideals are those very special communities, which we call liberal arts colleges.

In 1974 a faculty committee chaired by Dr. Edgar McKnight presented to the trustees of Furman University a new statement of the college's purpose along with an essay, titled "The Character and Values of Furman University," which, as I have indicated earlier, was authored primarily by L. D. Johnson, who had chaired a blue-ribbon task force appointed by President Blackwell to develop a statement that would "identify and clarify [Furman's] character and values to its faculty, administrators, staff, students, and other constituencies."

To anyone who wonders whether and why education really matters, I recommend a careful reading of both statements. To those gathered here this evening who are students or teachers at Furman, allow me to remind you that our joint commitment has been forcefully asserted in the following phrases: "Furman University…aspires to be a community of scholars which introduces students to the methods and concepts of liberal learning and prepares them for the lifelong process of becoming educated. To achieve this purpose Furman attempts to educate men and women to become responsible citizens and intellectual leaders in the human community. To this end, students at Furman are given opportunities to develop inquiring minds and healthy bodies, an appreciation for intellectual discipline, and an open-minded delight in freedom of inquiry and pursuit of truth. By stressing the arts and sciences, by fostering Christian character, and by emphasizing the value of a broad foundation for specialized careers, Furman aims to develop individual excellence and to prepare students for living as well as for a livelihood."

Defined in these terms, education *clearly* matters. Education *really* matters.

I believe, then, that knowing who one is matters and that knowing all one can know about human beings and their varied environments, past and present, really matter.

I also believe that a sense of living and working, giving and receiving, planning and building, as a vital member of an identifiable community, really matters in one's intellectual and psychological growth and development as a person, as a human being relating happily and productively to other human beings. Speaking in the simplest of terms I can think of, I believe that it really matters that one *belong*, that one belong to some group of persons with reasonably compatible beliefs, aspirations, goals, and commitments; with reasonably compatible views regarding order, law, degree, and those other forces that ultimately govern human conduct and make it possible for us to live in political and social units.

I had the good fortune to grow up in a real neighborhood — one of those old-fashioned neighborhoods that one sometimes sees in a movie set in the 1930s and 1940s. Our street was lined on both sides by single-family houses with just enough space between them to provide a driveway and a three-foot strip of grass or swept dirt. Front yards were small, but most of them attempted to be decorative. There were shrubs and flowers. Front porches with swings, rocking chairs, and pots of ferns and begonias were where the family gathered after supper. Back yards were larger; they were places where children played, where mothers hung the clothes to dry, and where fathers cultivated small gardens in the summer and collard and turnip green patches in the fall. In most of those single-family houses, one would find an assortment of aunts, uncles, and other relatives who had sought refuge from the Depression or from other unfortunate family circumstances. The only elementary school I ever attended was exactly one and a half city blocks from our house. The only high school I ever attended was exactly three and a half blocks from our house. Three grocery stores and a drug store with a soda fountain were less than a ten-minute walk away. Indeed, which grocery store one shopped at was sometimes used as an indication of how well off you were financially. One store was known to be managed by a man with a kind heart who dispensed easy credit. The church I attended, and which I joined when I was a young boy, stood on the crest of a hill precisely six houses away from our house. Behind our house were acres of open fields, rolling hills, a little creek that cut its way through large rocks. There was also a little branch (a Southern term for a brook) alongside of which tall weeping willows actually grew aslant. I lived in that community until I was eighteen years old. My family, my friends, my teachers, my role models, some of my aunts, uncles, and cousins, people whom I loved, whom I feared, and some of whom I strongly disliked — they were all there. I felt secure; I felt that I was a part of a place, a person within a place who functioned constructively or destructively in that place. Ever since I first read any of his poetry, I have felt that Wordsworth was right: The child *is* father of the man, and that community (a complex of working-class, uneducated people struggling against or submitting to poverty, ignorance, and a hundred and one different prejudices) played a major role in fathering me.

Furman University is the community in which I have lived out my adult life. As I indicated earlier in these remarks, when I arrived here in 1957, the

Furman University that had moved to Greenville in the middle of the nineteenth century had, in a sense, been achieved. Within a year, Furman would move to a new campus, and everybody talked about new buildings, new resources, new opportunities. A few people dreamed of and talked about a new potential, and they charted courses for the future. As I said to you earlier, when I returned to Chapel Hill after a four-hour day in which I was "interviewed" by Dean Bonner and Dean Tibbs, enjoyed brief conversations with Jim Stewart and Al Reid, and experienced a remarkably formal meeting with Dr. John Laney Plyler, Anne asked me what I was going to do about the job. I responded that I felt I had to take it because Furman seemed about to become just the kind of college we wanted to be a part of. And so we came, in a hand-me-down car, with our two boys and a five-month-old daughter, and an unfinished dissertation. And we have been a part of the fellowship of this community for thirty-two years, and that has really mattered.

When L. D. Johnson, assisted by a number of his colleagues, wrote "The Character and Values of Furman University," he composed a classic description of the community he hoped Furman would become and always be. It seems to me appropriate that we listen to his words tonight:

> Furman is a person-centered community, emphasizing the prime worth of persons and encouraging concern for others. Development of proper regard for the rights and feelings of others constitutes one of the Christian college's higher callings. Christian love requires us to view others as persons to be respected rather than as objects to be used, and to treat them as we would like to be treated. Concern for persons is expressed in the academic community through continuing efforts to: express sincere interest in the spiritual, emotional, physical and financial needs of all persons in the Furman community; build a sense of community through open communication among administrators, faculty, staff and students; express appreciation of loyalty to the community, and recognize unusual efforts on its behalf whether at academic, administrator, service, or student levels; encourage students and faculty to make commitment to academic and personal achievement; cultivate pride in and appreciation for the community's heritage, the contributions of predecessors who have given shape to the institution; [and] appropriately involve all members of the community in the process of decisions which affect the community's life.

I believe that when L. D. and his colleagues wrote those words, they were expressing what they hoped Furman would become. I further believe that Furman has achieved that kind of community identity and that the qualities set forth in this statement make Furman the unique institution I believe it to be. Being a part of such a community has mattered, *really* mattered, to me. To have known and to know, to have worked with and to work with John Plyler, Gordon Blackwell, and John Johns; Francis Bonner and L. D. Johnson; Ernie Harrill, Marguerite Chiles, and Tank Hardaway; Winston Babb, Carlyle Ellett, Don Clanton, and Sandy Molnar; DuPre Rhame and Arnold Putman; Tom Flowers and Lindsay Smith, Schaefer Kendrick, Al Sanders, and Bill Leverette; Theron Price and T. C. Smith; John Hoskins and Currie McArthur; Al Reid, Jim Stewart, and David Smith — has mattered in my life.

In my final few moments, I find myself becoming uncomfortably personal; but in order to be true to the task that making this lecture set for me, I can't avoid the situation. For I must tell you that loving and being loved really matter in my world — and, I believe, in everybody's world. Having said it, I'm not sure how to elaborate upon the point. Indeed, when I first walked into the maze of reflection and thought through which I had to work my way in order to provide these remarks to you tonight, when I first asked myself, "John, what *really* matters in your life?", the answer came to me very quickly — "Anne, the children, our family, my mother. I have to start with them." They are, for me, in this life, the ultimate community from which I derive the joy that fuels my life. I love them, and they love me. All the unpleasant responses that we have made and will continue to make to each other within the complex of the events and activities of our lives are merely accidental. The love we have for each other is fundamental. They have loved me when I have been vain, stupid, unkind, unfair, trivial, and morally and ethically shallow. They have nurtured me and sustained me.

I am, therefore, fearful for a society that, for a while at least, has seemed to think that "relationships" will provide a firm and strong enough foundation for happy and fulfilling human lives. I just don't believe it.

I have come to the end of my contribution to the L. D. Johnson Memorial Lecture Series without a single direct reference to the life of the spirit. I have told you that I believe that making an honest and continuous effort to know and understand one's self really matters; that working hard to educate one's self to know as much as one can know about the natural, political, social, and human world into which we are born and in which we must live really matters; that being a part of a community in which the concern of others for us and our concern for them fosters our personhood really matter; and, finally, that loving specific persons and being loved by them really matter. I have focused my attention upon what really matters to me in the world in which I live and work and have responsibility for others.

So I have avoided the largest of the issues — what *ultimately* matters. And as I tried to find a way to explain to you briefly why I had chosen to limit my consideration this evening to human relationships, I ran across the following statement from a famous modern philosopher, and he says it for me just beautifully: "To know and to serve God, of course, is why we're here, a clear truth that, like the nose on your face, is here at hand and easily discernible but can make you dizzy if you try to focus on it hard." I am grateful to Garrison Keillor for helping me explain why I chose not to risk the dizziness.

# Albert Blackwell
## Religion
*October 8, 1990*

If my assigned topic for this evening had been "What Matters Most to Me," I could have entertained you with a list of my consuming loves, with the music of Mozart very near the top and football at the bottom. One measure of what matters most to us is the amount of time we devote to our various pursuits. By this measure I would have to say that it matters a great deal to me to have things working properly, and since we all know that things do not work properly on their own, I spend a lot of time coaxing things to work and trying to keep them in working order. I mean things like the furnace and the back screen door. I want pianos to be in tune, cars to start, and windows not to stick. I hate the wobble in my daughter Jody's bicycle wheel and the warble in her Walkman. As a result, I spend prodigious amounts of time trying to remedy these mechanical ills, and I enjoy it. My ideal recreation is to stroll the aisles of a well-stocked hardware store.

If anyone is interested, you can find a clue to this compulsive behavior on my part in Auld Hardware, that wonderful relic of another century at the joining of Rutherford Road and Poinsett Highway. Ask the proprietor, Al, to show you the octagonal rotating bolt case at the back of the store — the one with a small brass nameplate reading "A. R. Brown, Erwin, Tennessee. Patented May 7, 1901." Albert Rosecrans Brown was my grandfather. He spent his early career as a traveling salesman, driving his buggy over Eastern Tennessee and western North Carolina, taking orders for W. W. Woodruff & Company, Wholesale Hardware, of Knoxville. Later, he established and operated a general store in Erwin, A. R. Brown and Company. My mother, Olive, worked in the family store office and tells me that my grandfather's favorite department was always hardware. And so, as we say, I come by my compulsion naturally.

If, I say, my assigned topic for this evening had been "What Matters Most to Me," I would tell you all this. But the L. D. Johnson Memorial Lectures committee has headed off this risk. They have not licensed me to speak on "What Matters Most to Me," but have assigned me the very different topic — "What Really Matters?" I have before me here my two lists under these different headings. Give me just a moment to compare them. No, they are not identical. In truth, they have only a little overlap. From this we may conclude several things. First, the L. D. Johnson Memorial Lectures committee is a wise committee. You are to be spared the indignity of having me unfurl my list of pet peeves and petty preferences as if it were a chart of the moral universe. Second, since my list of what matters most to me is not congruent with my list of what really matters, I am apparently not a saint — something that will not surprise the committee and, I suppose, is good for me to learn. Third, my challenge for this evening is something more difficult than autobiography, though autobiography will be involved, and something much more valuable as well — assuming that I can find something intelligible to say.

What really matters is not to make things work but to do the right thing, and as filmmaker Spike Lee has recently shown us, this sometimes requires that we bring the normal working of things to a halt. To be more exact, I prefer to say that what really matters is to *be* the right thing. What really matters is to try to be a good person.

At this point I can almost hear some of my colleagues thinking, "Oh this is rich, Albert! The committee gives you six months' advance notice for this lecture, and you bring us together to serve up a platitude: 'to try to be a good person.' Spare us! Unfurl that list of peeves and preferences you mentioned and let's be out of here. 'To try to be a good person' — really, is this truism the best you can do?"

Well, this does seem to be the best I have been able to do. But is it a truism? I do not think so. If an assertion is a truism, then it permits no live alternatives. But here our culture offers us a host of live alternatives. To say that what really matters is to try to be a good person is *not* to say that what really matters is to try to be a rich person, a famous person, an established person, a churchgoing person, an educated person, a person of taste, a talented person, a competitive person, a clever person, a well-liked person, a well-trimmed person, a well-toned person, an odor-free person, a sexy person, a fast-lane person, a Marlboro person, a person who's come a long way, baby, or a low-cholesterol person. Barbara Ehrenreich, writing in (of all places) *Lear's* magazine recently asked:

> Since when is breakfast cereal a *moral* issue? Morality is no longer a prominent feature of civil society. But…as virtue drained out of our public lives, it reappeared in our cereal bowls, and our exercise regimens. We redefined virtue as health. And considering the probable state of our souls, this was not a bad move. By relocating the seat of virtue from the soul to the pecs, the abs, and the coronary arteries, we may not have become the most virtuous people on earth, but we surely became the most desperate for

grace.... To say we want to be healthy is to gravely understate the case. We want to be *good*....

Somehow, we need to find our way back to being healthy without being. Health is great. It makes us bouncier and probably happier. Better yet, it can make us fit *for* something: strong enough to fight the big-time polluters, for example, the corporate waste dumpers; tough enough to take on economic arrangements that condemn so many to poverty, to dangerous occupations; lean and powerful enough to demand a more nurturing, less anxiety-ridden social order. Health is good. But it is not, as even the ancient and athletic Greeks would have said, *the* good.

In light of Ehrenreich's observation, our challenge for this hour is to shed some light on the good — on what makes a person good, and not just healthy and happy. The key to this pursuit is to be found in the word Ehrenreich employs four times in her account of our present moral predicament — the word "virtue." For, as the ancient and athletic Socrates, Plato, and Aristotle defined them, the virtues are those qualities that make us good.

Here we see the real wisdom of the L. D. Johnson Memorial Lectures committee in focusing our evening on the question of what really matters. For, while I have been tinkering with things for about half a century now, humankind has been working at the question of what makes us good for some four millennia and more. Whereas my peeves and preferences are but idiosyncrasies, a myriad of persons and societies have left record of their struggles with the question of what really matters. And so we do not have to start our inquiry from scratch, or settle for my subjective judgments.

Now, to be sure, we do not have to accept the traditional virtues just as we find them or adopt them uncritically. One advantage of a perennial and ongoing tradition is that the centuries allow us time to examine it and expose and discuss its weaknesses, and a vital tradition embraces salutary changes with every new generation. Professor Jaroslav Pelikan of Yale tells us that tradition is the living faith of the dead, while traditionalism is the dead faith of the living. Emphasizing the difference between tradition, in this organic sense, and moribund traditionalism, I would like to say that I consider it foolish solipsism to ignore our traditions, to assume that because they are old they lack relevance in our time. My assumption is exactly the opposite: Our time, like every time, needs the accumulated wisdom of our race.

The tradition I want to invoke this evening goes back through Mary Wollstonecraft, Lord Shaftesbury, Aquinas, Augustine, the Apostle Paul, Cicero, and a host of others to the classical Greeks who defined and debated the virtues as those qualities that make us good. According to this tradition, what really matters is to live a life of virtue. And so we need to try to understand what virtue is and to specify particular virtues.

One of the things that matters to me, though we might debate whether or not it really matters, is to see what Frank and Ernest are up to on the cartoon page of each morning's newspaper. Sometime during the past summer, one of these characters — so utterly without redeeming social merit that I find them irresistible — was in his typical slouch across the desk from an employment agent. The agent says to him, "Well, you're the first applicant who has listed as a qualification that you are biodegradable." We laugh at this because biodegradability is a human quality all right, but it is not an aptitude, not an excellence, not a virtue. Likewise, our lives express many qualities, some universally human, some peculiarly our own, giving variety and color to our social world. But which of these many qualities deserve to be called virtues?

Before we go too far, let me grant that "virtue" is, or has become, a pretty stuffy word — more the subject of parody than an object of respect. Mark Twain once described an acquaintance as "a good man of the worst sort," and we all know what he means. The last time I heard the word "virtue" used in ordinary conversation, someone quipped, "I'm afraid her virtue is showing." It was not a friendly remark. Yet the last decade has seen a renaissance of academic interest in this term and the traditions behind it — though as with many of our academic interests, it has been rather more theoretical than practical. Thus, we confirm Henry David Thoreau's observation that there are nine hundred and ninety-nine patrons of virtue to every virtuous person.

Traditionally, virtue has meant strength of character, with the particular virtues as the admirable qualities, the habits of heart and mind and will and imagination, that constitute good character. Exactly what these qualities are has been the subject of perennial discussion. Differing cultures, eras, philosophical schools, and individual persons have produced different lists, of different lengths. As a way of trying to simplify this complex situation, Greeks, Romans and Christians alike have labored at refining a list of "cardinal virtues" — from the Latin *cardo* or "hinge" — upon which all the other virtues pivot. By the thirteenth-century writings of Aquinas, four classical virtues stemming from Socrates had been joined with the three Christian graces immortalized by the Apostle Paul to yield the seven cardinal virtues of the classical-Christian synthesis.

According to this tradition, then, what really matters is to live a life of prudence, justice, temperance, and fortitude, faith, hope and love. A good person's distinguishing qualities pivot on these hinges — not to the exclusion of other qualities, to be sure. Socrates was an ironist and a wit. Aquinas's genius at systematic presentation amounts to artistry. But though a good person's life may be witty, ironic, artistic, and a thousand other engaging qualities besides, its goodness does not rotate about those qualities. They matter less than the cardinal seven.

Immediately, a host of questions occur to us. Is this the only possible list of pivotal virtues? Does not the very number seven suggest arbitrary selection and manipulation? Even granting this classical-Christian list, who is to define what constitutes justice or faith? And are not these cardinals too confining to distinguish the life of a good person of real flesh and blood and tears of sorrow and joy? I want to come to this last question at the end and suggest a fuller list of qualities, less confining and more cordial, that for me define the highest ideal for a good life, for what really matters. But before I do, let me try to respond to some of the more obvious questions concerning the very idea of virtue: briefly, then, six of the more common objections to the tradition of the virtues, and then to close, a larger constellation of qualities that I believe make us good persons and are therefore what really matters.

The first objection is that the virtues are only abstractions, far removed from the heartbeat of our lives. Well, concrete is abstract until it is mixed and molded. Fortitude is abstract, until we see it in Mahatma Gandhi's moral determination, deterred by no force on earth. Humility is but a word, until we see the salutary effects of Mother Teresa's submission to what she believes to be God's will. Temperance is a percussive sound, until we succeed in cutting our twenty-two gallons of gasoline a week back to fourteen. Hope is merely eternal, until we write Representative Liz Patterson a letter concerning gun control or the death penalty. A kinder, gentler nation is windy rhetoric, until we stop spending the peace dividend on the military and adopt a kinder, gentler budget.

Father Divine used to say that we need to "tangibilitate" the gospel. So we need to tangibilitate the virtues. As for the Christian gospel, it came already tangibilitated. Christ did not counsel his followers to be generous, but told them "Give to everyone who begs from you." Christ's spiritual genius was in being concrete, vivid, indelibly memorable — and himself embodying the principles he taught. The Christian term for this is incarnation: that, in Christ, God's eternal Word became not words, but flesh. Now, I am a Christian because I was born one — because Albert Rosecrans and Tuppy Leanna Brown in eastern Tennessee, and Ransom Lemuel and Mary Lousetta Blackwell in central South Carolina, and their children Olive and Hoyt, my parents, were Christians. But I continue to embrace my Christian tradition in part because I find this doctrine of incarnation ineluctable and compelling.

We will do well to consider a second objection to the tradition of virtue, namely that it is a sure source of the deadly sin of pride. Pride is especially a danger for people like me who have known lives of comfort, acceptance, and plenty, insulated from the importuning temptations associated with affliction, rejection, and impoverishment. I feel well warned by the realism of William Thackeray, in his novel drawing its title from this cardinal sin, *Vanity Fair*. "Think what right have you to be scornful, whose virtue is [but] a deficiency of temptation." Our challenge, I think, is to keep alive our capacity for righteous indignation without toppling over into self-righteousness. The hinge virtue here is temperance: We must temper our scorn with honest self-reflection. A life of virtue is thus a precarious balancing.

In thinking of this ideal, and this danger, I think of the friend whom I, together with my valued colleagues who have preceded me in this series of lectures, am privileged to memorialize. L. D. Johnson managed this moral balancing as well as anyone I have known. Many of us shall never forget how, in defense of things that really matter, his scorching oratorical gift could give vent to righteous indignation. Yet none of us knew our finitude and mortality and tendencies to pride more existentially than L. D. Johnson, and more than most of us he refused the hypocrisies by which we attempt to hide our self-righteousness.

In L. D.'s Christian tradition and mine, the principal voice warning against the pride of virtue is the Apostle Paul's. Quoting the psalmist of his own beloved tradition of Judaism, he writes to the Christians in Rome: " 'None is righteous, no, not one.' For all have sinned and fall short of the glory of God." Paul seems to have believed that if we measure our lives by the requirements of moral perfection, then one of two results is inevitable: Either we will deceive ourselves as hypocrites, or we will despair over our failures. The Christian term for this human condition is original sin. I am a Christian because I was born one. But I continue to embrace my Christianity in part because I find this doctrine of original sin thoroughly realistic.

A third objection to the tradition of virtue is that it is too relativistic to offer us guidance. We speak of justice as a rational virtue. But as Alasdair MacIntyre asks in the title of his most recent, most valuable, and almost unreadable book, *Whose Justice? Which Rationality?*, even within our own cultural tradition we have to consider the justice of Jesse Helms and the justice of Jesse Jackson. Not to mention Jesse James. Then, we encounter concepts of justice in other cultures that bewilder us with their alien moral and legal traditions. Our college's commitment to pluralism leads us to encounter other traditions deliberately. But how are we to keep a footing in this shifting sand?

I believe that our pluralism can lead to health if we first of all agree to live with our deepest differences. We must be prepared to begin with arguments over what should be argued. For that fundamental argument, I believe, the virtues offer a possible beginning point. Our dialogue might run something like this:

> What is justice?
> Whatever justice is, it seems to matter doesn't it?
> But your notion of justice is so different from ours!
> If our views are so different, then perhaps we'd better pursue this question together.
> But in this way justice is so uncertain and elusive and slow in coming!
> Yes, but injustice is so painfully immediate and palpable; had we not better get started?

So our pursuit of justice presents a formidable and neverending prospect. But given the urgency and complexity of the injustices to be overcome, what else can we do, and what else might we expect? Thoreau again: "Oh, ye who would have your coconuts wrongside outwards!"

The requisite virtues here would appear to be fortitude and faith. We may define classical fortitude as persisting in the pursuit of virtue in spite of difficulty. Faith is not so easy to define and is subject to more abuse. William James tells of a schoolchild asked to explain faith. "Faith," replied the child, "is when you believe something that you know ain't true." But biblical faith is not believing something that you know ain't true. Biblical faith is trusting something that you think *is* true. Faith is daring to trust our convictions enough to put them to the test of action and experience. Such trust involves risk and requires courage, as Paul Tillich insists in his little theological classic *Dynamics of Faith*. Even Christ himself, when called good by an over-eager contemporary, replied "Why do you call me good? No one is good but God alone." And yet Christ taught "You therefore must be perfect, as your heavenly Father is perfect." Biblical faith, as I understand it, is this maintaining of commitment in the absence of certainty, and I continue to embrace Christianity in part because I find this doctrine of faith ennobling and enabling.

We citizens of the United States, with our pathological tendencies to privatism, must take especially seriously a fourth objection to the tradition of virtue, namely, that it is too individualistic. Here, it depends on which advocate of virtue we consider. It is true that some of the Stoic philosophers who lived during the decline and disintegration of classical Greece and amidst the impersonality of imperial Rome, having little control over the larger political and social life of their cultures, tended to limit their applications of virtue to individual life. But even Epictetus, the former slave of Emperor Nero's secretary, addresses the question of social obligation directly, with advice that we ignore today at approximately the cost of the recent Savings and Loan bailout: " 'What place, then,' " say you, " 'shall I hold in the state?' " Whatever you can hold with the preservation of your fidelity and honor. But if, by desiring to be useful to the state, you lose these qualities, how can you serve your country, faithless and shameless?"

Aristotle, near the root of the Western tradition of virtue, saw virtue not as individualistic, but as embedded and embodied in the life of the city-state. Likewise, in Lord Shaftesbury's publication of 1714, *An Inquiry Concerning Virtue*, tiny in size but vast in influence, he introduces his principal term in a public, not a private, context: "AND in the Case alone it is we call any Creature *Worthy* or *Virtuous*, when it can have the Notion of a publick Interest, and can attain the Speculation or Science of what is morally good or ill, admirable or blamable, right or wrong."

And Mary Wollstonecraft in her pioneering book of 1792, *A Vindication of the Rights of Woman*, presents virtue in the widest possible social dimension: "It is then an affection for the whole human race that makes my pen dart rapidly along to support what I believe to be the cause of virtue." Wollstonecraft argues that women should be granted equal access to education and social opportunity, and thus equal access to what she calls the "grand end" of human beings, namely, "the dignity of conscious virtue." But she bases her argument not in concern for individual rights, not even in concern for gender rights, but in her passion for human well-being. "To render women pleasing at the expense of every solid virtue," she writes, "is to degrade one half of the human species." It is to rob our species of one half of its potential virtue. Needless to add, this is a robbery our species can ill afford.

It has been said that one distinguishing mark of the virtues is that for a person to exercise these qualities is not to rob another person of them. This is not a completely simple proposition, but an example might help to make its intention clear. Winning cannot be a virtue by this criterion, for if I win, you must lose; cooperation, in contrast, sometimes makes the lists of virtues. This is one reason why the music of Mozart appears near the top of my list of things that matter most to me, and football at the bottom — though the main reason, I must confess, is simply that the music of Mozart sounds better. My striving to catch a wisp of Mozart's sublimity at the piano need not inhibit your attempt to do the same. Indeed, we can combine our attempts in Mozart's piano music for four hands. But though football is a team sport (and even I can appreciate some of the game's finesse), still if Furman is to win, The Citadel must lose.

The biblical term for the ideal society of virtue is the kingdom of God. From the beginning of Israel's story to the final biblical images of the closing of the age, God's kingdom is a state of social solidarity. At the creation of the Israelite nation in the exodus narrative, Israel is called to be a people holy to the LORD. We get a good glimpse of what this entails in chapter 25 of Leviticus, where Moses stipulates that in this sanctified society the poor are to be given whatever they need, freely and without begrudging; that no interest is to be charged those whose needs are met through loans; that Israelites are not to enslave each other and may redeem themselves from servitude at any time they can provide fair payment; that every third year, a tithe of produce is to be stored to provision sojourners, orphans, widows, and Levites; that every seventh year, all unpaid debts are to be canceled and all servants released, with sufficient provisions of flocks, grain, and wine to get them started again; and that every fiftieth year, all agricultural property is to be redistributed to restore ownership to the original families. This is not creeping socialism. This is human solidarity sprung full-grown from the mind of Yahweh.

Similarly, in the concluding act of the biblical drama, contrary to the notions of many, Christians are not privately snatched up to be with their Lord. (Perhaps you have seen the bumper sticker, "Caution: In case of the Rapture this car will be unoccupied!" This is not a slogan of Christian faith but a specimen of Christian snottiness.) Rather, God's holy city comes down to be the dwelling place of a holy people. And all in between the exodus and the new Jerusalem, the biblical concern is less with getting a few individuals into heaven than with introducing a bit of heaven into human society. I continue to embrace my Christian tradition in part because I find this doctrine of the kingdom of God steeped in hope for society and profoundly motivating.

Commentaries have suggested that the "kingship" of God is a better phrase for the biblical concept than the "kingdom" of God. I agree, as the word "kingdom" inevitably suggests a sacred place rather than a sanctified state of mind and heart and society. But the kingship of God invokes a fifth criticism of the tradition of virtue, namely, that the tradition is too hierarchical. The problem is not simply the masculinity of "kingship." Many have already remedied that problem by employing the phrase "God's sovereignty." (For me the word "sovereign" always brings to mind the image of Queen Elizabeth I.) The problem remains. It is the converse of the problem of individualism, namely, that the image of divine sovereignty throttles mutuality and threatens human liberty. This is a fundamental issue. Is virtue decreed to us, or is it our creation?

Allow me to speak briefly in support of a hierarchical view of virtue, though my opinions here have been chastened by the significant debates over this issue in our time. I believe that as arithmetic is given, in a way that mathematicians must acknowledge; as gravity is given, in a way that physicists must accept; as the overtone series is given, with which musicians must cooperate; so the moral structure of the cosmos is given, which we must honor if human well-being is to prosper. Our particular laws are not given. These we must discover and invent, as a composer must discover and invent a melody. But I believe that the fundamental moral structure conditioning all our ethical discovery and invention is given, and like the physicist who pretends exemption from gravity, we ignore this fundamental givenness at our peril. The reality by which our particular moral laws are tested comes from the creator God patterned with moral grain. With respect to this fundamental givenness, it is true that we exercise no reciprocity; we enjoy no absolute freedom.

The result of our absolute dependence upon this divine sovereignty, however, is the most thoroughgoing mutuality, embracing all creatures, great and small. As number transcends the idiosyncrasies of mathematicians and undergirds the American Mathematical Society; as gravity transcends the quirks (and quarks) of physicists and binds the American Physical Society; as the overtone series transcends the preening of musicians and accounts for the harmonies of the Emerson String Quartet; so the givenness of the cosmos transcends and morally unites all creatures in the most comprehensive mutuality. No other mutuality is as deeply grounded. We say that we are bound together by economic interdependence, and so we are, but recession strikes and we turn on one another with protective tariffs and cutthroat competition. We say that we are bound together by dependence upon a common planet, and so we are, but already we are reading science-fiction accounts of spacecraft commandeered by a few, determined upon abandoning a fouled planet Earth to save themselves by colonizing elsewhere in the galaxy. We say that we are bound together by our common humanity, and so we are, but our century does not have to be told the atrocities inflicted when some group decides that another group is inhuman, subhuman, or anti-human.

Our profoundest mutuality, I believe, is that we are all children of the cosmic God, from whom, as the psalmist recognizes, there is no fleeing:

> Whither shall I go from thy Spirit?
>     Or whither shall I flee from thy presence?
> If I ascend to heaven, thou art there!
>     If I make my bed in Sheol, thou art there!
> If I take the wings of the morning
>     and dwell in the uttermost parts of the sea,
> even there thy hand shall lead me,
>     and thy right hand shall hold me.

What image shall we use for this mutuality of our common cosmic parent-hood? It is more profound than that of common paternity, since paternity is sometimes subject to ambiguity. Our mutuality is at least as profound as that of the common divine maternity suggested in chapter 8 of Proverbs.

Perhaps the question of hierarchical threat to our freedom and independence is especially intense for us as US citizens, born under a Declaration against "absolute Despotism," and living under a Constitution that secures "the Blessings of Liberty to ourselves and our Posterity." Matthew Arnold once said that "freedom is a good horse to ride — but to ride somewhere." So, I think, with our constitutional liberties. Our Constitution's legal guarantees of liberty were written against the moral background of the Declaration of Independence, with its language of inalienable rights endowed by the Creator, granted by "the Laws of Nature and of Nature's God." Precisely what these rights are, and exactly how they are best secured, continues to be a matter of struggle and debate in our country, as it has been for over 200 years and will continue to be as long as our republic shall endure. Yet these debates and struggles have, for the greatest part, shared the assumption of our nation's founders that human rights are not accidental — not merely the product of chance or human taste or arbitrary choice — but, rather, despite their obscurity and ambivalence, are finally patterned by the God-given moral grain of the cosmos.

So too with the virtue required if human rights and dignity are to thrive. James Madison was particularly explicit and eloquent in expressing this article of republican faith:

> I go on this great republican principle, that the people will have virtue and intelligence to select [representatives] of virtue and wisdom. Is there no virtue among us? If there be not, we are in a wretched situation. No theoretical checks, no form of government can render us secure. To suppose that any form of government will secure liberty or happiness without any virtue in the people is a chimerical idea.

Our horse of legal freedom, Madison believed, must be bridled with civic virtue, lest it turn maverick and run away to our mutual disaster.

As for the particular civic virtues Madison had in mind, we may see them personified in George Willoughby Maynard's nineteenth-century paintings in Pompeian style, which anchor the four corners of the lavish Jefferson Building of the Library of Congress in Washington. They are Fortitude and Justice, Patriotism and Courage, Temperance and Prudence, Industry and Concord. Freedom, we may notice, is not among these democratic virtues. Freedom never appears among the traditional lists of virtues. Freedom is a good horse to ride, but to ride somewhere.

In summary, the tradition of virtue has argued that the qualities making us good — in this case, good citizens — are not random or arbitrary. They are complex and elusive, but they are not, in Madison's word, "chimerical." Martin Luther King, Jr., expressed this conviction like a refrain in his sermons: "The universe swings on moral hinges." This is, of course, a confession of faith — a declaration of commitment in the absence of certainty, an affirmation of trust in something that we think is true, trust sufficient to put our convictions to the test of action and experience. More particularly, Martin Luther King, Jr., was declaring faith in a sovereign God of justice and mercy. I continue to embrace my Christian tradition in part because I find the doctrine of God's sovereignty insusceptible of doubt, and because I observe that belief in God's justice and mercy is reflected in reality as healing and wholesome.

Now, before I recommend the particular virtues with which I would like to conclude, a sixth and final problem with the tradition of virtue. Are the virtues not too nearly impossible? How many of us can aspire to be a Martin Luther King, Jr., or a Gandhi or Mother Teresa? Not I, certainly. And so, finally, I am not a Stoic, but a Puritan, a forgiven sinner.

This little confession brings us to that most beguiling of subjects: sin. We learn a lot about ourselves in realizing how much more fascinating the deadly sins are than the cardinal virtues. Also seven in number, the deadly sins may be listed with the aid of a mnemonic device employing their first letters: L for lust, A for avarice, S for sloth, V for vanity, E for envy, G for gluttony, A for anger, and S again for sins — LAS VEGAS. You see, already our interest is picking up! Some of you will recall Garrison Keillor's remark at Furman a couple of summers ago as the Southern Baptist Convention was preparing to assemble in Las Vegas. Keillor claimed that the Baptist intent was "to put the fun back in fundamentalism."

Well, I hate to disappoint you, but I am not going to talk much about the seven deadly sins tonight. I can do no better than to recommend Henry Fairlie's irrepressible book, titled *The Seven Deadly Sins Today*. Fairlie serves up his moral theme with more ginger than I have found in any other book I have ever read. But, frankly, I believe that for most of us in this room our sins are not the colorful big seven. Nor are our sins those of unconcern and indifference, represented in a *New Yorker* cartoon picturing the three monkeys who traditionally have seen, heard, and spoken no evil, but who are re-captioned for our age: "Wherever. Whoever. Whatever." We are not unconcerned or indifferent; we are just so damned busy. Ours are the skimpy sins of distraction and neglect. The traditional Christian confession concerning sins of omission, things left undone, was certainly worded for people like me. Mine are not the flashy sins of Las Vegas, but the daily distractions of middle-class life. I intend to write Representative Patterson about El Salvador, I really do, but right this minute I've got to find the right batteries for my VCR remote unit.

Instead of reveling in the seven deadly sins, I would like to suggest a list of seven cardinal distractions. I have borrowed this list in part from L. D. Johnson, and have arranged it alliteratively, again for purposes of recollection — though, of course, our problem is not in remembering these distractions, but rather in trying to put them out of our minds. Like the cardinal virtues, our cardinal distractions are four plus three: comfort, convenience, consumerism, and commerce, appearance, affluence, and achievement. These are distractions that constantly divert me from a life of mixing and molding and balancing the virtues that really matter.

Which brings me back to my love of making things work. The tension between my compulsion to keep things working and my awareness that these things are finally not what really matters, I think, explains why I so easily fly off the handle when stubborn things refuse to respond to my ministrations: when simply pulling out a bookcase yawns into a cleaning job greater than that recently lavished upon the Sistine Chapel ceiling; when paint intended for my ceiling performs a Jackson Pollock number on my floor. A little time spent at this is fine, I keep thinking, but do I really wish to dedicate my life to these stupid things? Recreation, yes, but vocation? And as my tolerant family can testify, sometimes in these moments my frustration rises to the level of the colorful sin of anger.

On the whole, however, this is not the dynamics of an heroic morality. I know that Nietzsche would be disappointed in me. But the Apostle Paul would not be surprised: "For all have sinned and fall short of the glory of God" — including, we must assume, even bland and usually mild-mannered professors of religion. Paul's advice to us is to place our faith in the ancient tradition of Judaism — taught by the peacemaker Abigail and the prophet Nathan to David; taught by David to all who have read and sung and prayed the seven penitential psalms; taught by the great eighth-century prophets; taught by John the Baptist, crying in the wilderness; taught by Christ from the commencement of his ministry in Galilee, and exemplified by Christ in one of his seven last words from the cross. It is the tradition of repentance, forgiveness, and amendment of life.

Biblical religion is not a religion for moral heroes. Even Paul himself sometimes forgets this, as when he writes of Abraham: "No distrust made him waver concerning the promise of God...fully convinced that God was able to do what he had promised." Likewise the author of Hebrews, who writes, "By faith Sarah herself received power to conceive, even when she was past the age, since she considered him faithful who had promised."

Both of these New Testament writers seem to forget that Abraham's first response to the news that he and Sarah were to bear a son in their dotage was to fall on his face in laughter, and that an eavesdropping Sarah also laughed, and then lied about it and got scolded. Biblical religion is not a religion for moral heroes. It is a religion for persons aspiring to moral life who need to acknowledge failure. "I have not come to call the righteous," Christ says to the self-righteous who are criticizing him at a party, "but sinners to repentance."

Finally, of course, Paul gives this teaching of Christ central place. "Do you not know that God's kindness is meant to lead you to repentance?", Paul asks the Roman Christians. And then, in chapter 4 of his letter to the Romans, he reiterates his basic teaching: that though we are not righteous, if we trust the way of repentance and amendment of life enough to put it to the test of action and experience, that the God of righteousness and mercy will forgive our wrongdoing. Though we are not righteous, says Paul, we are "reckoned" so (Revised Standard Version), or "counted" so (King James Version and New English Bible), or "considered" so (Jerusalem Bible), or "accepted" as so (Today's English Version), or "credited" with being so (New International Version). Whatever the best English translation, the Greek word recurs in this one chapter ten times. It appears to be important.

Paul seems to mean by this repeated phrase that repentance cannot undo the temporal consequences of our wrongdoing. Uriah, for example, murdered by King David, cannot be brought back to life to kiss away Bathsheba's tears of lamentation. But repentance can lift the eternal burden of guilt and issue in renewal of life, as when David, to the astonishment of his servants, "arose from the earth, and washed, and anointed himself, and changed his clothes; and he went in to the house of the LORD, and worshipped; he then went to his own house; and when he asked, they set food before him, and he ate. Then David comforted his wife, Bathsheba."

The Christian doctrine summarizing this process of repentance, forgiveness and amendment of life is salvation by grace through faith. Its summary by the author of The First Letter of John could not be more concise: "If we say we have no sin, we deceive ourselves, and the truth is not in us. If we confess our sins, God is faithful and just, and will forgive our sins and cleanse us from all unrighteousness."

Many of you will recall a bestseller of about a dozen years ago, titled *I'm OK and You're OK*. That book prompted the chaplain of Yale University at that time, William Sloane Coffin, Jr., to remark that while the book might offer therapy to some, it represented poor biblical theology. Coffin threatened to counter with his own book, titled *I'm Not OK and You're Not OK, and That's OK*. I continue to embrace my Christian tradition in part because

I find this doctrine of salvation by grace — through trust in Christ's way of repentance, forgiveness, and amendment of life — a painful but healing doctrine.

The virtues enter this healing process at two points: at the beginning, when honestly comparing our lives to these transcendent ideals leads us to repentance; and at the end, when these ideals guide us in our attempts to amend our forgiven lives. This second role of the virtues explains why Paul, the great preacher of salvation by grace through faith, gives us list after list of the virtues that should guide the faithful — and also some lists of juicy vices to avoid. His lists include the four classical virtues: prudence (or discernment), temperance (or self-control), justice (or righteousness), and fortitude (or steadfastness and endurance). And Paul originates the triad of Christian graces: faith, hope, and love. But this list of the traditional seven by no means exhausts Paul's recommendations of virtue.

This past summer, to celebrate our twenty-fifth wedding anniversary, Marian and I took off on a lark to satisfy one of our frustrated passions. I am referring to our shared interest in amateur star-gazing. Knowing that we would have to escape the humid haze of our eastern summers, we simply took down the *Almanac* and looked up the driest place in the country for the first week in August. It was Death Valley. (No, no — the important Death Valley, way out West.) So we picked the second driest place, Boise, Idaho, and sure enough, we had one good and two wonderful nights to view the stars, though the smoke of range and forest fires kept us on the move. Marian worked at the constellations on the macro level, and I wrestled with our son Christopher's sixteen-power telescope to search them at the micro level. In one of the moments that gives me goosebumps even in recollection, we focused attention on the constellation of the seven sisters, the Pliades — singled out by both the book of Job and the prophet Amos as a particular splendor of God's vast creation. Among and around the points of light visible to the naked eye our little scope disclosed a glorious cluster of scores of additional stars.

And so it is through the lens of New Testament writings. Among and around the seven cardinal virtues and graces we find a score of ancillary virtues to guide the faithful — repentant and thankful enough for their forgiveness to wish to amend their lives. Are these Christian virtues, then? Heavens no, no more than the stars are Christians stars. These are a constellation of transcendent virtues, radiant above us all, brought nearer and made clearer by the lens of Judeo-Christian Scripture. I would like to close by surveying (in alphabetical order) this constellation of qualities that really matter.

*Compassion* really matters, virtually defined for Christian tradition by the Samaritan's care for the stripped traveler, beaten and left for dead in the road to Jericho. *Fidelity* really matters, such as the Apostle Peter taught by failing at it so miserably, and the Galilean Marys exemplified by being last at the cross and first at the tomb. *Forbearance* really matters, such as Christ repeatedly showed toward his non-comprehending disciples who, despite their slowness of heart, had in truth left their homes and followed him. It really matters that we *forgive* one another, seven times in a single day, if such be the need. *Gentleness* really matters, like the gentleness mitigating the imagery of postexilic prophets when they begin comparing Israel to an untrained calf or a wayward son or daughter, whereas before the sufferings of the exile they had upbraided the Israelites for being greedy cows and lusty stallions neighing after neighbors' wives.

*Graciousness* really matters, like the graciousness transforming the tense meeting between Peter the Jew and Cornelius the Gentile, thus accounting for my standing before you this evening as a Gentile grafted into the religious tradition of Judaism. *Harmony* really matters, echoing the harmony of spirit among the disciples at Pentecost so strong as to overcome the discord of nationalities that has disrupted human solidarity since the tower of Babel. *Honorableness* really matters, like that of Joseph of Arimathea, who withheld consent from the dishonorable proceedings of the legal body of which he was a member, and asked Pilate for the body of Christ to give it an honorable burial. *Human affection* really matters, such as bound Ruth and Naomi, David and Jonathan. *Humility* really matters, like the intrepid humility of Abigail as she walked into the profanity of David's anger to soften his implacable will and domesticate his savage heart.

*Joy* really matters, the luminous joy of Paul's letters, even as he is buffeted by imprisonments, beatings, and stonings, in danger from robbers, traitors, and the sea, amidst toil and hardship, insomnia and anxiety, all in glad service to his God. *Kindness* really matters, such as the naive barbarians of Malta showed in kindling a fire for the shipwrecked Paul and his shivering companions. *Liberality* really matters, like that of Job, who not only gave to poor widows and wayfaring street people, but withheld nothing they desired. *Meekness* really matters, such as allowed royal David's Son to suffer the little children to come to him. *Mercy* really matters, such as commuted the sentence in the only capital case to come before Christ, that of the woman caught in adultery.

*Patience* really matters, resembling that of the sower of kingdom seeds who waits for them to sprout and grow, he knows not how, into the blade and the ear and the full grain in the ear. *Peace* really matters, like the peace restored to the warring factions of the church of Corinth through Paul's urging of reconciling love. *Purity* really matters, like the Canaanite woman's purity of heart that willed one thing despite two abrasive dismissals by

Christ, finally to win his wonder for her great faith. *Reverence* really matters, such as Christ taught his disciples — "Dear Father, Hallowed be your name. Thy Kingdom come" — and prayed amidst his own anguish: "Nevertheless, not my will but yours be done." *Self-examination* really matters, lest we presume to remove a splinter from our neighbor's eye with a landscape timber in our own.

*Sympathy* really matters, like that mysterious shaft of sympathy cutting across the gloating victory-song of Deborah to illumine the camp of the enemy, where we see the mother of Sisera, awaiting in desperate self-deception the return of her murdered warrior son. *Tenderheartedness* really matters, such as Mary and Martha witnessed in Christ as he wept on the way to view the dead body of Lazarus, their brother and his friend. *Thankfulness* really matters, like that of the one leper of ten, and he a Samaritan, who returned alone to thank Christ for his healing. *Truthfulness* really matters, as Ananias and Sapphira learned too late to save them from the falsehood that poisoned their hearts. And *wisdom* really matters, godly wisdom, she who in Proverbs 8 heartens us with the promise we hardly dare to trust: "I love those who love me, and those who seek me diligently find me."

What really matters, I believe, is our setting distractions aside to mix and mold and balance these virtues in our lives.

Our listing of virtues has come largely from the Apostle Paul, and so let us give Paul the concluding word: "Finally, dear friends, whatever is true, whatever is honorable, whatever is just, whatever is pure, whatever is lovely, whatever is gracious, if there is any virtue, if there is anything worthy of praise, think about these things. And the God of peace will be with you."

# James Smart
## History
### February 10, 1992

Several of my predecessors in this series have described the emotions they experienced when preparing to address the topic "What Really Matters?" in the context of the L. D. Johnson lectures. Typically, they spoke of contrasting feelings of pleasure and anxiety. The pleasure, they said, sprang from being forced to think seriously about matters of ultimate concern, whereas the anxiety stemmed from fear that their observations might strike the audience as inane or even as downright foolish. My own emotional response to this assignment has been simpler and more one-dimensional: I have been utterly terrified!

My terror proceeds in part from the difficulty of conceiving an adequate answer to the question at hand. Saying what really matters is rather like defining the universe and giving two examples of it. My problem was further compounded by my great admiration both for L. D. and for those colleagues whose penetrating comments from this lectern over the past decade I appreciate deeply but cannot hope to equal. Moreover, each of the eighteen previous speakers has, by staking out his or her own territory, effectively narrowed the range of possibilities available to all successors. Since none of us wants to plow fields already broken, the task becomes more formidable with each passing year.

The difficulty lies not in conceiving possible answers but rather in choosing among the plethora of possibilities that come to mind. A great many things matter. How do you select a single bloom from a whole garden of radiant flowers, when focusing on only one or two can wrongly be interpreted to mean that thousands of other blossoms are lacking in beauty or value? Our task is less a labor of generation than of elimination. And, in candor, the best answers were enunciated centuries ago. Hear, for example, these words from the Old Testament: "He has showed you, O man, what is good; and what does the LORD require of you but to do justice, and to love kindness, and to walk humbly with your God?" (Micah 6:8, Revised Standard Version).

Nothing I can say could compare to the profundity and the simplicity of that statement from the prophet; and a wise person, having quoted these words of Micah, would sit down and be silent. Not once in my fifty-seven years, however, has anyone ever accused me of wisdom, and I see no reason to open myself to such a charge tonight.

I shall pursue the subject at two different levels, first considering briefly several topics that seemed too important to leave out but which, for various reasons, were not selected for extended development. In the second and third parts of the lecture I will attempt to probe more deeply into two concerns that matter a great deal to *me*, though admittedly, may seem less urgent to some who hear this presentation. I suppose that my adoption of this procedure represents my modest attempt to apply the instruction I received from Theron Price, L. D.'s long-time friend and colleague. Perhaps twenty years ago, when discussing an Asheville minister whose sermons reached Greenville on Channel 13, Price laid down the dictum that a good public address should reflect both "horizon" and "penetration." I interpreted the first characteristic to mean an intelligent survey of some larger landscape, while by the second I think he intended a more microscopic investigation into one or more features of the terrain.

## Many Things Matter

From the standpoint of personal happiness and well-being, my own experience suggests that nothing matters so much as the choice of a life partner. This is true whether that partnership is embodied in traditional marriage or in one of the less conventional forms that are now becoming more common in our society. Virtually everyone who is fortunate enough to live above the subsistence level will experience most of the variables that contribute to a happy life — friendship, social acceptance, success, pleasure, security, beauty, and the like — as well as those factors that militate against happiness — rejection, pain, failure, deprivation, etc. More than any other factor, what tips the balance to overall well-being or toward general unhappiness is, in my opinion, the quality and character of that person whose hand you hold as you walk the road of life. To those of you who are young and who covet a happy life, it matters greatly whom you choose to share it with.

The mention of a partner leads logically to another important life component, namely, home. By "home" I do not mean merely a physical shelter secure from natural elements and social dangers, though this is essential. "Home" is much more: a space sanctified by familiarity, enriched both by what we put into it and draw from it to the point where it functions as one's personal center of the universe. Our mental health needs that kind of center, a loved and loving place we can navigate in the dead of night without turning the lights on. It helps to provide the psychological balance needed to avoid being swept away by the rising tides of rapid technological and social changes. Home really matters, and it matters that an estimated three to six million Americans lack permanent shelter of any kind and that American economic trends over the past decade or so have made it increasingly difficult for countless young families to achieve home ownership. The emotional well-being of our society makes it imperative that we find ways to overcome these unfortunate patterns.

Certainly, good health matters — as does the fact that some thirty-seven million of our fellow citizens are without health insurance and therefore stand in jeopardy of being denied access to the care upon which good health in part depends. It matters a great deal that people find opportunities for meaningful work, work that is adequately compensated to sustain individuals and families in an acceptable living standard. Surely, it also matters that at the present time over nine million persons in our potential workforce are denied any employment and that in the midst of this affluent society, millions more eke out a meager existence from minimum wage salaries, which fail to lift the earner above the poverty level.

Perhaps you feel, as I feel, individually powerless to do much to rectify such staggering social ills as unemployment, the housing shortage, or insufficient access to medical care. Consider, then, something else that matters that is within the power of every individual to provide. I am speaking now of small gestures of kindness, sympathy, or appreciation — the gestures that a poet (I think it was Robert Browning) once described as "little, unremembered acts of kindness and of love." (If it wasn't Browning, it was another overly sentimental nineteenth-century English writer and, in any case, one of my colleagues will correct me as soon as I leave the platform.) True, Victorian sentimentality is now out of fashion. But there is more at stake here than just minor courtesies that cover society with a veneer of civility. For some time now, studies from both medicine and social psychology have noted that these acts of consideration constitute an important form of psychic nourishment. To be deprived of them adversely affects not only the emotional status of an individual, but his or her physical status as well. The process starts in the crib. To grow and develop properly, the newborn infant requires both mother's milk — or some acceptable substitute — and the mother's affectionate handling, her fondling, her stroking. Infants who are denied such ministrations become dangerously unhealthy and may develop the sometimes fatal syndrome known as "the failure to thrive." UN health officials who visited refugee camps along the Iraqi-Kuwaiti border last summer reported that despite abundant food and adequate shelter and medicine, the camps were filled with sickly children, many at the point of death, simply because their distracted, disoriented parents were not able to provide the emotional stimuli required. Tragically, these babies "failed to thrive."

As we mature from infancy through childhood and ultimately become adults, we do not outgrow our need for stroking. Instead, mother's literal strokes are sublimated into the symbolic, ritualized strokes of social behavior: handshakes, words of greeting, smiles, polite exchanges of pleasantries, asking a friend "How are you?" and taking the time to hear the answer. Small gestures? Yes, but vitally important to our psychic health. Indeed, one social psychiatrist, writing for a popular audience back in the sixties, dramatized their importance by reducing this concept to a striking epigram: "If you don't stroke me, my spinal chord will shrivel up." Most of us could cite personal examples of how thoughtless associates have damaged our spines, but I prefer to take the positive approach and describe a case of the opposite kind. When Lynn McKnight (Edgar and Shirley's daughter and a friend of our daughter since the sixth grade) was attending Furman, she came waltzing into my office one rather dismal afternoon and announced with her customary effervescence, "I just came by to give you a hug." She then proceeded to do so. This unexpected act of kindness not only made my day and my week; it brightened my whole term and even the entire academic year. Lynn has long since forgotten that incident; her action was a part of her character, and her thoughtfulness came as naturally as her breathing. But I have never forgotten it, and fifteen years after the fact I am a healthier, happier person because of it. Small gestures of kindness, sympathy, appreciation — these things really do matter, and they are within the capacity of each and every person to bestow.

So many things matter: justice, international peace, the environment, friendship, the proper nurture of children, the enjoyment of beauty, the elevation of one's mind. It is impossible to list all the things that matter, let alone to discuss them. Permit me, then, to abandon this more generalized treatment and turn to the two topics that I wish to elaborate in somewhat greater detail.

## Perspective Matters

Perspective means different things in different contexts. In painting, for example, it refers to those techniques used by artists to create the illusion of the third dimension (depth) on a flat, two-dimensional surface. Its achievement is based upon a precise mathematical understanding of spatial relationships. The artists who first worked out the "laws of perspective" were Italians of the early fifteenth century — Masaccio, Brunelleschi, Ucello, and others — who thought that perspective represented one of if not the greatest achievement(s) in the history of painting, a judgment with which few twentieth-century artists would concur.

Perspective also has a special meaning — in fact, several special meanings — in the study of history. At its core, however, historical perspective denotes the awareness of the qualitative difference that separates the past from the present. Those who lack historical perspective can only conceive the past as a previous version in time of present realities. For example, children prior to a certain point in their intellectual development are unable really to think historically. You may tell them stories from long ago and far away, but young children envision the conditions you describe as earlier examples of the way things are now. Even those scholars who study and write about the past have not always been able to place it in proper perspective. Many of the medieval chroniclers, who did numerous things quite well, were generally deficient in this regard. When they described the Roman emperors and their foremost generals, it is clear to us that their mental images of the great men of antiquity were really drawn from the kings and feudal lords of their own age, whom they merely projected backwards in chronological terms. For the discovery of true perspective in history, as in painting, we are primarily indebted to those perceptive Italians of the Renaissance era.

You may be relieved to hear, however, that although I have mentioned perspective in these more specialized contexts, these are not the senses in which I plan to explore the concept. Instead, I want to draw upon two uses of perspective from the language of everyday experience. First of all, perspective means one's personal point of view. It reflects the unique, individual vantage point from which each person necessarily looks out upon all external reality. However clearly our sights are fixed upon the object of our gaze, we are still seeing it from a single, limited perspective. We cannot view both sides of the mountain simultaneously, or as I learned on a visit to Wilmington last summer, if you really want to inspect the battleship *USS North Carolina,* you must not only come as close as possible at times, but also on occasion get as far away from it as you can. Proper appreciation requires a macro as well as a micro perspective; proximity can distort reality just as much as distance. (This helps to explain why counseling is often essential even in the best of marriages, and why historians are generally more adept at analyzing Athens in the time of Socrates than the presidency of Ronald Reagan.)

Our view of experience is subjective, and we can no more divorce ourselves from our individual perspectives than we can cease being ourselves. The best we can do is to move around a lot to secure different vistas, and perhaps we can even reach a sort of cumulative perspective forged by abstraction and generalization from a lifetime of observations. But in the final analysis we are stuck with life's subjectivity. This was certainly obvious to all of you long before I mentioned it tonight, so why bother to bring it up at all?

There are two reasons. One is that it is often the most obvious truths that we are most apt to ignore, just as natives treat with disdain some local attraction that tourists drive thousands of miles to enjoy. As evidence that this particular lesson is often forgotten, I cite the language of current political discourse in this election year. How often do we hear supporters of one candidate or another inveigh against "special interests." When I listen closely to learn the meaning of this pejorative term, it frequently turns out to be nothing more than some group that the speaker doesn't belong to — minorities, labor unions, the AMA, the anti-abortion movement, or whatever. Conversely, political speakers seem quick to consider groups to which they do belong as legitimate vehicles for promoting the national interest and the common good. What is such discourse, if not either a willful or an inadvertent denial that all politics initiate from individual perspective?

But if occasional reminders are needed that personal viewpoints lack the force of revealed truth, there is an even greater need for an opposite kind of warning. Far too many persons in our society — students, workers, citizens — seem to be unaware that their unique perspectives, while never absolute truth, constitute a priceless possession unobtainable from any other source. And among the foremost moral obligations owed by every individual to the larger community is the obligation to share his or her insights, to make private perspective available for consideration in public scrutiny.

In some ways I am here merely echoing what was said far more cogently by John Stuart Mill in his 1859 essay *On Liberty*. In that work Mill argued that all social progress — whether in the form of intellectual advance or improvements in the conventions of daily living — was directly dependent upon the activity of diverse individuals who dared to develop their unique ideas and experiences, which could then be examined by society as possible alternatives to established opinions and patterns of living. There is, perhaps, a slight shift of emphasis from Mill's argument to my own. Mill emphasized the *right* of the individual to pursue diversity and the corresponding absence of any societal right to use compulsion or control to prevent it, whereas my own stress is on the *moral duty* of the individual to be forthcoming with one's own opinions and viewpoints. To withhold my perspective from the common scrutiny is just as much a crime against my society as to refuse my contribution to the common tax or to the legitimate common defense.

One is deluded when one believes that what he or she says or doesn't say makes no real difference. Evidence to the contrary was provided by the recent experiments of a social psychologist at Smith College. After a series of ugly racial incidents at Smith, the psychologist arranged a number of conversations about race with different campus groups, raising questions in each group about attitudes toward people of different races. What the participating groups did not know was that the researcher was accompanied by an undisclosed confederate, who in each session was always the first person to respond to the questions. Perhaps you can anticipate the outcome: If the confederate took a strong stand against racism, then others were more inclined not to tolerate racist views. Conversely, if the first speaker voiced racist sentiments, others took this as permission to express a similar outlook. The investigator concluded that it was of the utmost importance for administrators, faculty, and students to communicate clearly their commitments to openness and racial equality.

Last summer, when I read the account about Smith College, I was reminded of an episode at Furman during the preceding spring, an episode that occasioned my saddest moment ever as a member of the Furman community. Some of you will recall that a senior woman had given a lengthy and candid interview to the campus newspaper in which she described what life was like for an acknowledged lesbian on the Furman campus. The young woman in question had taken two courses with me, and I was (and am) fond of her. Although I choose not to use her name on this occasion, the *Paladin* story included both her name and her picture, a striking testimony to the courage of her convictions. Subsequent issues of the student newspaper included numerous letters and comments from readers on the subject of gay and lesbian rights. Some defended their peers of differing sexual orientations, while others denounced them. Among the latter was one "Hotline" telephone caller who left the message that provoked my sadness: "I don't think they have any rights. I think they should all be killed."

I cannot be certain whether the caller expressed a genuine hatred and contempt, or whether he or she was really an unusually vicious prankster deliberately trying to be outrageous. But in any case, I could not help but wonder, in light of the experiment at Smith, whether my own silence on the controversial subject of homosexuality had unwittingly helped to give permission for the caller to express such a view and how many people would, in turn, take this expression as sanction for its repetition.

Before leaving the subject of perspective, may I treat just one additional meaning of the concept? Perspective also refers to the ability to see different aspects of a subject in proper relationship to each other and to some larger whole. This kind of perspective matters, too. If we hope to live sanely, let alone wisely, we cannot guide our lives by isolated facts, however significant, or singular insights, however valid. Facts and insights must be integrated into a more coherent general understanding. This is one of the lessons we try to teach in History 11, and I am confident that our colleagues make the same attempt in courses ranging from art to zoology.

I have been particularly struck by the absence of perspective as I have watched segments of the American public celebrate since 1989 the collapse of communism in Eastern Europe. It was my impression watching President Bush's State of the Union speech a few weeks ago that none of his remarks called forth such jubilant, bipartisan cheering as his ringing declarations concerning the death of communism. To be sure, the fallen regimes were brutal, totalitarian structures behind which for decades stood a naked and ruthless Soviet imperialism. The removal of such regimes and the enlargement of freedom for these populations are indeed appropriate causes for rejoicing. But lest our celebrations take on an unseemly character, let us remember that the founders of the socialist ideal — from Babeuf and the "Conspiracy of Equals" during the French Revolution, through Saint-Simon and Blanc and Owen, and including Marx and Engels and Lenin himself — were dreamers of a noble dream. Their goal was to liberate the oppressed, to empower the weak, to provide for the impoverished; and it is not at all clear to me why I should be glad that this part of the great experiment has failed. Even such a dyed-in-the wool capitalist and social Darwinist as Andrew Carnegie confessed that socialism was a noble ideal, which, for better or for worse, was too lofty to be realized, given the imperfections of existing human nature. Assuming that Carnegie's evaluation was correct, I still fail to see why we are supposed to regard this as *good* news.

I hope to be both clear and emphatic in stating that among the economic systems that have operated during this century, capitalism has no peer as a mechanism for producing goods. The only qualification that I feel compelled to add to that statement is that in no instance have we ever witnessed a pure, unmixed model of any economic type, whether capitalism, socialism, or communism. Having thus qualified the description, I have no qualms in asserting as demonstrated truth the superiority of private capital, the profit motive, and the free market in creating the most plentiful supply of consumer products. But, having acknowledged this fact, we need to place it in some larger, more comprehensive perspective.

In building that larger perspective, we might start with the observation of Jesus that life does not consist solely of things possessed, that is, of consumer goods. We should also be reminded that Adam Smith, the venerated critic of economic controls and defender of the market economy, listed among the legitimate functions of government the provision of certain public works and services that cannot be readily provided by private initiative alone. And we should certainly be able to see what I fear is being overlooked in the current national euphoria, namely, that to establish the defects and failings of the collectivist economic ideal is *not* tantamount to validating any and all features of our own system. It does not justify the unstated but implicit implications of our celebration that we should rest content with our current capitalist model despite its own glaring deficiencies, and that private profit represents an adequate mechanism for addressing all social needs.

Consider for a moment the contributions of the profit motive to some different aspects of our national life. I have already noted but will repeat for emphasis that the desire to make a profit is an extremely effective stimulus to the creation of goods and services, and that is very important. (Or to employ the vocabulary of this lecture series, that really matters.) But what happens when the profit motive enters the religious life of the nation? It generates not saints or prophets, but religious hucksters who bilk the poor and the unsophisticated; it calls forth not Mother Teresa, but Jim Bakker and Robert Tilton. And how has the profit motive functioned to foster education? For example, can anyone name a single distinguished institution of higher learning created and sustained by the incentive of financial gain? To the best of my knowledge, there is none. The most eminent centers of learning, both here and abroad, were founded to promote religious/humanitarian/educational objectives or to serve public needs, and they have always operated as non-profit corporations — to the frequent dismay of their business officers. Please be assured that the American educational landscape is dotted with numerous post-secondary schools, mostly business colleges, owned by private investors and intended to earn profits on invested capital. At their best, such institutions afford basic job skills for society's economic and educational underclass, a function of undeniable social value. But at their worst, these schools have been thinly disguised vehicles for raiding the public treasury and manipulating disadvantaged youth. To be fair, I should also mention that some interesting experiments are now underway in Florida, in which profit-driven educational contractors have taken responsibility for operating public schools, pledging to do so at lower costs and with better educational outcomes. The initial reports have been promising, and perhaps these attempts will demonstrate that there is an educational context in which the profit motive has utility. But, for now, I can only conclude that while private profits serve us well in supplying crops and steel and VCRs, such incentives are not the answer for society's educational needs.

Whether the profit motive has been more of a help or a hindrance in the field of health care is an extremely complex question, and one on which it seems to me the jury is still out. At most, I can hazard a tentative judgment that its effects have been mixed, serving society well at some points and poorly at others. Our system of primary care has always centered around private physicians who operate their practices as profit-making businesses, and in my opinion the results have generally been beneficial. Those of us with funds and/or insurance receive splendid treatment, while the contributions of state and federal governments and the charitable impulses of individual doctors have seen to it that many of those who can't pay are not totally excluded from the system. On the other hand, certain disclosures over the past few months have raised serious questions about the compatibility of profits and the public interest in health care. I am thinking here of such things as the outrageous markups on medical supplies, which the profit-driven Humana Hospitals levied upon their patients; the excessive prescribing of diagnostic tests by Florida physicians who were silent partners or owners of the laboratories performing the tests; the apparent falsification or concealment of data by drug manufacturers to secure FDA approval for inferior or dangerous products; and the all too common practice in private treatment centers for substance abuse and psychiatric care of gearing programs of treatment to their patients' insurance benefits rather than their medical needs. And above and beyond any such bill of particulars loom the larger issues of access to health care and the total proportion of social wealth that we can afford to invest in health services.

Few people would deny that our nation is confronted by a healthcare crisis and that fundamental choices must be made in the immediate future. My plea is simply that we consider these choices within the framework of the broadest possible perspective. We should not select among alternatives because of our own vested interests, whether as providers or consumers, nor should we choose options on the purely ideological grounds of a preference for private entrepreneurship. Let us instead adopt a resolutely pragmatic approach, defining to the best of our abilities what problems are to be addressed and what mechanisms seem best calculated to resolve them. I think this is what it means to see things in relation to each other and to some larger whole, that is, to see them in perspective.

## The Faith of Our Fathers Matters, As Does the Culture of Our Peers

Much of my life revolves around three institutions that matter a great deal to me. One is home and family: 18 Starsdale Circle, Bonnie, Susan, Jim, and Rusty. Another is Furman University and, in particular, its history department. The third is Greenville's First Baptist Church, where over the past three years Bonnie and I have developed particular affection for an incredibly lively and stimulating group of people who constitute the Don and Trudy Rose class on Sunday mornings. I share with the fellow inmates of each institution many common values, but nevertheless retain certain personal inclinations, which at some times are unique to me and at other times typify the views of minority or majority subgroups within the larger communities. One of the things that sets me apart to some degree within all three institutions is the way I have chosen to handle the problem of retaining an historic religious faith while living and actively sharing in the culture of the twentieth century, a culture that is in many respects antithetical to religion.

Within the academy and within the church there are some individuals who hold that faith and modern scientific learning are mutually exclusive, and that one can profess allegiance to one or the other, but not both. Those within the religious camp who take this position usually apply it by rejecting much, if not all, cultural development from the eighteenth century to the present. Their counterparts in the academic community take the opposite tack, arguing that since all of the world's great religious traditions — Judaism, Christianity, Islam, Buddhism, Hinduism — were products of a pre-scientific age, they must now be consigned, as Lenin consigned his Menshevik opponents, to "the garbage heap of history."

Neither of these alternatives satisfies me. Along with many others in both camps, I take seriously the faith of my fathers, but I am determined to live in the twentieth century, perhaps even, with luck, in the twenty-first. To do so requires those of us who are so disposed to take up the difficult task of reconciling faith and learning in an intellectually honest way, without resorting to double truths or logic-tight mental compartments. Anyone who thinks such an undertaking is easy has simply failed to understand the nature of the issues at stake. Had we lived at an earlier period in Western history, the reconciliation of religion and culture would have been less problematical simply because from the fifth through the seventeenth centuries, the great intellectuals who shaped our culture were themselves Christian theologians and philosophers, or at least were persons who identified with the dominant tradition of a theological worldview. But this changed dramatically with the scientific revolution of the late seventeenth century and with the new generation of intellectuals who emerged in the eighteenth-century Enlightenment. This was the generation of Voltaire and Diderot, Hume and Holbach, who not only moved decisively outside of their inherited religious traditions, but who also marshaled their considerable powers of logic and persuasion to assault the very foundations of traditional religious belief. David Hume, for example, virtually destroyed the credibility of miracles and reduced one of the classic arguments for the existence of God — namely, the argument from design — to a shambles, concluding that, at most, a reasonable person might affirm that the Creator of the universe bears some remote resemblance to human intelligence. Hardly adequate grounds for holding fast to the faith of our fathers! And from Hume's age to our own, the difficulties of harmonizing our religious beliefs with what we know about nature and humanity have increased exponentially.

That's the bad news for those of us who want to live as Christians in a post-Christian culture. Now for the good news — the gospel according to Jim Smart. The good news is that, despite the problems, historic faith and contemporary culture can be reconciled, and those who argue the opposite need to take a closer look at the historical record. Speaking as an historian, I can assure anyone who may be interested that reconciliations of theology with other branches of knowledge are not only possible, but that they have in fact been worked out by the ablest religious spokespersons of every age and culture right down to the present. Such syntheses of religion and culture are never so perfect as to compel universal acceptance, but they are guaranteed by the integrity of their framers, and they merit the serious consideration of honest, intelligent observers.

Let me illustrate the evidence upon which this claim is based by a very partial roll call of contributors. (I will speak only of my own faith community, Christianity, and of my own culture, that of the West, because these are the ones of which I have some understanding. I nevertheless assume that scholars from the other great traditions have performed similar tasks for their own communities of faith.) Reconciliations of faith and learning are as old as Christianity itself. One can argue that, in some ways, Jesus himself initiated such efforts by placing the new revelation of which he was the bearer squarely in the context of the Jewish law and prophets. Not long thereafter, Paul the apostle fused Hellenistic learning with his gospel of the crucified and risen Christ. In the troubled days of the early fifth century, it was the lot of Augustine to reconcile faith in divine providence with the harsh realities of the barbarian invasions and the collapse of Roman peace and stability. The thirteenth century called forth perhaps the greatest of all reconcilers, Thomas Aquinas, who harmonized Christian theology with Aristotelian logic and science and thereby built a new bridge between faith and reason. Such bridges cannot stand forever, and in the fifteenth century it was rebuilt by Marsiglio Ficino with a difference; this time it was Platonic thought at the other end of the span.

The seventeenth century was of crucial importance in the emergence of modern Western thought. Among its seminal thinkers were Descartes and Locke, who laid the epistemological foundations for the new culture, and Newton, who standardized the scientific methodology that would direct the study of nature for the next 200 years. Yet these three men, while doing so much to shape the new scientific culture, were all at pains to demonstrate its compatibility with their theological heritage, and all three died confident in their efforts. I will pass over the eighteenth-century religious apologists, conceding as I do so that their work was generally less impressive than that of their anti-religious antagonists. But in the nineteenth century, in the persons of Schleiermacher earlier and Kierkegaard later, theologians met the challenges of the Enlightened philosophers head on, each in his own way pressing the case for religious truth upon the cultured despisers of religion.

And so the work has continued into our own century in the capable hands of men like the church historian Walter Rauschenbusch, who deftly wove scientific perspectives into his theology, while simultaneously contending that our religious traditions, far from being obsolete, provided the only source of the insights and dynamism required to surmount the social ills of the industrial age. More recently, scholars like Paul Tillich and the formidable Niebuhrs have found ways not only to restate religious truths in a more contemporary vocabulary, but also to restore to religion its role as an important critic of existing cultural forms.

I want to end my "roll call of reconcilers" with the name of L. D Johnson, a friend and colleague who rejected exclusive residence in either Athens or Jerusalem, insisting instead upon joint citizenship in both cities. He embraced science and applauded its efforts to push back the frontiers of knowledge. He was deeply versed in contemporary literature, with its relentless focus on human absurdities, including those absurdities peculiar to religion. He had no fear of the modern social sciences, whether anthropology or sociology or experimental psychology. But he also believed that the Christian gospel was as timely in the twentieth century as it had been in the first, and that the fundamental realities of sin and redemption are not altered by the passing of time or the changing contours of culture. Had he not combined the best of modern scholarship with the timeless values of religious truth, he could not have played the role that he filled among us, to wit, that of a rather gaunt, balding apostle to the bruised and skeptical spirits of the late twentieth century.

In my defense of faith in an age of doubt, please notice that I have spoken only historically, not theologically or philosophically. I have suggested that reconciliations of religion and culture can be made and that they have in fact been made across the centuries. What I have not done is to prescribe the form that such a reconciliation should take or even to suggest a methodology for creating the form. This is because I believe that integrating one's total life experience into a coherent worldview is a highly personal undertaking, which taps into the very foundations of one's being, a task that each individual can only perform for himself or herself. We can share encouragement and insights, but in the final interpretive act each soul stands naked before God and conscience. It cannot be otherwise.

But if I dare not offer some sort of "paint by the numbers" plan, I would like to conclude by making three suggestions about the spirit and posture from which such individual and personal efforts may best begin. I know that I have already taxed your patience, and I shall try to be brief.

First, we need to be clear about whose responsibility it is to resolve conflicts between knowledge and religious faith. Such responsibility does not rest upon the shoulders of secular intellectuals; their sole duty is to use the tools of their intellectual disciplines in a responsible manner to uncover whatever facts or insights the process can yield. If their conclusions are upsetting to our theological notions, then that is our problem, not theirs. I find few things so infuriating as the inability or the unwillingness of religious communities to recognize this obvious reality, whether it be the Inquisition forcing Galileo to recant, or creationist groups demanding that their views be treated as equally plausible as the evolutionary hypothesis, or the Shiite Imams calling for the assassination of Salman Rushdie. The only question the religious community is entitled to ask when conclusions are advanced is "Does this conclusion square with the best evidence in this field of inquiry at the present time?" And if it does, then we may need to take a fresh look at our own religious views and to rethink the possible relationship of faith and knowledge at this point. But the obligation to do so is our obligation. To ask scholars to tailor their findings to fit our conceptions is the height of folly and invites contempt toward religion from educated people.

A second suggestion is that syntheses of faith and learning are best constructed upon what is known, rather then upon matters still cloaked in mystery. The alternative course, majoring upon the unknown, seems to me to have led some religious apologists over the past three centuries down a dead-end street. When scientists or philosophers have advanced new explanatory theses, some theologians have rushed in to say, "Yes, but…you still can't explain this or that phenomenon, so we must retain theology to explain what is still mysterious." They give us a sort of "God of the gaps," whose chief function seems to be to preside over the unmapped regions of nature and the human psyche and whose very plausibility seems predicated upon the imperfections of human knowledge. If such a deity did indeed exist, one might expect this god jealously to defend his assigned territory. In other words, this god would have a vested interest in perpetuating human ignorance. This approach has not worked in the past and most certainly will not work in the future. If religious faith deserves preserving, it must perform some worthier task than being hailed in to cover the gaps in our knowledge.

Finally, a word about the fundamental assumption from which attempts to harmonize the faith of our fathers and the culture of our peers begins: the assumption that God is the author of all truth, and that the believer therefore welcomes truth from all sources and is unafraid to follow the truth wherever it leads. It may lead me to abandon positions taken previously. It may lead me to modify my theology, or to alter my political principles, or to adopt different attitudes toward individuals or social groups. It may well impel me to the most wrenching and painful of personal examinations. But if I truly believe that behind all truth stands the one immortal, invisible God, the creator and sustainer of life, how can I do otherwise, and how can I fear the outcome?

# Gerda McCahan
## Psychology
### March 9, 1992

I'm very thankful to be here. With a few changes in things, I just might not have made it. But I did. So tonight we're together, and things are good, and things are good for Furman.

I am also very glad to be home again. When I come out here somehow I'm back in touch with twenty-five years of my life that were more fun than I could ever communicate to you. This was an interesting place to be, and I was here at an interesting time. And it's great to be back and have that feeling of being home.

This is not a scholarly presentation. I know that might be a great disappointment to those who have come for intellectual stimulation and for all the things that go with it, but in the last two years I have had some experiences that were certainly not what I would have predicted. I would not have embraced them willingly, I assure you, if I had been given a choice. There is nothing that will really change your point of view about life more quickly than to have someone look you straight in the eye and say, "You have a life-threatening illness." WOW!! You know all through the years it is somebody else who has a life-threatening illness. Then, all of a sudden someone looked at me and said, "You've go it!" Just as suddenly, it had such a strange effect on me and those I love.

Tonight, I am going to try to talk about my experiences and the effects that reverberated through my family system. For me this has been a period of considerable learning. In other words, I have not been stagnating and I have not been "depressing," as Classer might say. Taken all together, I have found this to be an extremely interesting two years. It was as though I was at the center of a kaleidoscope and the kaleidoscope shifted about a quarter of a turn. Every piece was there, but the design had become different. All of a sudden, the things that I had always depended upon, always thought would be the same and had been the same for years, were different. Things that were rocking along suddenly had an urgency to them that I had not really anticipated. When that happened, everything was so different, I found, that whether I intended it or not, it became a serious consideration for me personally to think again about *what really does matter* and *what has mattered to me*. You may say, "Well, kid, you're a little late. You cannot do anything about it when you are so soon old." But somehow there was a great need to get things together in my head and in a new way.

Anybody who is a clinical psychologist has studied lives for years. You have done case histories; you have counseled people; you have listened to stories; you have done everything possible to understand a person's life, but when you start looking at your own life, then you have another set of problems. How do you approach the data? As a professional, I'll level with you. I think my data is ninety-five percent collected. I think if one has collected the data for this life, it behooves us to do something about interpreting it. It is even possible that we really must interpret it. The urgent question became how am I going to approach that data? Do I dare to look at it in a new way? I've looked at it many times before in different life stages. Do I really want to look at it now? How do I feel about that?

It was a very interesting situation for me. I finally said to myself, "Well, I guess it is time to interpret the findings." And the funny part of it is that there was a real inner pressure to do that — a pressure in me to see it, to look at it, to review it, to decide what I had done about it. And that meant that when Betty invited me back to say something about what really matters, I had the best of all possible conditions to keep me on track. I had a deadline and I made a commitment. Of course, when I was supposed to do this in October, they put me in the hospital in the middle of the night. I didn't make that deadline but I have made this one. I want this one put up as a gold star — *I made it*. Rejoice with me!

My first task was to have a way to look at my life data: successes, failures, triumphs, and sorrows. I'm going to tell you a little bit about how I looked at the data. I don't know whether my method would work for you or not. I don't know whether it sounds interesting to you or not, but this is the methodology that I finally found comfortable for myself. I think it worked for me.

There is another aspect of this project. You know I am a "pro." People are my business. But is this different? Am I more than that? Even if I am trained in working with people, is data collected laboriously at the experiential level basically different? Must I develop a different approach? Will I have to see it differently? Of course. What tends to happen is that you go back to values and to ideas that really have gone with you through most of your life.

So what began to come back to me was the parable of the talents. You see, if you work with students, you beat them over the head with the parable of the talents for years. If you have children, you beat them over the head with the parable of the talents. You have been given so many talents. What will you do to turn your potential, or talent, into usable abilities? My kaleidoscope shifted. My entire point of view in looking at the parable changed. I began to think about the end of the parable when the Master comes home at midnight. All of a sudden, I was not thinking about developing ability or competence. I was beginning to think about answering the question "What did I do here with all that was given me?" It was a different perspective. Before the Master comes home at midnight, I really wanted to do some thinking. I needed to think my life through again.

Now, with midnight a tad closer, I found that I identified three big questions that really concerned me. First, I accept myself as a biological organism operating according to natural law. I know about neurons and the way they work. (Not as much as John Batson knows, but that's all right. I'll let him carry that for me.) The main question here is, is that all we are: a marvelous organism blessed with a highly developed brain, a skillful prehensile hand, and a stereoscopic eye? That's a possibility. Are we working out a genetic code, which is something remarkable and perhaps recognized as more remarkable as we know more about it? Am I, Gerda McCahan, individual, unique? Or is what I am a functioning brain existing only when that brain functions and that's it?

Well, all you've got to do is take one of these magic pills to be convinced. They've got a pill that will make you do anything. And I am proof of it tonight. Right? So believe it. There's a lot of chemistry in whatever is our individuality. The question is, is there anything else? In other words, is that all there is to it? Or are we something more? Go back to things that you have grown up with. You remember that the psalmist says we are a little lower than the angels. Does that mean that we are a little more than just the functioning of a nervous system with a certain cortical level that permits us a certain repertoire of behaviors? Is there anything individual about us that exists beyond that? If that's the case, then you have to ask, "Is this life a trust?" Were we given this life? Does it involve a task? Well, there have been several days that I've thought it was a task. Many days I have thought that is was a task more than anything else. And you have had those same days. It's a task, I am sure.

Is life a special gift? And if it's a special gift, do we have any responsibility for it? Or do we just take it and tear off the wrappings and say, "One more thing to put up on the shelf." Is it a gift? If it's a gift, what is the gift? Having gone over this question, I came to the conclusion, (maybe because I am eccentric, perhaps because I am egotistical) that I am special. I think that I am unique. I also am perfectly well aware that you can make a very good case for physical monism. But *I choose* to live life the way I see it. Is that basic self-esteem or conceit? I don't know. Yes, I think that I am a biological organism, and I think the human organism itself is a most remarkable miracle and each of us is a unique replication (a contradiction in terms surely, and yet applicable in this situation). Anyone whose work is people has to stand in awe of the human organism.

If life is a gift and we have accepted it, we need to look at what we have been given. What are the dimensions of it? The first is this marvelous miracle that is our biological self. The second dimension is that this human self cannot develop or even exist alone. Whatever the eternal scheme of things is, we are part of a community of selves interacting, affecting, and stimulating each other. If we don't have other selves or cannot relate to them, we don't get along, So the second part of the gift is the significant others who make up your life. Who are they? They are probably somewhere between five and eight in number, and you can probably identify them. They are significant people who have shaped the person you are and are becoming at this moment. Significant others, relationships, caring involvements, that's a second aspect of the gift of life.

The third that we must not forget is the supportive environment that permits us to become. Have you looked at those children in Bangladesh? The starving babies in Ethiopia? The number of people who are hungry in Greenville, South Carolina? Theirs has not been the supportive type of environment that we have had. We have had something special — a special gift.

And the fourth thing we have been given is a certain amount of time. All of life exists in a capsule of time in which all the dynamics that we have talked about interact to work out the miracle that we call development, which is the story of our lives. In many ways what is most remarkable about this gift is that we aren't completely programmed. Now, take some of the fishes, and some of the rats, and the baby sea turtles who find their way to the sea by the light of the moon. They are pretty well programmed, aren't they? In other words, they do what they are supposed to do, and when they finish they get the heck out of here. But we are different. In the way our life is structured, we have control. We can and must make choices. We are given the opportunity to become, and we are given the opportunity to exist in a way that we create ourselves. We create our lives.

So assume that I've got to deal with a biological organism, with some significant others, in a supportive environment, in a capsule of time. I have been assigned an interesting task and given the tools to create a self. I admit that I am more aware that there is a time capsule now, my own specifically.

With all of that awareness, what am I supposed to be doing? What am I supposed to have done? I think there are two major tasks that we're responsible for in this life. Sometimes we do well; sometimes we do badly. We have this personal, necessary contribution to make to our own development.

Without our contribution it won't happen. This gives us a very special responsibility and a very special mandate to do something that's unlike other organisms on this earth.

The first of the tasks is the *development of self.* When a baby comes into this world she/he is a bundle of potential. And anybody who has one, has seen one, has loved one, has lived with one, and/or has raised one knows that you're watching a special, individual self develop. It is not just a *tabula rasa* who comes to live with you; it's that rascal that won't go to sleep at two o'clock in the morning. It's the one that is exactly like Uncle Bob (whom you never could stand). This person comes here already a person. Actually, what we're seeing through the life span is the struggle to turn potential into attainment.

Because our potential is great, it comes out on "useful" things, like IQ tests, where people persist in telling you that you're not doing as well as you can do. It doesn't matter if you lucked out on two or three test items. You're always being told about your potential. And some young person says, "If it's really there, give me some way of using it." What we do during most of our lives is struggle to change potential into attainment of various kinds. When it becomes attainment, then it's useful. Then we can do something.

That struggle to turn potential into attainment takes a lot of effort. It is a marvelous ride up the hill for a while when time is on your side. After a while you find that it's not necessarily more than an even break, and when more time passes you find that maybe you're going downhill a little bit, not doing quite as well.

This struggle goes on from the time you discover your fingers and your toes to the day like today when I suddenly found that I couldn't get out of a wheelchair in the hospital. That was a humbling experience. I don't know if you've been hauled around by anybody lately, but don't do it if you don't have to. If you can get up, then get up yourself.

There is another fascinating part about this, (and I'm not going to give you a course in developmental psychology, despite my temptation to do so). What's fascinating is the whole process of learning and developing a relationship with our self. First you've got to discover your body; then you've got to learn to control it; then you've got to make it skillful; then you've got to accept it. Did you know that most people in this room never really accepted themselves as a body? All of you here have something you don't like about yourself. You didn't like it when you were ten or eleven or twelve. You may think you've got a big nose, although nobody else has noticed its size. But you think that you've got it. Or you may be a person who's too tall or too short or too fat or too thin or just, like me, too big. Do you know that it was in my last year of my teaching that I found out that some students had never gotten used to the fact that I'm over six feet tall. Never. One student confessed to me that she walked down the hall as a freshman and said, "I hope to God that I do not ever get into that woman's class; she scares me to death!" (And all this time I thought I was such a nice person.) Students found that it was great when I got a bar stool and an overhead projector and sat down to teach. Everyone breathed a sign of relief. We were now getting on the same level. Just today, I had three people (at least) talking about how tall I was. Well, I want to tell you that after seventy-two years it's an old story, but one I live with comfortably at last.

That's the kind of thing I mean; there are some people who never really learn to live with their body. And there are some people who integrate body and mind to a point that's a joy to see. I found that out years ago when I had three football fans at home. I joined them and began to look at professional athletes somewhat differently. (They are rather nice to look at, incidentally.) What's so interesting is when they do what they do, you see marvelous integration of mind and body. The biological organism is working perfectly. Have you ever watched one of them run — not when he was being knocked down by somebody, just run — perfectly? Some people seem to become a physical monism. Many of us aspire to make it work that way because the most efficient way to work is when mind and body are integrated and working together. Right? And then there are other people who just kind of live in their bodies almost in spite of their bodies, like Gandhi.

As you get older, ladies and gentlemen, you feel more that way. You don't run nearly as well — not at all, if you can help it. If you can't open the pickle jar or can't get the pill out of the child-proof package in the middle of the night, you begin to say, "I am different from this body. It is not working right." So you see that there is an integration period when the mind/body relationship grows toward oneness followed by a period where you begin to lose a little bit of that feeling and you find yourself saying, "I am a little separate from that body that doesn't respond so well to my commands." I don't know what this change in perception means, but I'm telling you that's what happens. Perhaps it's the last line of perceptual self-defense, turning the unacceptable changes into the "not me" to guard self-esteem. It happens because we find ourselves as somewhat separate from the "physical me." We are not all physical. This perception lets us be something more than what we are physically able to do.

To summarize, we go through some programs to develop a self, from discovering our fingers to "Now I lay me down to sleep." We have to learn to live with our bodies, and we perceive the mind/body relationship differently, in different degrees of closeness, at different times in our lives.

The second task is the impact we make on other selves and what they give us, a transcendence of self through interaction. Life is never a solitary venture. You're always stimulated by another self. Because human beings are not isolated organisms, they have to have somebody else who gives to them and who gets from them. In a sense, the developing of the self becomes a process of transcending self, receiving, and giving. You suddenly find that it's not so much what you do and how you get your work done or what your paycheck is. You begin to find that in receiving and giving in relationships, you contribute to the development of other selves. Sometimes you do it in work. People who teach are constantly doing that, in fact are dedicated to it. Thus, besides the period of developing self, we have the other major task of transcending self.

In adulthood, it's in the transcending of self that we gain our greatest satisfactions. What do I mean by transcending self? I mean a willingness to give of yourself and to receive no personal reward. If you have been a helper for a number of years, and all of a sudden you become the helpee, that is a new and shaking experience, uncomfortably like a return to childhood. So, in a sense, it is the interactional variable that supports development of individual selves and all selves. The power of impact, as one's self makes its mark on another self or selves, defines the second task. In that sense, what did you do? What did you give? How did you care? How did you receive what people gave you? That dimension is all part of the way that the self is continuing to grow. I am emphasizing the fact that, in adulthood particularly, there is a mutual give and take between us that makes for real growth — the growth of self.

What kind of things am I talking about? I am talking about daring to commit, to enjoy and to appreciate beyond your own self-interest. That means that you are going to work like heck as a volunteer on something for which you will get no personal reward. In other words, to see a person or a project grow, to see it get better, to see something happen that you couldn't do by yourself is so exciting; it's wonderful. All of a sudden you are able to do something with people that you couldn't do by yourself, but with people of like mind you can. It happens, and there is a joy, a feeling of satisfaction that adds to you as a person, that makes things brighter, that makes things more fun.

Actually, what I am saying is that somewhere along the line you've got to commit yourself to something bigger than you are. Two things happened to me ten or fifteen years ago, but only now can I see what happened. All of a sudden "my blood ran purple." I forgot all the things "they" did wrong or failed to do, and I began to see all the things "they" did right. I really liked that. And then when people said that Greenville did something, that was really good; I felt as proud as punch. You would think that I owned the place. These days when I come back out to Furman and people say, "What are you doing out here?", I say, "I'm one of the owners and I've come to check up on you rascals." When you succeed, I have fun because I belong to you and you belong to me. When you do it well, whatever it is, I love it. I can sit on the porch and enjoy, and you have had the responsibility of getting it done.

The third task I want to talk to you about is one I don't like to talk about now. The *third task* is using your time. Embarrassing, isn't it? I once worked with an industrial consultant who told me about the importance and the perils of planning. He said when you go into the office in the morning you're supposed to have a plan as to what you intend to get done that day, and I knew that I had done that several times in my life. Not exactly every day as I should have, but several times at least. He said, "You'll find that there is one problem with the plan. You go into the office and something else that you never planned happens and at five o'clock you look at your watch and you haven't done a damned thing you had planned for the day. The 'to do' list is untouched. And you are horrified by what happened to the time." He referred to this experience as "Operation Surprise," meaning that everything you planned, all the things you planned to do that made good sense, had gone out the window. He said, "I'll tell you one thing that will make life more comfortable for you. Be sure you make a list of the things you actually did during that day. If you don't you might go stark-raving crazy."

Everything that we are doing is based on time. Everything that we are doing is limited by time. Time is all we've got. Did you know that all there is to life is right now, is this instant with you and me and the interaction between us? The beginning of my sentence is already in the past and the end is in the future. This is life, tiny increments of a flying present. This is all there is to it.

Where does it go? Look at time. Don't fence yourself out. That self of yours deserves some time. I have decided that retreats serve very good purposes, and maybe we ought to retreat in our own ways more frequently. Be sure you have some "think time." But if you don't assign time on the calendar for it, forget it; you will never have it. Watch out for committing an enormous amount of time to things that don't matter. When I went back over things I had done, some things that I had worked so hard on and put so much into came to nothing, and other things that I did impulsively worked. Think what you put your time into. It is important to guard some time for yourself. You deserve it. You need it. The fact is, somebody expects you to turn potential into attainment, or do something that shows what you have been given. Leave time to refuel. You can give and give and give, and after a while you give yourself away. You need time for the growth of self.

On the basis of this framework, what have I found? I'm going to be embarrassingly honest with you tonight, because I think at least if I've gone this far to emphasize methodology, which everyone knows is universally boring, in examining my life, then I ought to let you know my conclusions. They're not all positive, but there are some conclusions that seem to fit the data and have some validity for me.

1. I did not achieve my potential. I came closer in some areas than others. Some potential I never even used at all. What I found is that the problem was not my lack of motivation, but my lack of energy to support the implementation of my ideas. To really achieve your potential you have got to have the organic energy to power it. A high energy level goes with attainment. And I'm one of those people who was born tired and is going to die of a relapse.

2. I did commit myself to some things beyond myself. And my own interest grew with
those commitments and with the experiences I had with them. I'm glad that I committed myself to some things beyond me. Sometimes it was to people; sometimes it was to projects. Sometimes it was to plants! They are so quiet; they even die quietly, whereas as a psychologist you always know that your client is going to protest in some way.

3. I also committed myself to caring about people. That's a risky business, because they disappoint you sometimes, but sometimes they are the most exciting projects that you can be involved in. I'm glad that I did that. That was a good investment.

4. I took the risk of loving a lot of people. That is always risky. Every now and then I got clobbered, but sometimes it was real fun to watch them and love them and see them become. That was great. Sometimes I won; sometimes I lost. And sometimes I was sorry that I had picked who I picked, but that's all right. Sometimes I made a difference.

5. I found that when I looked at my life, it made a meaningful whole to me. I don't know if it would make a meaningful whole to

you, but you don't have to make any judgments since you're not the peer review group who is going over the paper.

6. I found there were definable chapters in my life where certain things began, had a middle, and an ending. And then I went on to another chapter that was quite different. Usually those chapters were defined by geography, where we were living. When we moved, everything changed and another chapter began. Age was the other dimension. At a certain age things became a little different with different roles and expectations. I found that was rather important.

7. I also found there were some recurrent themes that would appear in one life stage and appear in another form later on. They usually were associated with values. They expressed themselves in different ways in different chapters. In these recurring themes, I could see a kind of structure. My life was not a layer cake or a bunch of things put one on top of the other. I could see some longitudinal structure, and that was comforting to me. There was evidence of a warp as well as a woof.

8. I found that some important decisions were made impulsively and some turned out to be as good as the ones that were well planned, but I will not make a case for impulsivity. I consider that luck.

9. I also found that I had a lot of weaknesses. Sometimes I was a jellyfish. There were times I should have been a much better fighter than I was, and I regret that. I've ducked some issues I should have faced. I know that, and I must accept responsibility.

So that's where I am. This is sunset. But sunset, instead of being a stage of stagnation, has been a very interesting growth period in my life. I have enjoyed every day of it. Except, of course, when Dr. Gluck didn't get out the powerful chemicals, or we needed to look again at the recipe. Those days were not as good. But I have been given two beautiful years by Dr. Gluck and the remarkable staff of the Cancer Treatment Center of Greenville Memorial Hospital.

What has been special about these two years? Heavens, I have had time to observe. Most of my life I didn't have time to observe. I was too busy doing, just as you are doing. Now I enjoy. I listen. I commiserate. I sit on my porch. I like it. It's delightful. I have time to appreciate. And the people

I love come by and help me appreciate them. I don't have any papers to grade!! I look at you carrying those papers, and each time I say, "Dear Lord, retirement is beautiful." Everything else I did at Furman I loved, but I am glad not to be carrying those papers. Sometimes I take a nap without guilt. And that's a delight. That's what is interesting about this sunset.

Let's talk a minute about sunsets. There are different kinds. Some are short and fiery. Some are gray and dismal. And some are long and golden. I'm going for that one. I'm hoping that when the sun is set and the stars are out and the Master comes home at midnight, somehow all will be well.

**Editor's note:** Shortly after this lecture, on August 17, 1992, Gerda passed away.

# Thomas O. Buford
## Philosophy
*October 26, 1992*

What matters most? Preparation for this lecture is not the first occasion for my thinking seriously about that question. Once, in the family room of our home on Abingdon Way our children had tried my patience to the limit. Standing with Michael Novak on the "edge of nothingness" and welling up from deep inside my personal history, I blurted out, "I expect you to be trustworthy, loyal, helpful, friendly, courteous, kind, obedient, cheerful, thrifty, brave, clean, and reverent!" They sat there in stone silence, and I thought to myself, "My word, Buford, you are still a Boy Scout!"

In addition to the daily interest in the question "What really matters?" that rearing three children forced on my attention, I remember one other occasion for giving this topic careful attention. The president of a small Baptist college in Texas asked me to visit him in Dallas to talk about a post in academic administration at the school. I flew out to Dallas; unfortunately, our meeting was delayed until the next day. His flight was grounded by a sudden sandstorm (visibility was only 100 yards at the airport of his departure). I should have known then and there that I wasn't interested; I've never liked Texas sandstorms, particularly when combined with rain. Mud pellets fall from the heavens, and windshields on automobiles look like warm chocolate chips stuck on them and oozed. He arrived and we talked the day through in his room at the hotel. As we reviewed the challenges and opportunities facing the academic life of the college, my interest waned and his promises waxed. In late afternoon, as it came time for my flight, we drove to Love Field, and he walked me to the departure gate. Then he said, "Tom, Southern Baptists and Texas Baptists have provided you a rich legacy, a church community, an education. It is now time for you to pay back something to them. You are obligated to take this job." Though stunned by such a bluntly stated moral argument, I told him I would give it serious consideration. When I returned home and discussed the opportunity with Dee, we decided not to take the job. In my letter to the president, I thanked him for his hospitality and for considering me for the position, and I declined the offer. And with specific reference to his moral argument, I said that what matters most to me can be placed in the following descending order: God, my wife and family, being a Baptist Christian, philosophy, being a Texan, and last being a Southern Baptist. I haven't heard from him since. Though they do not exhaust my values, these particular ones have not changed; neither has their configuration. Still at the top of the list, God matters most.

I wish that affirmation were enough for me; unfortunately, it is not. Once I say "God matters most," perplexities arise; I find myself faced with a nettle of questions and some insight. It is one thing to say God matters most, but it is another to say what that means for everyday living. Surely it must have something to do with one's life if one says God matters more than anything else. But what does God have to do with life? How is "what matters most" related to, involved in, anyone's life? My family matters to me next to God. They are related to, involved in, everything about me. No choice, pattern of behavior, no standard I employ or goal I have affects my life as pervasively as does my family. If God matters more than that, then God must affect my life work deeply, more pervasively than they do.

It's easy to say that God does so since God is Creator, and I am God's creature living in the created world. Certainly God matters most in that sense. Yet Deists say as much, and their God becomes an absentee landlord. In that sense, my family, by playing an everyday role in the way my life goes in who I am, matters more than the landlord whose ownership is clear but who chooses not to get involved. But the God of my faith is involved, is not on Mount Olympus, not in some distant heaven. God, what matters most, must be involved. But how? What are the marks of that involvement? They must be here, there, somewhere in our experience as persons living in this world.

This issue has perplexed me since I was a child and I found my way into Christianity through a small Baptist congregation in Overton, Texas. At each main juncture in my life when I made decisions that affected the course and pattern of my life, I have enveloped them with prayer. Yet, in the envelope, the decision was mine alone. Through prayer I was in dialogue with God, yet at the point of decision God seemed to have something else to do. I can recall that the decision to go to graduate school and not to law school was an act of Promethean defiance. At least that's the way I thought of it. Who is this God with whom I commune in prayer but who ignores me when my going gets tough? I'm sure Job is only smiling.

Nevertheless, the issue remains. How are we to think of God's relation to persons, particularly when we believe God matters most? Walk with me through my thinking about that affirmation; let's consider one perplexity and then an insight.

# Perplexity

## Meaning of the Affirmation

Where shall we start? We can begin by clarifying what "God matters most" means. Humans are related to God in a way unlike their relation to anything else. That relationship constitutes the place of humans in the created order in a way no other does. The writer of Genesis could have had that point in mind when the words were penned that humans are made in the image of God. The *imago dei* claim means more than humans are listeners for God's commands, obedient servants, and good stewards of the created order. Through their relationship with God humans not only exist, but also have an identity, are knowable, and find ways of living that are good and just. Without God humans would not exist, not have ways that are good and just, not have an identity, and not be knowable. God is, as metaphysicians say, the ground of the existence, identity, self-knowledge, and moral life of persons. I cannot address all of these beliefs; most are outside the issue of this lecture. I want to focus only on one topic — who I am, or personal identity.

Let's be clear about what identity means in this context. It could mean the nature of the persons or the way of life of persons. Sometimes the distinction is made between the person and the personality of the person. We will simply assume that persons as persons are creatures of God. But I am interested in the way of life of persons, the personality of the person and how God is related to it.

## The Source of Identity

There are two ways of thinking about one's life so far as identity is concerned: Identity is based in someone or thing other than oneself, or it is based only in oneself. The first is not new. It is found in Greek society. The words "Know thyself" meant that one's way of life is formed by one's place of responsibilities in society, and a wise person will learn that and act accordingly. The second is modern. Most Americans who hear the words "Know thyself" turn inward to seek there who they are, the way of life that is best for them.

These two ways of viewing the roots of personal identity have an interesting implication for how modern Christians understand their relation to God, specifically their identity. It places them in a perplexity regarding the basis of their identity. If we follow the Bible, books written in the context of traditional societies, we must believe identity is rooted in someone or something not ourselves. We must consciously affirm that someone or thing, not ourselves, constitutes our identity and directs our lives. But as modern Americans who are deeply individualistic, we believe our identity comes from ourselves. We believe we must be self-directed and autonomous.

## Identity as an Antinomy

This perplexity has a logical pattern. It is what philosophers call an antinomy. As an antinomy it is composed of two statements that are contradictory, yet both are true. That is logically odd. Let me explain. On the one hand they are contradictory. That means that if one is true, the other must be false. For example, if I say, "My identity is constituted by and gained only through God," and if what I claim is the case, the statement is true. And if that statement is true, then the statement "It is not the case that one's identity is constituted by and gained only through God" must be false. Simply put, "One's identity comes only through God, and it is false that one's identity comes only through God" cannot both be true nor both be false. One must be true and the other false. That's what I mean when I say that they are contradictory. On the other hand, any American Christian would recognize they are both true. That's what makes an antinomy odd. The statements are contradictory, and yet both are true. That is logically odd. Here, we have two true but incompatible views of "Know thyself." To gain the depth of this perplexity, let's consider each one.

The ground of personal identity is God. Early Christian understandings of this claim were first formulated in the context of and influenced by traditional societies whose root value was honor. And it was in such a society that "Know thyself" became prominent. Consider the cultural context in which these words first gained their meaning. The words "Know thyself" were inscribed over the entrance way to the oracle at Delphi. What did that mean for the Greeks? Living in traditional societies and believing that goods are limited, the Greeks, along with their Mediterranean basin neighbors, believed that the highest value for any person was honor. Honor is one's place in society, one's status and role in society. Honor comes to one through the eyes of others. A change of place cannot come by one's own efforts; it is either given at birth or bestowed on one by a person of higher status. Born to a place in society and bound by its duties, a person spent his life learning his station and fulfilling its duties. And the way others viewed him was central to his understanding of his place. Society bestowed upon persons their identity. Though persons were numerically different (obviously they have different bodies) and they had their own thoughts, neither was as important as the identity that comes from one's place in society. "Know thyself" meant

"Know one's station and its duties"; such constituted wisdom, and ignorance of it constituted foolishness. To act on it properly constituted virtue.

Consider two examples from Greek culture. Socrates, who was perplexed by the report that the oracle at Delphi said that there is none wiser than Socrates, turned to conversations with others, including poets, artisans, and politicians, to learn the meaning of the oracle. The Socratic dialectic is a social act that will lead the perplexed from ignorance to knowledge to self-discovery. A clear example of the dialectic is Socrates' conversation with Euthyphro. Deep in the conversation Euthyphro defined piety as "that part of justice which attends to the gods" (Euthyphro 14). Socrates states his frustration. At the point Euthyphro could have defined piety as the imitation of the gods, the highest form of flattery, Euthyphro turned away and Socrates, disappointed, followed. That is, piety is gaining one's personal identity from the gods.

Next, consider Plato. In the *Republic*, humans find their true identity only in the Good, the source of all things being and being known (including humans). Plato encourages us to take the journey to the rational structure of reality and let reason guide us. As the mind moves from images to visible objects to mathematical objects to the forms and the Good, it does so rationally. The imagination, appetites, and the capacity for indignation hinder the rational work of the mind, so they must be subordinated to reason. The soul that completes the journey finds in the Good the way of life one ought to live; one finds one's identity. What is the relation of the rational soul to its rational object that constitutes one's personality, one's way of life? It is imitation, wherein the soul imitates the Good.

Before we move on, consider for a moment the meaning of the word "imitation," and we can better understand Plato's view. The word "imitation" signifies an appeal to a metaphor from crafting. To say that the good soul imitates the Good is parallel to the assertion that a portrait imitates the person it portrays. This implies a relation between the image and the original. If imitation is a relation, how should it be construed?

There are three possible meanings of imitation. First, imitation could mean resemblance. For example, a cloud and the head of a horse may resemble each other. In the relation of resemblance the two objects are mutually dependent. The relation is symmetrical, as in 1+2 = 1+1+1. This is clearly not what the image of God in man means. God and humans are not equal and mutually dependent. Second, imitation could mean copy. In this case humans are like God, but God is not like humans. That relation is asymmetrical. For example, it is true that "John is the father of Sue," but it is false that "Sue is the father of John." "Is the father of" is an asymmetrical relation. In a copy relation, the image is a window through which one sees the original. The value of the image derives solely from the original. The status of the image? It is totally dependent on the original. And its identity derives from its perfectly mirroring the original. Third, imitation could mean representation. In this case, humans represent God, but God does not represent humans. The relation is asymmetrical, as in the copy theory. But, unlike a copy, a representation is not a window through which one can view the original. Nor does its value derive solely from the original. Rather, the representation is an interpretation of the original, has value in and of itself as an interpretation, and its ends are internal to itself. The identity of the representation derives both from what it is like and from the ends internal to it, understood as an interpretation of the subject matter.

Now, back to Plato. Which of these meanings of imitation does he employ? A casual reading of Plato's writings leads one to believe that he held to the copy theory. The good soul copies the Good; the morally correct soul copies the moral ground of the universe, the Good. And this copying meant the subordination of the lower to the higher; the appetitive, spirited, and imaginative elements must follow their political leader, reason.

Both the social structure of traditional society and Plato's views significantly influenced early (as well as later) Christian thinking. Within this cultural and intellectual context, early Christian thinkers thought through their faith. They believed that humans are made in the image of God. That is, their identity as persons comes from and is dependent on God. They bear God's imprint, the *imago dei*; through it Christians find who they are.

Consider Augustine's view. In the first paragraph of his autobiography, *The Confessions*, Augustine wrote that our hearts are restless until they find their peace in God. His story is the story of every person. Lost in the fictional world of our imagination, dreams, pictures, and illusions we seek our identity in our own creations. But as creators of our world who depend on the imagination we only do it badly. The story of life is of the journey of the soul as it moves from its life captivated by the fraudulent imagination and a self-created but false identity to the life of peace that reason brings as it guides the soul to God. To know oneself, one must first know God. Guided by reason and subjecting our wills to God, our hearts find peace; in God we know who we are, what we are to do, and what we are to be. God constitutes the identity of the life at peace. But what does that mean? We are related to God, but how is that relation to be understood?

What is the relation of persons to God in Augustine's view? It is the relation of a copy to its original. (But it is also the ontological relation of participation. Both natural objects and moral actions are because they participate in the forms, the Good in God's mind. Humans are because they participate in God. Evidence for this is drawn from Augustine's use of

Neoplatonism as the scaffolding for his philosophy and theology. The world, including humans, imitates the eternal forms; God is the source of everything's being and being known.) Augustine follows Plato in accepting the copy theory. What of God do humans copy? God as the forms is the rational, moral ground of the rational, moral structure of the created order. And humans come to know God, in part, through their reason. The identity of the human personality, of the human life, lies in the rational grasp of God, the moral ground of the universe. Reason is king in persons, and all other dimensions of the soul must subordinate themselves to its rule. The lower must copy the higher for human identity truly to manifest itself. And a moral, well-ordered society should manifest this hierarchy as well. Upon finding themselves through God they also find their proper place in society. The meaning and value of a person's life are derived solely from God; the better the copy the better the life.

It would be interesting to trace the concept of *imago dei* through the history of Christian thought. But for now we can say that the views fall into two groups: those that find God's image in reason and those who find it in the moral life of God. Most Protestant and Catholic thinkers follow the former view. The latter view is adopted by some, including Borden Parker Bowne and E. Y. Mullins, in part at least.[1] Though they may differ, they adopt the copy theory of the image. Human identity consists either in reason or in moral patterns, both of which copy God's rational and/or moral nature.

Regarding the first of the two statements in the antinomy, it is true that humans gain their identity only through God, and that identity is achieved through the imitation of God. Let's turn to the other statement that made up the antinomy.

It is not the case that the ground of personal identity is God. One of the achievements of the modern world is the independent, autonomous personality. We have come to understand ourselves as masterless persons.[2] This idea has its roots early in the modern world. Consider Descartes; he claimed we can, independent of God, know for certain that we exist, and we call on God only to account for other human minds and nature and to guarantee the dependability of knowledge claims about the external world. "God is a logically necessary premise" (Hallowell 112). Locke develops further this view of man with his strong emphasis on the place of experience in the growth and development of knowledge. Having no innate ideas (read no *imago dei*), the mind is a blank tablet; what makes marks on the mind comes either through the internal or external senses. This means that persons are formed by the environments in which they live. Yet both Descartes and Locke hold to the view that there is a person persisting through the changing experiences. Rousseau rejects that as well. In his highly influential *A Discourse on Inequality*, humans change from a free, brute-like existence to an enslaved existence, as they acquire private property, language, and form society. Rousseau's humans are malleable, private, individual, alone, good; in them there is no essence. They can take on whatever form of life their choices and their environment allow them.

Consider the place of the masterless man in one social science. The anthropological studies of Gregory Bateson led him to develop a theory of social development that was heavily dependent on studies in cybernetics. The theory is not important, but why he needed one is. He studied two societies, the Latmul people and the Bali people. One was agnostic and the other was not. Western thinkers had assumed that all people are agnostic. That is, they are by nature competitive and warlike. Human relations are at bottom a matter of contest. Yet the Latmul people were agnostic and the Bali people were not. There seemed to be nothing about their nature as humans that required they behave one way rather than another. There seemed to be no internal master, *imago dei* or otherwise, that necessitated their behavior. Masterless man crafts whatever identity, life or personality, the environment, heredity, and evolution allow.

Modern autonomous persons possess independently of God both absolute value and equality, and they create their own identity by interacting with and learning from their environment, their heredity, and their place in the evolutionary flow. It is true that humans gain their identity without God.

To conclude this discussion of the antinomy, the perplexity, we face when we say that God matters most; we have two statements, both of which contemporary American Christians believe are true. First, the identity of our everyday lives requires God, and second, our identity does not require God. Either we are copies of God or we are not. Both are true. Yet they are inconsistent; if one is true the other must be false — an antinomy, a perplexity. If we take this problem seriously, we are in a state of philosophical wonder. We have walked together through some of the complexities of this perplexity. Now, let's consider an insight.

## Insight

Is there any way out of this bind? Possibly. Let me give you my insight into untying this deeply personal knot. Before we begin, however, let's agree that in our effort to untie this knot we maintain both the insights of the Judeo-Christian tradition and the insights hard won in the modern world; we may be tightening the knot.

## Rethinking the Antinomy

Where shall we start? One helpful way to work our way through this problem is to rethink the Old Testament, early Christian, Greek, and modern background to the antinomy. Possibly some inadequate interpretations of those sources led us to this perplexity, and reconsidering them could suggest a fresh, insightful approach to it.

The *imago dei* in the Old Testament — turn first to the Old Testament. How best understand the meaning of *imago dei* in Genesis? Consider again the meaning of "image" as a relation between God and man. Recall that early Christian thinkers interpreted it in terms of Neoplatonic metaphysics. "Image" in *imago dei* meant a "copy." What is copied is reason; God is reason and so are God's copies, humans. In the formulation that led to the antinomy, reason is that of God, which is copied in man. We see this in the work of Augustine, in particular. God is being, and for Augustine that meant the forms of Plato reside in God. That much we can know by reason alone. We also believe that God is will and memory. But it is the rationality of God that is supremely imaged in man. The stability we find in humans, that which persists amid their changing lives, is the rational being that remains because it participates in God as rational being. This requires that the imagination, the cause of a fraudulent world and false freedom, be subordinated to reason as the restless mind moves in its spiritual quest for peace in God. The copy view was held by Christians who defended and articulated their faith in terms of Neoplatonic metaphysics. It is not the view of the writer of Genesis.

What view did that writer hold? The God of the Bible is the Creator.[3] Consider the language the writer uses to speak of God and humans. The word used for God the creator is *yotser*; for creation, *yetsirah*; and to create, *yatsar*. God placed in humans a creative impulse that allowed humans "to imitate God's own creation" (Kearney 39). This creative capacity is *yetser*. These words have as their root, *yzr*, which means to "form, or fashion, and also, to form inwardly, to plan. It was used as the technical word for the potter's work" (Kearney 46). Central to their meaning is imagination. One cannot create what one cannot imagine, whether one is divine or human. By giving humans imagination God risked allowing man to emulate Him, to set himself up as His rival, to supplant Him in the order of creation" (Kearney 39). "The yetser, understood accordingly as man's creative impulse to imitate God's own creation, was arguably first realized when Adam and Eve ate of the forbidden fruit of the Tree of Knowledge" (Kearney 39). The ability to imagine is the basis for ethical consciousness and historical consciousness. The imagination allows one to "project a future order of human creation (i.e.

the sin of presumption and pride) and to recall the events of the past (i.e. guilt and remorse).… Imagination enables man to think in terms of opposites — good and evil, past and future, God and man. Thus bringing about the consciousness of sin and of time, the fallen imagination exposes man to the experiences of division, discord and contradiction" (Kearney 39-40). Thus, the image of God in man is the imagination; and the fall of man is attributed to the misuse of that image, the imagination.

Yet there is an essential difference between human and divine creation. It is found in the kind of creative act God undertakes. On the one hand, God creates *ex nihilo*. The word suggesting this is *Bara* and is found in Genesis 1:27, the first creation account. On the other hand, in Genesis 2:7, the second creation account, God creates with preexisting materials. Here "the term Yatsar is used in conjunction with Bara — 'He created (yatsar) him out of dust…and in the Garden of Eden he put the man he had just created (yatsar).'… Here the implication is that God creates Adam…from pre-existing matter" (Kearney 69). Of these two, humans resemble God's creative power only in the second sense. Humans create, but are limited by necessity to preexisting materials.

Interpretations of the place imagination ought to have in our lives formed two traditions, "the way of suppression" and "the way of integration" (Kearney 43, 46). According to the way of suppression, the imagination is condemned to evil. This seems to be what is implied in Genesis 6:5: "The imagination [*yetser*] of man's heart is evil from its youth." Such a negative reading marked a dominant tradition of Talmudic interpretation, "one that deems the yetser to be incorrigibly wicked and counseled suppression as the only remedy" (Kearney 43). Divine law is understood as "warranting a renunciation of the imaginative impulse," of the *yetser hara*, the evil imagination (Kearney 43). In addition, evil imagination is identified with the corporeal and sexual nature of man. In response, rabbinical teaching recommended death, self-denial, and other ascetic practices "as curbs to the erotic impulses of imagination" (Kearney 44). And the *yetser* was connected with idolatry. "Rabbi Jannai…declares that 'one who obeys his yetser practices idolatry' (Jer. Nedarim, 41 b)" (Kearney 45). What view of imitation is present in the way of suppression? It is the copy theory. Thinkers in this tradition embraced the Neoplatonic view of image. For Plato and his followers, including Augustine, images are far removed from the truth, and the imagination must be subordinated to and controlled by reason. (Ironically, the articulation of God's relation to humans, the *imago dei*, employed a metaphor formed by the imagination!)

According to the latter, the way of integration, the imagination is deemed to be that most primordial "drive" of man which, as sublimated and oriented towards the divine way (Talmud), can serve as an indispensable power for attaining the goal of creation: the universal embodiment of God's plan in the Messianic Kingdom of justice and peace.... Once redirected towards the fulfillment of the Divine purpose (yetser), the human yetser might indeed become an accomplice in the task of historical re-creation: a task which man undertakes in dialogue with God. In short, if the evil imagination epitomizes the error of history as a monologue of man with himself, the good imagination (yetser hatov) opens up history to an I-Thou dialogue between man and his Creator. This is no doubt why the Talmud declares that "God created man with two yetsers, the good and the evil" (Berach, 61a) and prognosticates that the Messianic treaty between the Lion and the Lamb will result from an "atoned," i.e. integrated, imagination (Gen. R. 48) (Kearney 46-47).

What view of image is employed in the way of integration? It seems to be representation. God creates humans as imaginative beings. But this capacity can never merely copy God's imagination. The imagination forms possibilities, or it is not the imagination. And possibilities are what is not yet the case and may never be. If humans are truly made in God's image, they can form possibilities that God has not formed and act on them even though God has not done so. Granted, human creation is always from preexisting materials; it can bring into existence what has not been there before. The image can only be a representation of God; it cannot be a copy of God. As representations, humans seek to create reconciliation between their ways and God's way. I concur with Kearney that the second interpretation best "conforms to the ultimate recommendation of the Torah as supreme guide for man in his efforts to integrate the inclinations of the yetser and reconcile them with the plan of God's creation" (Kearney 48-49).

The Greeks — what can we learn from the Greeks? We learn from them that the self is dyadic and that the distinctive capacity of humans is their ability to craft. That humans are known through something other than themselves was assumed in the traditional cultures of the Mediterranean basin, and this social condition found its way into their metaphysics. The Greeks assumed crafting as a distinctive characteristic of humans, but they did not argue for it.[4] However, we must reject their subordination of the imagination to the hegemony of reason. Without the imagination there could be no language, and reason would not have a field in which to do its distinctive work.

The Moderns — what can we learn from the Moderns? The masterless man of the moderns, such as we Americans believe in, is autonomous and

free, but only in a limited sense. It is easy to exaggerate the degree of freedom and autonomy we possess. All humans born into the world are born to
parents and in a social context. Those parents, that social context, and that
physical environment define them. We are free, but only in a limited sense.[5]

To see how this is so, we turn to Rousseau. Though Rousseau spoke of
the human machine, as did many others of his time (being heavily influenced by a French interpretation of the work of Isaac Newton), he believed
humans are autonomous. That is, they possess free will. Humans, unlike an
animal, contribute to their own behavior as free agents. Further, in the state
of nature, humans are free of political control (anarchic freedom) and free of
the control of other men (personal freedom; remember that in an honor
society humans are under the control of someone — even a king is under the
control of God). In addition to being autonomous, natural humans also
have the capacity for self-improvement. Though many of the philosophies
thought that humans will perfect themselves and their institutions, Rousseau
merely saw this as the capacity for self improvement. It is also the capacity
for self-destruction. The significance of this is that the future is open. There
are no necessary ends to which humans must work.[6] However, in society
only free will remains. Persons are under the control of other persons and
they are also under political control. This is what it means to live in a society. We can say that though humans are defined dyadically, they possess free
will.

Assessing the reexamination — what have we learned from our reexamination of the Hebrew view of the *imago dei* and from early Christian
thinkers, the Greeks, and the Moderns? (1) Human likeness to God is rep-
resentational and consists in the imagination; (2) the imagination implies
freedom (freedom of the will, we would say today); (3) humans are creators,
or crafters, who transform the commonplace into something it was not
before their work began; and (4) humans gain their definition both from
God and from their own creative work. But, more importantly, we have
gained a key insight, an insight that may shed light on how all these live
together. It is an insight drawn from art: creative-finding.

## Creative-finders

From the Hebrews and Christians, as well from the Greeks, we learn that
humans are crafters or creative-finders. The creative act of forming the self,
particularly the self-creation of the self-circumspect person, brings something into existence that was not there before. This does not imply that selves
are fictions of a romantic imagination. Selves can be differentiated from each
other, and that differentiation does not rest on the imagination alone. Their

individuality primarily rests in the "medium" that imaginative selves explore. By medium I include language, society, and the physical environment. But I also include the bodily life of individuals. The self created by a world class athlete and one created by a clumsy person are different selves. And it is not only in language that the difference lies. It is also in the body through which the person explores possibilities, suggested no doubt by language but also by the body itself. It is in the medium that the self finds possibilities. These possibilities as projected by the imagination are images, but what the mind imagines could not have occurred without the suggestiveness of the "medium." In addition, the medium sets boundaries to the possibilities of the creative imagination. The imagination can conceive of possibilities that the medium will not support. Succinctly, a cello cannot be made to sound like an oboe, and an oboe cannot be made to sound like a base drum. Though each of these instruments suggests to the composer a wide range of possibilities, they have their limits or boundaries. Thus, medium is both suggestive and limiting. Now we can say that any self is formed within a suggestive and limiting context that exists both within it and external to it, in the sense that we can say that our bodies exist external to our minds, but not separate from them.[7] So, as persons create themselves, they also find themselves, in this special sense of "find."

## Untying the Knot

With this background and insight, let's turn to the antinomy. As we have seen, the sticking point of the antinomy is that American Christians believe that self-identity is and is not a copy of God. However, if one considers the insight of creative-finding, one may have a way of thinking about this key sticking point that may loosen the knot. Again, the antinomy: Self-identity requires something other than the self, or self-identity does not require anything other than the self.

Consider the second of the two statements: Self-identity is not grounded on anything other than the self.[8] As we craft our lives, we bring into existence something that was not there before. There is no better way to recognize this than to see how we change as we successfully take on a challenging task. (Note what occurs if one avoids such tasks.) As we create ourselves, we bring into existence something new. In this sense our identity is dependent only on our capacity for self-creation. God did not do it, so we cannot claim it is dependent on God.

Consider the other statement: Self-identity is grounded in something other than the self. Again, consider the act of creating. As one works in a medium, exploring its possibilities and allowing it to manifest possibilities that one would not have known without the medium, one is finding what is available for artistic exploration. The crafted poem finds its identity through the medium. And the crafted self finds its identity through the suggestive possibilities of the medium its explorations helped bring to light.

For example, as persons craft their lives, they do so with the medium available to them. That is, within the biological possibilities they possess and the social opportunities available to them, humans find their lives. Persons can become musical only if they have the ear for it, the talent for it, appropriate educational opportunities, and the encouragement of their friends and family. And persons can become good people only within a context that will support and encourage goodness. Thus, it is true that we gain our identity through something other than ourselves. We do imitate that other, not as a copy, but as a representation.

This means that in the act of crafting ourselves, we find both statements are true. But under this interpretation something has now happened to the two statements. It is false that the only ground of self-identity is through something other than oneself. For what we understand of the act of crafting ourselves, we are both self-dependent and not self-dependent at the same time. Both are true, but now they are not contradictory.

The self-identity of Christians is both independent of and dependent on God. That is, in the crafting act we creatively find ourselves. And in that same act we find our self-identity in God. How can that be the case? God is Creator. Central to that creating activity is the imagination. It is in the act of crafting ourselves through the imaginative exploration of our world that we imitate, that we find God. In the act of self-creation we have glimpses. As the creative imagination is employed in constructing our story within the story of God we find who we are, what we are to do, and what we are to be.

## Personal Identity as Creative-finding

At the outset of this lecture, I said that what matters most is God. Now I can say what this means, at least in part. It means that God is creator and we are, by virtue of the imagination that most distinguishes us as humans, creators too. We are co-creators with God; not God's equals, but creators nevertheless. What, then, is our identity? We are creators in concert with God the Creator. But what form does this creator life take? Does this mean that I missed my calling when in my teens I went to college rather than to a conservatory to study music? No, not that. The creator life is deeply moral. I am to love God and my fellow persons. Or, to love mercy, love justice, and walk humbly with God. That takes imagination, moral imagination. It will not occur unless I creatively find ways to be that way and to make it happen. I ought to creatively find the Way. This is the life of responsible reconciliation of all aspects of life in society. One who creatively finds love, justice, and a humble walk with God also creatively finds reconciliation in the inner life, reconciliation in the outer life, and reconciliation with God — not integrated under a class concept or universal, such as logic would demand, and not reconciled as a copy might be reconciled to its original, but reconciled as different sounds of the orchestra, sometimes high, sometimes, low, loud, soft, themes and counter themes, melodic and discordant, all find their place in the music. Different, similar, odd, but reconciled and beautiful in the hands of the creative-finding of the orchestra.

And what about my sense of being alone at the decision points in my life? That came from a view of God and God's relation to persons that is faulty. We are not to copy God. That requires we know the original in its fullness. Neither in Christ nor in the world do we have that. Rather, in our creative-finding we are representations of God. That means we are imaginative co-creators with God and with other persons who deliberate, debate, argue, and choose, much as a writer surrounded with the art world deliberates, debates, argues, and chooses the theme, the language, the right metaphor for a story. We are creator-finders of our lives; that is ours to do. But we are not masterless persons either. We, as creative-finders, reconcile ourselves with God as we seek and find the way. We, as creative-finders, reconcile ourselves with others as we seek a just and loving society. We, as creative-finders, reconcile ourselves with the natural world as we seek to be responsible to the possibilities our natural medium provides us. So what I thought was God's abandonment was my part in the reconciling work of creative-finders. In that creative-finding moment, we are persons. In that creative-finding moment, we have our dignity. In that creative-finding moment, we grow in God's image. The creative-finding of reconciliation is God's gift, God's grace, God's love to persons. Christians find this grace supremely manifested in the Christ.

Let me rephrase my belief. What matters most is God, who created humans to be co-creators with the Creator, to be creative-finders in the art of reconciling society, nature, and God.

# Notes

[1] It is important to note that I have emphasized the rational aspect of God imaged in man. Augustine's view is richer than that, however. In humans one finds the Trinity. Humans manifest the Father in the Eternal Forms (which reside in the memory), the Son in thought, and the Holy Spirit in the will. My purpose is more philosophical than theological, and for that reason I have emphasized the rational aspect of God's image in humans. Also in this discussion I have focused on Augustine and omitted the one other major Christian thinker in the Middle Ages, Thomas Aquinas. He, too, believes reason and the will are the image of God in humans. The relation is also copy, but it is the copy of the cause in the effect. This difference does not alter my major contention that the *imago dei* is reason. For an overview of the *imago dei* doctrine, see Neibuhr 150-160. For twentieth-century Protestant thinking, see Tillich 258-259 and Brunner 88-89. For the moral view, see Mullins 258-259.

[2] Hallowell claims this is an "entirely novel conception" 111.

[3] In the following discussion I depend heavily on Kearney, *The Wake of the Imagination*. His is the most extensive examination available of the relation of the imagination to God as recorded in the Old Testament and as discussed in rabbinical literature.

[4] See Turbayne 7-66 for a defense of this statement.

[5] For a defense of this view, see Hampshire, *Innocence and Experience*, and Grassi, *Rhetoric as Philosophy*.

[6] See Rousseau's *Discourse on Inequality*. We see this later in the nineteenth century in Nietzsche, who says, "The sole source of values and truth in the world is the autonomous individual — all rests in the rectitude of his will" (Norton 92).

[7] A distinction does not imply the kind of difference that Rorty assumes to exist between the self and nature. See Rorty 5.

[8] This is not a rebirth of Cartesianism. Rather, humans can reflect on themselves without that reflection being mediated by another person and/or event or by the subject — object dichotomy.

# Works Cited

Brunner, Emil. *Specific Problems.* Vol. 2 of *Christianity and Civilization.* 2 vols. London: Nisbet, 1949/1955.

Grassi, Ernesto. *Rhetoric as Philosophy.* University Park: Pennsylvania State UP, 1980.

Hallowell, John H. *Main Currents in Modern Political Thought.* New York: Holt, 1950/1965.

Hampshire, Stuart. *Innocence and Experience.* Cambridge MA: Harvard UP, 1989.

Kearney, Richard. *The Wake of Imagination, Toward a Postmodern Culture.* Minneapolis: U of Minnesota P, 1988.

Mullins, E. Y. *The Christian Religion in its Doctrinal Expression.* Philadelphia: Judson, 1917/1954.

Niebuhr, Reinhold. *Human Nature.* Vol. 1 of *The Nature and Destiny of Man, A Christian Interpretation.* 2 vols. New York: Scribner's, 1941/1964.

Norton, David. *Personal Destinies, A Philosophy of Ethical Individualism.* Princeton: Princeton UP. 1976.

Plato. *Euthyphro, Apology, Crito, Symposium.* Trans. Jowett with introduction by Moses Hadas. Washington, DC: Regnery Gateway, 1953/1991.

Rorty, Richard. *Contingency, Irony, and Solidarity.* New York: Cambridge, 1989

Rousseau, Jean-Jacques. *A Discourse on Inequality.* Trans. Maurice Cranston. New York: Penguin, 1984.

Tillich, Paul. *Systematic Theology.* Vol. 1. Chicago: U of Chicago P, 1951.

Turbayne, Colin Murray. *Metaphors for the Mind, The Creative Mind and Its Origins.* Columbia, SC: U of South Carolina P, 1991. For the moral view, see Mullins 258-259.

# David Shi
## History and President of Furman
### November 8, 1993

The question put to the children of Israel was "How then shall we live?" Throughout human history, people have been encouraged to ask the same questions of themselves: What is the meaning of life, and how shall one live?

Yet, in fact, we rarely take time to think critically about the things that give genuine meaning to our lives. Instead, we tend to operate on automatic pilot or in overdrive, pursuing artificial goals that are largely defined for us by external forces. To cite but one example: A recent survey of some 200,000 college freshmen reveals that seventy-six percent of them indicate that "being financially well off" is their primary concern. Only thirty-nine percent said that developing a "meaningful philosophy of life" was important to them.

Yet the journey to maturity involves more than physical growth and career success — it also requires confronting the enigma of what *really* matters.

At Furman, we promote the education of the whole person, and this means we have an uncommon interest in the exploration of values. That is, we believe that a Furman education should involve more than the learning of fresh knowledge and specialized skills. We seek to ensure that students have numerous opportunities to focus on what is ultimately worthwhile. This means asking students to consider who they *are* and what they are going to *be* in life, not simply what they are going to do, but what they are going to be — inside themselves and among themselves. If there is one thing that we hope all Furman students will take with them when they leave this special place, it is a more deliberative sense of what a truly good life should entail.

Like most of you, I suspect, my sense of what truly matters is largely derived from my experiences in life and from my relationships with people — parents and relatives, spouse and children, friends, teachers, students, colleagues, teammates, and coaches.

I have also learned much about life and myself from my readings. At an early age I developed what has become an unshakable addiction to books. I love books. I read them, read about them, write them, review them, loan and borrow them, go to bed with them, even dream about them.

Books awaken us, instruct us, admonish us. They point us in new directions or give us the courage to stay a given course. They help us find our bearings, engage us in self-scrutiny, lead us to feel uneasy about our failures and limitations, and even inspire us to lead lives of moral integrity. In other words, the road to what really matters is paved with good editions.

To read the Bible as an adult rather than an acolyte is to discover new vistas of meaning. To have read Thoreau and Emerson, Emily Dickinson and Virginia Woolf, Tolstoy and Richard Wright as a young adult, when one's senses are most keenly and nervously alert, was enchanting.

A decade ago I wrote two books about the ideal of simple living in the American experience. The research for those books helped inform and reinforce my own sense of what really matters, and much of what I have to say tonight is drawn from those sources.

Ever since Thomas Jefferson asserted in the Declaration of Independence that the pursuit of happiness is our inalienable right, Americans have been feverishly stalking the good life.

We have come to assume that happiness is our birthright. "How to gain, how to keep, how to recover happiness," the genial philosopher William James observed in 1901, "is in fact for most men [and women] the secret motive of all they do, and of all they are willing to endure."

To their credit, Jefferson and the other founding fathers and mothers recognized that people would necessarily fasten upon different versions of happiness. Indeed, in the quest for happiness, as in love, we are often astonished at what is chosen by others.

Our perceptions of what really matters also change over time as we pass through the successive stages of life — childhood, adulthood, middle age, and old age.

What today I think really matters bears little resemblance to my scale of priorities as an adolescent or as a Furman student. That is one reason why Jefferson phrased it in terms of a "pursuit" rather than a guarantee. But if pursuing happiness is our true national pastime and great obsession, it remains a frustrating quest and an amorphous objective. We valorize happiness; we think we know how it feels, and we often claim to be happy, but what *is* it?

Is it made of gossamer and spider's webs? A crumpled sunbeam? Is it something we find or something we create? Is it a function of what we have or what we do or who we are or what we accomplish? Alas, we can no more define happiness than a terrier could define a rat. It is something that we each intuitively pursue.

Through the centuries, people have arrived at quite different definitions of happiness. Daniel Boone, for example, emphasized that "all you need for happiness is a good gun, a good horse, and a good wife," in that order. The cynical nineteenth-century American writer Ambrose Bierce offered a comparative version of happiness. In his *Devil's Dictionary*, he defined happiness as "an agreeable sensation arising from contemplating the misery of another."

Over the years people have often emphasized marriage as an essential ingredient for happiness. A Jewish proverb advises young men that they should by "all means marry someone. If you get a good wife, you'll become happy; if you get a bad one, you'll become a philosopher." In a similar vein of male chauvinism, H. L. Mencken asserted that "the only really happy folk are married women and single men." Others define happiness in terms of what to avoid. I once heard a country-western song titled "Happiness Is Seeing Lubbock, Texas, in Your Rearview Mirror."

Of course, philosophers over the centuries have been preoccupied with the study of happiness. Aristotle devoted the whole first volume of the *Nichomachean Ethics* to the theme of happiness. He concluded that happiness was "not a product of action," but a mode of life, a *way* of living consonant with a deliberately chosen ideal of the good life. Similarly, Thomas Jefferson and the other founding parents, all of them well grounded in classical philosophy, equated happiness with the living of a socially virtuous and useful life. To be happy in a Jeffersonian sense was to be a moral person living the just life of a social being.

As time has passed, however, this classical conception of goodness has given way to a more modern version of happiness as self-fulfillment. We tend to engage in a kind of idolatry of the self, remaking the world in our own image. Self-esteem used to involve a fundamental sense of self-worth. It rested on the daily acts of effort, sacrifice, care, and accomplishment, which are the bedrock of character.

Now, its prevalent meaning has narrowed into merely feeling good about oneself. "Don't worry; be happy!" jazz singer Bobby McFerrin crooned in 1989. Ten million people bought the record and its beguilingly simple formula for happiness.

Every age has its illusions. Ours has been that happiness is synonymous with "smiley face" decals. Fun and "feeling good" are presumed to be as readily available as a prescription medicine or a do-it-yourself video. Each day we are bombarded with such pop-psych advice. Feel-good books such as *How to Be Happy Alone* explain how to be your own best friend. You can achieve happiness, we are told, by eating less or eating more, by undergoing liposuction or cosmetic surgery or hair implants. You can rub yourself with crystals or follow the teachings of L. Ron Hubbard or your personal fitness trainer.

The popularity of this therapeutic culture suggests that we've become so self-centered that we have lost contact with the traditional sources of insight that help us understand what really matters: the wisdom of elders, the claims of religious faith, and the nurturing warmth of nuclear families.

Remember what the role of the self is within the Judeo-Christian tradition. Witness the book of Job, the Epistles of Paul, the Confessions of Augustine — all of these sources cast stern suspicion upon those who promote the sufficiency of the self.

We read in the book of Matthew the great commandment to love God with all our soul, heart, mind, and strength. The second commandment is that we should love our neighbors as ourselves. Those two imperatives wonderfully complement one another and eloquently define a full and meaningful life.

Yet such an elevated notion of happiness is not sufficient for most of us. Instead, we tend to equate a good life with more and more goods. To be sure, the assumption that happiness is a function of our material possessions is not altogether false. Aristotle recognized that a good life required at least a modicum of prosperity.

Most of us, however, are not willing to settle for a little prosperity. We want more and more of it. Caught between the promise of prosperity and the reality of inequality, we are forever denied the serenity of contentment.

Our treasures multiply, but peace of mind eludes us; our pleasures increase, but not our satisfaction. Our reach continually exceeds our grasp. We relentlessly seek some good we lack, some place or position other than we have. Of course, such ambition can be quite stimulating and creative. But like all virtues it can become self-corrosive if taken to excess.

Since the early 1950s, public opinion surveys have consistently reported that only a third of Americans characterize themselves as being "very happy." We crave happiness, yet most of us remain strangers to it.

Our therapeutic outlook deceives us. Life in the fast lane nourishes the conviction that more money and newer things are better and necessary ingredients of the good life, and that nearly every need can be met, every anxiety relieved, every want satisfied, by the getting and spending of money.

Yet there are rumblings underneath the glitzy surface of our self-indulgent ethic. The three most frequently prescribed drugs in this country are an ulcer medication, a hypertension reliever, and a tranquilizer.

Stress has become one of the nation's leading public health concerns. The director of behavioral medicine at the University of Louisville recently observed that "our mode of life itself, the way we live, is emerging as today's principal cause of illness."

Fully half of all illnesses in the United States are stress-related. And stress is by no means limited to adults. College counselors have noted a surge in stress-related disorders, from anorexia to depression to grade anxiety. Suicide rates have also risen steadily during the last twenty years, especially among young people and women.

But how do we rediscover what really matters? That is the rub, isn't it? In the abstract it is easy to see and admire the virtues of enlightened living. But how do we get back on course? Where do we find a valid new compass?

Unfortunately, there is no magic formula or checklist I can provide you to follow in making such decisions. There is no universally applicable *summum bonum*, no Aristotelian mean or Platonic form of the good, no perfect prescription for a good life. We have to map our own path to what really matters, for each of us starts from a different state of confusion, and each day brings new challenges.

We must choose for ourselves what really matters. In this regard, life becomes a continual negotiation, a perennial compromise. A good life is typically composed of a mosaic of elements: home, family, faith, career, recreation, self-culture, civic duty. These elements involve all four elements of personhood — the physical, emotional, spiritual, and communal.

To achieve such a fragile coalition, we must strike and restrike a delicate balance between conflicting needs, goals, duties, responsibilities, and directions. The crucial thing is to press constantly against our own limitations and force ourselves to make conscious — and often painful — discriminations about what really matters.

Of course, our own frailty and inertia war against such continuous self-scrutiny. Like St. Augustine, we resolve to improve ourselves — tomorrow. As he once prayed, "Lord, give me chastity — but not yet."

The great challenge of living is in learning how to spend each day wisely. I cannot tell you how to spend each of your days nobly, but I can offer some basic guidelines derived from my own false starts and revised opinions.

Any uplifting philosophy of living, it seems to me, must first resonate with a sense that there are transcendent sources of meaning beyond ourselves, some set of purposes beyond the merely human and the individual.

One tangible aid in helping us to clarify our sense of what really matters is to keep a personal journal. If we lived in the seventeenth or eighteenth centuries, most of us would use a diary for daily reflection.

Today, however, few of us do. Why? Most often, people tell me that they do not have time. How painfully ironic that is! A diary, after all, allows us to achieve some stillness in the midst of the chaos of our daily lives. It takes us on a journey of self-discovery or can provide a repository of intimate confessions.

Far more than a mundane record of daily activities, a journal can be a place to take stock about what really matters. It also can help us diminish a sense of loneliness and focus our thoughts on what really matters. Pope John XXIII once acknowledged his own need to focus on what really mattered when he wrote in his own personal journal: "I must strip my vines of all useless foliage and concentrate on what is truth, justice, and charity."

If honesty is the first chapter in the book of wisdom, then the benefit of a diary is that it forces us to be honest with ourselves, honest about our values, our priorities, and our actions, for nothing is so difficult as not deceiving oneself. We look into ourselves and are able to accuse, convict, or condone. But a person does not achieve a fulfilling interior life solely by turning within and reflecting upon the mysteries found there. We also need to embrace the life outside ourselves.

Human beings have a fundamental need to be part of communities of spiritual and ethical purpose that transcend the individual. We all need to feel a part of a genuine community, a community of persons linked not merely by one kind of relationship — work or friendship or family — but many, interlocking kinds of connections. And we must recognize that, at times, we must put the needs of the whole above our own interests and concerns.

This is what Jefferson meant by civic virtue. A people who will not sacrifice for the common good cannot expect to have any common good.

To shift the locus of our concerns from the self toward connectedness with the world, we need to cultivate deeper personal relationships. A recent survey reported that seventy percent of Americans recognize that while they have many acquaintances, they have few close friends, and they perceive this as a serious void in their lives.

The moral of this fact is that we can all afford to invest more in intimacy. Of all the circumstances that most contented people share, loving relationships seem the most characteristic and the most important. Perhaps this is what Charlie Brown meant when he announced that "happiness is a warm puppy." Love does not make the world and its problems go away, but it does provide a context that commits us to the world and confronts its problems.

We must love this world in all of its chaos, misrule, and confusion — and we must realize that this messy human condition offers an arena for hope, creativity, and fulfillment.

Only through love can we pass from the prison of the self to the freedom of connectedness. Love renews and transforms our spirits. Love, in sum, is the primal and central core of morality, the virtue out of which all other virtues ripen.

We often assume that our understanding of what really matters arrives in the form of an epiphany, a shattering revelation. More often than not, however, what really matters is not limited to some cosmic moment or some profound moral dilemma, but rather is present in the ordinary circumstances of living, being, and doing.

Over the years I have come to treasure both the joys and sorrows of the family routine and the lyric intensity of its simple pleasures. It seems to me that there is no substitute for human relationship and presence, for listening, for sharing silence and wonderment and caring and suffering, for being part of an enterprise larger than life.

Some of you, I suspect, have by now grown impatient with me. You perhaps feel like James Russell Lowell, who after leaving a lecture by Emerson, groused that the speaker began nowhere and ended everywhere. Similarly, you may feel that I have still left the question of how to live, what to cherish, and what to do still hanging sullenly in the air.

So let me conclude with two very succinct prescriptions for a good life that I have personally found especially compelling. They were both compiled in the 1830s by two New England friends, William Henry Channing, who served as the chaplain of the House of Representatives, and Ralph Waldo Emerson, the lapsed Unitarian minister who became a profound poet and philosopher of Transcendental persuasion.

In a poem titled "My Symphony," Channing wrote,

To live content with
small means; to seek
elegance rather than
luxury, and refinement
rather than fashion;
To be worthy, not respectable,
    and wealthy, not rich;
    to study hard,
    think quietly,
    talk gently,
    act frankly;
to listen to stars and birds,
to babes and sages with open heart; to bear all cheerfully,
do all bravely, await occasions, never hurry.
In a word, to let the spiritual, unbidden, and unconscious, grow up
through the common.
This is to be my symphony.

Similarly, in answering the question of what really matters, Emerson once replied,

> To laugh often and much: to win the respect of intelligent people and the affection of children, to earn the appreciation of honest critics and endure the betrayal of false friends: to appreciate beauty, to find the best in others, to leave the world a bit better, whether by a healthy child, a garden patch, or a redeemed social condition: to know even one life has breathed easier because you have lived.

Such commonplace recipes for a good life offer a means to sustain, enlarge, and assure us. They provide the threads that can seam our days with significance. Such ideal versions of what really matters can be achieved only partially and rarely, but their essential dignity and dimension provide us with inspiriting standards to pursue.

Emerson later wrote in his own journal that "life is a selection." The pungent lesson of my own life experiences is that we can all afford to select more carefully than we do.

# Jeffrey S. Rogers
## Religion
### January 24, 1994

My topic is one to which L. D. Johnson returned repeatedly while he served Furman University as its chaplain. The peculiar nature of this college as a member of an unusual species of academic institutions, both fully fish and fully fowl, professing simultaneous commitments to a religious orientation and to the relentless pursuit of knowledge and the fearless encounter with truth, wherever and in whatever forms they might be found.[1] In particular, what follows is a reassessment of the "Baptist Issue" at Furman as a reflection of my own attempt to understand better and to articulate more clearly what it is that really matters about the kind of higher education in which Furman has been engaged across two centuries.

I am aware that more than a few people associated with Furman believe that the "Baptist Issue," so called, no longer matters. Many people believe that the action in 1990 by the Board of Trustees, which eventually resulted in the severance of relations between Furman and the South Carolina Baptist Convention, settled the "Baptist Issue" once and for all. In fact, however, that action settled only the issue of governance. Its sole purpose was to save a good little liberal arts college from being flushed into a septic tank of willful ignorance and intellectual dishonesty.[2] The Furman Trustees have stated repeatedly and unequivocally that by their action they had no intention of altering the fundamental (and decidedly *not* fundamental*ist*) nature and character of this university or its relation to its heritage. That heritage is decidedly — and, for some people at Furman, embarrassingly — Baptist. So what is Furman's "Baptist heritage"?

The sad truth is, the Furman community does not have a clue. We haven't the foggiest idea what our "Baptist heritage" is or could be. We have been utterly unable or steadfastly unwilling to come to grips with this institution's Baptist identity. Our failure is at the root of L. D. Johnson's criticism of Furman twenty-five years ago when he found himself in the uncomfortable position, according to his own account, of praising Bob Jones University, Oral Roberts University, and Wheaton College — not schools that Furman has recognized as its "peer group" at any time in its history, for good reason. But he pointed out that what they have done well that Furman has not done so well is (1) formulate a clear sense of institutional identity in relation to their professed religious orientation, (2) express that identity clearly and without reservation, and then (3) set about the business of being who they know themselves to be.

Furman, on the other hand, allowed its identity as "Baptist" to be determined principally by an external relationship with the South Carolina Baptist Convention, rather than by an internal and communal self-understanding and commitment. The result has been that Furman has never adequately accounted for its Baptist identity, especially in the light of its constant tension with the state convention. It is time for a free Furman to come to grips with the Baptist identity with which it was born and with which it has grown and sometimes even prospered for more than a century and a half. To that end, I offer five points and two proposals.

Point number one: When the Furman Board of Trustees amended the university's charter in 1990, it took the *most Baptist* action in the history of that body. In some quarters, that action continues to be depicted erroneously as a move by Furman "against the Baptists." It is time to lay that misconception to rest. Every member of the board who voted for that precipitous and lifesaving move was a South Carolina Baptist. Many of them were ordained ministers, and all of them were elected by South Carolina Baptists. The top administrative officials of this university were at that time all South Carolina Baptists. Baptist alumni/ae of Furman mobilized themselves, among them attorneys from North and South Carolina who found the legal escape route that Furman's own respected counsel did not believe existed. In other words, it was Baptists who threatened Furman's freedom and integrity, and it was Baptists who rose to the occasion to ensure Furman's freedom and integrity. Only through ignorance or dishonesty can the trustee action of 1990 be depicted as "Furman against the Baptists." More correctly, it was "Baptists for Furman."

The historian William Brackney has suggested that there are three "identification factors that all Baptists share."[3] The truth is, if Baptists can be characterized by a single feature, it is that we disagree with each other on almost everything. But consider the second of Brackney's three points of common ground among Baptists. If in place of "church" or "local congregation" you will read "college," you will recognize the quintessentially Baptist nature of the action of the trustees. Brackney writes,

> Baptists also share a stubbornness about the self-governance of their *local congregations*. From their inception, Baptists have resisted ecclesiastical or political control external to the *congregation*. When associations, societies,

and conventions posed a threat to *congregational* autonomy, *local congrega-tions* criticized the presumption of authority or discipline and if necessary, withdrew. The spirit of individual religious liberty has been easily trans-ferred to *congregations*, and given a controversial issue or uncomfortable leadership in an association or society [or convention], *churches* often affirm their autonomy above all else.[4]

As Brackney has indicated, when autonomy — the cornerstone of Baptist polity — is threatened, Baptists vote with their feet. In October of 1990, the majority of members of the Furman board lived up to their Baptist identi-ties by their radical affirmation of autonomy in the face of impending ecclesiastical and political interference in the life of this institution. Point number one: When the Furman Board of Trustees amended the university's charter, it took the *most Baptist* action in the history of that body.

Point number two: Furman University is a direct descendant and prin-cipal inheritor of an international and endangered Baptist tradition. This institution was spawned in one peculiar stream among the many and fre-quently conflicting currents that make up the wider Baptist tradition numbering in excess of thirty million adherents worldwide.[5] In the United States alone there are what are known as American Baptists, Bible Fellowship Baptists, Regular Baptists, General Baptists, National Baptists, North American Baptists, Liberty Baptists, General Six Principal Baptists, Old German Baptist Brethren, Pentecostal Free Will Baptists, Primitive Baptists, Southern Baptists, Seventh-Day Baptists, Duck River and Kindred Association Baptists, World Baptists, and Two Seed in the Spirit Predestinarian Baptists. And that doesn't name them all.

The peculiar stream in which Furman stands is the oldest Baptist stream in the American South, designated by some historians the "Charleston tra-dition." That's a helpful designation, as long as you remember that there is nothing uniquely "Charlestonian" about it. It was one branch in a Baptist watershed whose upper reaches were in England, Wales, and the Netherlands. And before it arrived in the 1680s on the banks of the Ashley and Cooper Rivers in the area of what we now know as Charleston, this branch had splashed and bubbled its way through the Middle Atlantic colonies and the colonies of New England. The "Charleston tradition," so called, was one manifestation of an international current in Baptist life that was neither parochial nor provincial. Were it not so ungainly and infelicitous we should call it the Charleston-Philadelphia-Rhode Island-Boston-Maine-England-Wales-Netherlands tradition. It is an old and historic Baptist tradition. But it has also been for nearly two centuries now an "endangered" tradition. Typically characterized as "genteel" and "cultured" (especially by those who want to be counted among its descendants), this Baptist stream stands in clear contrast to the camp-meeting revivalism that swept into Baptist life in South Carolina in the early 1800s.[6] To begin to realize the considerable differences between the old "Charleston tradition" and the newer revivalistic strains, which to this day pervade many Baptist circles, one need only visit the Furman Room on the second floor of our library to see there exhibited Richard Furman's austere black pulpit robe, modeled on the Geneva bands of Presbyterianism and worn by Furman when he pastored the historic First Baptist Church of Charleston, a position he held for thirty-seven years, from 1787 to 1824.

When reports of widespread camp-meeting revivals in North Carolina and Kentucky began to sift into the Charleston area, Richard Furman and his fellow Baptist ministers did not greet them enthusiastically. Furman had been an outspoken critic of what he considered to be the lifeless condition of religion in the American South in the late 1700s. And First Baptist Charleston had on more than one occasion welcomed to its pulpit the great George Whitefield, arguably the greatest evangelist of the eighteenth century, whose preaching was legendary for its revivalistic effectiveness. But he was not overly efficacious among the Charlestonians, it appears; and the emotional histrionics of the camp meetings was not what Richard Furman had in mind when he spoke of a "revival of religion." In addressing the evangelistic fervor of those meetings, Furman observed to the Charleston Association in 1800 that it was "an important point in religion" to "strike the proper line, both in judgment and in practice, between Christian zeal and wild enthusiasm." He continued, "Let it be our earnest care to choose the happy medium which truth and duty point out in these cases, and in every other where we are liable to run into dangerous and hurtful extremes."[7] There is an epitome of the "Charleston tradition" in Baptist life: "Choose the happy medium which truth and duty point out." Richard Furman deserved to wear that very Presbyterian robe, don't you think?

Furman and other leaders of the old Charleston Association bequeathed to Furman University a peculiar Baptist tradition that values truth and duty above enthusiasm, emotionalism, and manipulative strategies of evangelism. This university's historically critical stance — its frequent resistance to many of the prevailing winds of Baptist life — is this institution's Baptist birthright as a child of the so-called "Charleston tradition," the Charleston-Philadelphia-Rhode Island-Boston-Maine-England-Wales-Netherlands tradition. Point number two: Furman University is the descendant and inheritor of an international and endangered Baptist heritage.

Point number three: The institution that became Furman University was conceived in tension with the South Carolina Baptist Convention.

When Richard Furman and a handful of others determined to use the state Baptist convention, organized in 1821, as the vehicle for establishing an educational institution, they were very careful in the way they expressed the relation of that institution to the convention.

Consider to the following prescription in Article III of the convention's constitution:

> It is designed to be understood, distinctly, that the course of education and government [of the school] will be conducted with a sacred regard to the interests of morality and religion, according to the conscientious sentiments of the founders; *yet* on principles of Christian liberality, and in favor of the rights of private judgment.[8]

This is a pregnant statement; and if ever a womb contained twins, this one does. The constitution that mandates Furman's founding intends to stamp the school with the convention's "interests of morality and religion"; and *yet*, simultaneously, it intends to preserve the institution's "liberality" — its broadness of mind and spirit — and the primacy of "the rights of private judgment." Good luck.

The problem that this pregnancy eventually posed is that the "South Carolina Baptist Convention" only exists for several days each year when messengers from "cooperating" Baptist churches in the state convene for what is called the "annual meeting." So the convention's "interests of morality and religion" depend in the end on who shows up for the annual meeting each year and which expressions of "morality and religion" succeed in a popular vote at that meeting. Unfortunately, to quote the one whose legacy this lecture series honors, "Popular morality, like popular religion, is nearly always a shallow imitation of the real thing."[9] Framed more specifically to the issue of college and convention relations, the point is, as L. D. Johnson once put it, "Only people who are involved in and knowledgeable about education ought to be making decisions which vitally affect its future."[10]

In other words, the tension that has marked so much of this institution's history with the convention was part of its genetic makeup. Furman did not "grow up" to be in tension with the convention; Furman was conceived in that tension. The relationship between the two ultimately failed because the convention came to be dominated by a Baptist tradition that neither knows "liberality" nor respects "the rights of private judgment." Point number three: This institution was conceived in tension with the state Baptist convention.

Point number four: The curriculum of Furman University has been from the beginning essentially secular. People have asked me this question:

"How can Furman be a 'church-related' or 'Christian' or 'Baptist' college while offering an essentially secular curriculum?" My answer is this: "How can Furman do anything else and still be Furman?"

When we in the late twentieth century read Furman's founding documents, which speak of "a seminary of learning" and of "the gratuitous Education of indigent, pious young men, designed for the Gospel Ministry," we immediately think of professional, theological training for ministers.[11] And when we do, we commit a grievous error of anachronism predicated on a lack of historical perspective and an ignorance of Baptist polity. In Baptist polity, the cornerstone of which is the autonomy of the local church, a Baptist congregation may ordain to the ministry anyone it darn well pleases — educated, uneducated, male, female, heterosexual, homosexual, industrious, indolent, whatever. Others of us can scream and shout and stamp our feet and throw ourselves down on the floor in a tantrum, if we want. We can refuse to talk with that congregation; we can refuse to pray with them; we can refuse to minister with them in the name of Jesus Christ; but the one thing we cannot do is stop them. That's Baptist polity at work. There is no denominational apparatus that can control ordination or anything else in a local Baptist church.

In principle, then, no professional training for ministers is required. In fact, many Baptist congregations pride themselves on the lack of education and preparation their preachers have received. They believe in "God-called" preachers, they say, not "man-made" preachers. They ascribe to a position articulated by one Gilbert Beebe in 1833 that "a Theological Seminary, for the preparation of young men for the Ministry, is a workshop of the Devil, and the hotbed of all kinds of delusion."[12] I know that attitude well. It ran deep among some in the congregation I pastored when I was fresh from a fine little workshop of the devil and hotbed of delusion.

Our "genteel" and "cultured" Charlestonians of the late eighteenth and early nineteenth centuries saw it as nothing less than a recipe for disaster that Baptist polity provided for the proliferation of illiterate and unschooled clergy. They looked down the road and saw marching toward them a legion of Baptist ignoramuses, ordained to preach the gospel, yes, but entirely inadequately prepared to be intelligent and articulate leaders in churches and communities. So they committed themselves to "ministerial education," which was not dedicated to the production of a class of religious professionals, but to the preparation of persons, "first among equals" in Baptist parlance, who could provide intelligent and articulate leadership.

Accordingly, when the first Furman opened its doors, it was a college preparatory academy. It was advertised "to afford instruction to Students, that shall prepare them for the higher classes in the most respectable Colleges of the United States, and also, to impart instruction in Theology to young men designed for the Gospel Ministry."[13] There was a clear distinction between two programs. First, there was the college-prep program, which overlapped with existing college curricula since its goal was to prepare students to achieve *advanced* standing in "the most respectable Colleges of the United States." You might notice that there is nothing new about pretentious national ambitions in Furman's promotion of itself; they have been with us at least since the 1820s. Second, there is a separate program in theology for those preparing for the ministry. Outside of the "Theological Department," the Furman Academy and Theological Institute offered an essentially secular program of education with no admixture of "religious instruction" in the typical areas of college prep or collegiate study in the early nineteenth century.

This clear distinction between a collegiate education and theological training can be traced directly to the beginnings of Baptist higher education in this country. In 1795, Richard Furman received a letter from Jonathan Maxcy, then president of Rhode Island College, founded in 1764 as the first Baptist College in America and known since 1805 as Brown University. Maxcy wrote to Furman that students intent on going into the ministry should receive "an education in this college, in the languages, arts and sciences, and then let them spend two years [in a "College of Divinity"] in the study of the Scriptures, attending lectures of the professors, writing sermons, and preaching, etc."[14] It cannot be more clear that Richard Furman and other Baptists in South Carolina agreed with Maxcy's educational philosophy and Rhode Island College's practice of it. Furman and others in the Charleston area helped raise funds for Baptist students from South Carolina to attend Rhode Island College. And it was Furman who successfully nominated his fellow Baptist Jonathan Maxcy to become the first president of South Carolina College, now the University of South Carolina. In other words, the church-related Furman University and the state-supported University of South Carolina were initially built on one and the same conception of a college curriculum.

Persons who expect Furman's curriculum and its faculty to be more like those at Bob Jones, Oral Roberts, or Wheaton than like USC or UNC or Virginia simply do not know Furman's history. Nor do they really know *Baptist* history, because Baptists stand among the great secularizing traditions in all of Christendom. Baptists have systematically desacralized almost everything about the Christian tradition. In England, Baptists rejected the divine right of kings and so helped to strip the monarchy of the trappings of the sacred. Baptists rejected the ancient and hallowed traditions of church government to claim that a democratic model borrowed from the philosophical and political world and conveniently read back into the New Testament was the only acceptable form of government for the church. Baptists rejected the sacred calendar of the Christian year and demanded that church and state alike mark time by a secular calendar. Baptists reduced the holy "sacraments," through which God's grace was mediated to the faithful, to mere "ordinances," commands to be obeyed.[15] The list could continue.

"How can Furman offer an essentially secular curriculum?" "How can Furman do anything else and still be Furman?" Hear L. D. Johnson: "There is no distinctively Christian methodology which religion provides for the work of the natural scientist, social scientist, humanist or artist.... Theological controls of non-theological disciplines are no part of authentically Christian education."[16]

That, my friends, is an authentically *Baptist* voice speaking out of a framework that has thoroughly desacralized the natural, social, and personal worlds and that has furthermore rejected all hegemonic truth claims, even religious ones. My father put it this way when in a similar role to L. D. Johnson's he called on Lutheran colleges to be unapologetic about their embrace of the secular as well as the sacred:

> By "secular" I mean three things, all of which are related and intertwined. First, "of or pertaining to [the] temporal."... Secondly, I mean by it "non-ecclesiastical." Thirdly, by "secular," I mean "without consciously conceived religious presuppositions."... The "secular" is that sphere of life which has (in Bonhoeffer's phrase) "abandoned the idea of God as a working hypothesis." Now you just do not need the idea of God to build bridges, to manage an economy, to teach calculus, to discover the DNA molecule, or to make love. Quite honestly, God as a "working hypothesis" will only get in the way in these matters.[17]

We Baptists, especially, must cease and desist from our self-serving hypocrisy about the secular dimension of our world.

Thanks to the wisdom of its founders and the faithfulness to the Furman tradition of those who have governed this institution since, Furman's collegiate curriculum has never been determined by ecclesiastical methods or models. It has always consisted of a blend of contemporary educational and cultural currents, local needs, and the particular capabilities and interests of its faculty and administrators. Point number four: The curriculum of Furman University has always been essentially secular.

Point number five: From its beginning, Furman has provided a non-sectarian context for education. Furman has always offered an education in an institutional setting that supports, encourages, and challenges students, faculty, and staff to grow in knowledge and in faith, to grow in truth that is based in empirical knowledge and to grow in truth that transcends the empirical, to grow in spirit as well as in intellect. As L. D. Johnson put it in response to an inquiry from a Baptist pastor, "In the final analysis the justification for a church-related institution of higher learning lies in the fact that it offers a 'plus' in addition to academic excellence."[18] Not a substitute in content, but a "plus" provided by the context.

This "plus" is entirely consistent with Furman's liberal arts ideals. Furman is committed to challenging the members of its community to fashion intelligent and reflective lives of character and service. An indispensable part of that fashioning involves engaging and being engaged by the profound insights and lofty aspirations of the great religious traditions of our world as well as the powerful ideas and empowering methods of secular disciplines. One can certainly choose to live in ignorance of those religious traditions or those secular disciplines, but the Furman education was intended from the beginning to alleviate the poverty of life and shallowness of character that such ignorance typically brings.

The nature of the educational context that Furman provides has been from the outset non-sectarian. In his Harvard dissertation, titled *Baptist Colleges in the Development of American Society*, Donald Potts has pointed out that provincial sectarianism played no role in the founding of the earliest Baptist colleges in this country, including Furman. He writes,

> Throughout the antebellum years, Baptist higher education was largely nondenominational in its aims and its functions. Sectarian sentiments were notably absent in the recruitment of students and solicitation of funds, even when these objectives were pursued in the Baptist press. Contributions of Baptist colleges to the general public were of greater significance than their service to denominational interests. Yet by the late 1840s and increasingly so in the 1850s forces were at work that presaged a change in the nature of these institutions. Sectionalism and denominationalism began to erode the inclusive character which predominated prior to the Civil War.[19]

Indeed, according to the original "Rules for Government" of the Furman Academy and Theological Institute, students were to be admitted "without regard to sect or denomination."[20] The faculty were to be "of irreproachable morals, competent in attainments in science, and *if not Baptists*, friendly at least in their feelings and sentiments to the Baptist denomination."[21]

There are two primary reasons for this non-sectarian orientation of Furman. The first reason was pragmatic: Creed or doctrine or affiliation was not an issue because the collegiate curriculum did not deal in creeds or doctrines or affiliations. The second reason was principled: Furman's founding tradition was fully invested in religious liberty.

Baptists have not always spoken with a unanimous or even a consistent voice on the issue of freedom of religion, among other freedoms, despite the power of much Baptist myth-making on this point.[22] But there are streams of Baptist life — and Furman University was born in one of them — that championed religious liberty and that were instrumental in building that liberty into the constitutions of fledgling states and a nascent nation. Furman's founders had the integrity to recognize that one cannot demand freedom of religion for oneself without demanding freedom of religion for all others, including those whose religion is very different from — even anathema to — one's own. They recognized, furthermore, that there is no freedom *of* religion where there is not also freedom *from* religion. To compel a person to be religious violates the principle of religious liberty every bit as much as the compulsion to be of one particular religious orientation. That is why L. D. Johnson responded to a Baptist pastor that while Furman has an obligation to make a clear institutional affirmation of the nature of its religious orientation, it must do so "without any coercion of those who live in the institution to adopt that affirmation for themselves."[23] That is an essentially Baptist perspective on religious liberty within an institutional context.

There is room in the Furman community for believers of every hue and flavor — and for non-believers as well — not "in spite of" Furman's Baptist heritage but *because* of Furman's Baptist heritage. For students, there are no religious requirements either for admission or for graduation. For faculty, the founding documents provide us with three criteria, none of which is doctrinal or sectarian: evident quality of life, evident professional competence, and a willingness to work within a Baptist frame of reference characterized by "liberality" and the primacy of "the rights of private judgment" as well as "the interests of morality and religion." Point number five: From its beginning, Furman has provided a non-sectarian context for education.

Five points. Now two proposals.

Proposal number one: Furman University must undertake a program of rediscovery and education of itself. We must educate trustees, administrators, old faculty, new faculty, and prospective faculty, students, alumni, friends, and parents about the nature of Furman's Baptist heritage and identity.

Now that we have been released from the political necessity — or expediency, whichever it was — of reducing the Baptist heritage of Furman to the history of the South Carolina Baptist Convention, we can set aside the bankrupt rhetoric and failed reality of a narrow-minded denominationalism to rediscover the national and international web of history of which Furman is a part. Furman's tradition associates it in history with Brown, Bucknell,

Chicago, Colby, Colgate, Regents Park Oxford, Richmond, Rochester, Wake Forest, and many others. It remains to be seen whether Furman will follow the path taken by some of these institutions and relinquish its distinctive and historic character. That is possible, but it is not inevitable.

Furman has survived, and in recent years even thrived, precisely because its birthright combination of an essentially secular curriculum and a non-sectarian context in which faith and learning alike are valued has enabled it to occupy an important niche in the ecosystem of American higher education. To suggest, as some now do, that Furman should reject the religious dimension of its character and identity — and thus abandon its niche — is to call on the institution to make a potentially suicidal move in a viciously competitive and unforgiving post-baby-boom environment. The future of this institution cannot be built on an ambitious wish and a godless prayer. It can only be built on a compelling vision; on analytical and self-critical assessments of the institution's strengths, weaknesses, opportunities, and threats; and on leadership that can articulate and implement programs, policies, and procedures that are consistent with that vision and those assessments.

Because Furman has tacitly accepted a petty and ignorant caricature drawn by cultured despisers of Baptist life and by uninformed proponents of it, too many members of this university's community do not recognize the remarkable asset that this institution's Baptist heritage is as we attempt to assess Furman's present, envision its future, and articulate and implement that which is necessary to get us from here to there. This university has some educational work to do.

Proposal number two: Furman University must develop, implement, and coordinate programs that will facilitate its interconnectedness with a national and international Baptist constituency. The point here is not to limit ourselves to Baptists, but to begin by extending ourselves to the remarkable opportunities that already exist for Furman. The range of possibilities is enormous.

For example, one of the major shortcomings of a Furman education right now is that we provide our students with inadequate experience for living and working in much of American and international society because of the ethnic homogeneity of the Furman community. And yet Furman has a natural Baptist connection to more African-American, Hispanic, Latino, Korean, and Vietnamese churches in the United States than exist among any other Protestant group. In other words, Furman has a ready-made national and international network in which this university's involvement and commitment to education could produce win-win opportunities of global and historic proportions.

For a second example, it is unfortunate that after the split with the convention, Furman's first attempt to cultivate friends among Baptists was perceived by many as little more than an thinly veiled appeal for funds. As well intended as this effort was, it did not connect with the essentially personal nature of the budgeting process in Baptist churches and the implications of Baptist polity for church-relatedness to institutions such as Furman. But Furman has the resources to prosper within the framework of that process and polity, even though we haven't fully utilized them yet.

To give just one illustration, Furman's Church-Related Vocations Program, orchestrated by Dr. Jim Pitts and Dr. Vic Greene, has won national recognition and is presently being imitated by colleges and universities in a number of states. We should be promoting that program with personal contacts in every church — Baptist or otherwise — with a history of relatedness to Furman. In churches from Georgia to New York, I run into Furman alumni/ae and Furman families who want to know more about what we are doing at Furman about "what really matters" to them. We should be working in those churches the way that Head Football Coach Bobby Johnson's staff is working right now in high schools in South Carolina, Georgia, Florida, and Tennessee building relationships and identifying prospects for Furman University. The issue here is not about an ideological or political attempt to keep Furman "Baptist" or keep Furman "Christian." The issue is utilizing a remarkable resource that Furman has at its disposal to keep it fully enrolled and to keep it competitive and among the ranks of the selective liberal arts colleges in this country.

For a third example, the accidence and even the substance of Baptist life in much of the United States and around the world is in a period of transition and reformation in which there has been a vacuum in place of academic institutional participation and leadership. Here again, Furman has a ready-made national and international network in which this university's involvement and commitment to education could produce win-win opportunities of global and historic proportions.

These are only three of many possible examples. But two things must happen before Furman will be able to take advantage of the enormous opportunities that our Baptist connection offers us. First, knowledge must replace the ignorance on this campus about Furman's Baptist heritage and identity. And second, and even more importantly, the buck must arrive and stop on the desk of the new president of Furman University. Had we but world enough and time, coyness on the "Baptist issue" would be no crime. But we don't, and it is. Whoever he or she turns out to be, the new president must be prepared to initiate and oversee the development, implementation, and coordination of programs that will facilitate interconnectedness with a national and international Baptist constituency that remains an integral part of Furman's best hope for greatness in the future.

Sooner or later, in one way or another, people and institutions alike typically set out on what the historian Jaroslav Pelikan has called "a quest for a tradition." Where we do not have a tradition, we will invent one; where we do not like the tradition we have, we will reinvent it. In Furman's case, we need neither invent nor reinvent. We need only rediscover, reinvigorate, and embody more confidently a peculiar tradition that has served this institution marvelously well across two centuries. But the challenge before us is enormous. It remains to be seen whether the Furman University community will have the wisdom and the maturity, the fortitude and the stamina to affirm the twins in the womb. In time we will know whether the reassessment I have offered will be interpreted as a birth announcement or a eulogy for a great and historic tradition at a free Furman.

Can a free Furman sustain a regard for "the interests of morality and religion" while cultivating the principles of "liberality" and the priority of "the rights of private judgment," and especially so in a community and a larger world in which competing "interests of morality and religion" are locked in mortal combat and "liberality" and "rights of private judgment" are under siege? Can a free Furman maintain the dynamic balance of an essentially secular curriculum and a vital religious heritage while powerful and destabilizing forces of imbalance whirl around us and among us? I have no doubt that L. D. Johnson would agree with me that these are questions that really matter. They do not arise out of my pet convictions or your pet convictions, but out of a deep concern for the well-being of this institution and for the well-being of the world in which we live. It is there, at the intersection of concern for the institution and concern for the world, that the future of Furman must be built.

This institution's Baptist heritage is one of the substantial assets we have at our disposal in the building process. But we must not make like the foolish servant who was content to preserve his asset in the ground. To "preserve" a heritage is to pickle it, to can it, to kill it. A heritage is to be embodied, not embalmed, to be lived out at risk, not saved under glass as an icon or an artifact. The issue of Furman's governance is settled, but the "Baptist issue" — Furman's distinctive heritage — remains before us. Birth announcement or eulogy? Asset or artifact? The action or the inaction of the Furman University community will decide. May God grant us wisdom and maturity, fortitude and stamina for the challenge ahead of us. It really does matter.

# Notes

1This lecture is dedicated to the late Rev. Louis V. Rogers, Lutheran pastor and college chaplain, biologist and anthropologist, actor and activist, with gratitude for the love and the vision. *Ad majorem gloriam Dei.*

2I am indebted for this last turn of phrase to Dr. Robert Bratcher, a remarkable Baptist scholar, teacher, and prophet, who was never one to be intimidated into silence or lulled into appeasement.

3William Henry Brackney, *The Baptists* (Denominations in America 2; New York: Greenwood, 1988) 21. The three factors that Brackney identifies are the authority of the Bible for faith and practice, the autonomy of the local congregation, and believer's baptism by immersion.

4Ibid.

5Ibid., 293-96.

6For an overview of Baptist history in South Carolina see Helen Lee Turner, "The Baptists," in *Religion in South Carolina* (Columbia: University of South Carolina, 1993).

7Cited in James A. Rogers, *Richard Furman: Life and Legacy* (Macon, GA: Mercer University, 1985) 110.

8"Constitution of the Baptist State Convention in South Carolina." In *Minutes of the State Convention of the Baptist Denomination in South Carolina,* 1822: 5.

9L. D. Johnson, Address at Furman University Opening Convocation, 18 September 1974. Unpublished manuscript. South Carolina Baptist Historical Collection, Furman University.

10L. D. Johnson, "College-State Convention Relations," unpublished ms., n.d., 3. SCBHC.

11"Constitution of the Baptist State Convention in South Carolina." In *Minutes of the State Convention of the Baptist Denomination in South Carolina,* 1822: 5.

12"Popular Institutions," *Signs of the Times,* 13 February 1833; cited David B. Potts, *Baptist Colleges.* 124.

13*Charleston Courier,* 3 and 5 January 1827; cited in McGlothlin, *Baptist Beginnings,* 64.

14Cited in Harvey T. Cook, ed., *A Biography of Richard Furman* (Greenville, SC: Baptist Courier, 1913) 86-87.

15For an exception, see the statement of the Council of the Baptist Union of Great Britain and Ireland, March 1948, which employs the language of "sacrament" and affirms that believer's baptism and the Lord's Supper "both are 'means of grace' to those who receive them in faith" (reproduced in Walter B. Shurden, *The Baptist Identity: Four Fragile Freedoms* [Macon, GA: Smyth & Helwys, 1993] 87-95). The more typical position is evident in a paper adopted by six North American Baptist groups in May 1964 (reproduced in ibid., 67-78); it explicitly rejects the sacraments' "mediating in any way the saving grace of God to the individual."

[16]Johnson, "College-State Convention Relationships," 8.

[17]Louis V. Rogers, "The University as a Model of Metropolis," unpublished address to the Southeastern District Convention of the Lutheran Church (Missouri Synod), Williamsburg, VA, April 1968: 8.

[18]L. D. Johnson, letter to the Rev. Dr. Julian Cave, 16 March 1966. SCBHC.

[19]Potts, *Baptist Colleges*, 244.

[20]*Minutes of the State Convention of the Baptist Denomination in South Carolina*, 1826, p. 14.

[21]Ibid.; emphasis added.

[22]See the essays in William G. McLoughlin, *Soul Liberty: The Baptists' Struggle in New England, 1630–1833* (Hanover, NH: Brown University, 1991), which illustrate, among other things, that "the manner in which the concept of religious freedom evolved, both in the southern colonies against the Anglican establishment and in the northern colonies against the Puritan establishment, had less to do with ideology than with the very practical exigencies of finding spiritual self expression within the limited bounds available to the dissenters within these establishments (ix-x). It is not surprising, then, that "the story of Baptist dissent" exhibits "ironies, inconsistencies, and contradictions within the concepts and practice of toleration and religious liberty" (xi).

[23]L. D. Johnson, letter to the Rev. Dr. Julian Cave, 16 March 1966. SCBHC.

# A. V. Huff, Jr.
## History and Vice-president for Academic Affairs and Dean
### January 30, 1995

In good rabbinical tradition, if I were to reduce my subject tonight — "What really matters within the university community" — I could put it in a phrase. What really matters is the life of the mind, as viewed from the Delectable Mountains. The first part, "the life of the mind," should give you no trouble. The second part, "as viewed from the Delectable Mountains," may puzzle you a little. That reference should separate out the "real Baptists" in the audience.

Deeply embedded within Western civilization, which is both our geographical and principal cultural heritage in the academy, is the importance of the mind — of rationality — in understanding ourselves, our society, and the nature of the universe as well. We associate the rational tradition with the ancient Greeks, and well we might, though even a cursory reading of Homer and certainly *The Bacchae* by Euripides reminds us on what a narrow cultural base Greek rationalism operated. Unfortunately, the Greek intellectuals never agreed on precisely how mind related to matter. Plato represents one major tradition; Aristotle represents the other. The Greeks bequeathed us their dilemma, and we still struggle with it. In theory (*theoria*), we struggle with it in academic settings like Furman; and in practice (*praxis*), we struggle with it every day, as we confront issues such as religious fundamentalism and the role of government in society. But the major thinkers of the classical age would have agreed with the ancient Greek metaphor *kupia he psyche tou anthropou* — mind is the mistress of man. And, for us, their intellectual descendants, the mind is crucial to the understanding of ourselves and the world in which we live.

But there is another, equally important source of our heritage — the Hebrew and Christian traditions, especially at a place like Furman. The Hebrew and Christian communities, too, held the life of the mind to be of special significance, though the Hebrews refused to divide human beings into discrete parts, such as body, soul, and spirit, of which the Greeks were so fond. The heart of the Hebrew Scripture, the Torah, is found in Deuteronomy 6:4ff. It begins: "Hear, O Israel: the LORD our God, the

LORD is one." Then it continues, as restated by Jesus in Matthew 22: "You shall love the LORD your God with all your heart, and with all your soul, and with all your mind."

In his letter to the Roman church, St. Paul wrote a kind of midrash on that last portion of the *Shema*: "I appeal to you, therefore, brothers and sisters by the mercies of God to present your bodies as a living sacrifice, holy and acceptable to God, which is your rational worship. Do not be conformed to this world, but be transformed by *the renewing of your minds*, so that you may discern what is the will of God — what is good and acceptable and perfect."

Therefore, the life of the mind in the context of Hebrew and Christian faith is not only understanding and self-knowledge, but it is also *vocatio* — an important part of our *calling* as the children of God. However, the academic community, even in a Christian liberal arts college, is not church. Yet, as surely as we gather for worship around an altar or flesh out that worship in feeding the hungry or visiting the prisoners, so too, for those of us who are God's people, our desks become altars in the reshaping of our minds in the pursuit of truth. To paraphrase the writer of the Letter of James: "Faith without knowledge is dead." Or to invoke a more respectable authority than yours truly, St. Anselm put it this way, the life of the mind is *fides quaerens intellectum* — faith in search of understanding.

When much of the long-forgotten Greek heritage began to reenter Western culture in the twelfth and thirteenth centuries, St. Thomas Aquinas reordered the role of faith and reason, assigning each to its own proper sphere. Reason took supremacy over the natural world, up to and including the question of the existence of God. Faith took over at that point to lead us into theological truth. However uneasy, the medieval synthesis of faith and reason obtained. So far, so good.

Then, the time-bomb embedded in the Greek view of the mind went off. An explosion of knowledge occurred in the Renaissance that challenged the assumptions of the medieval synthesis. In the sixteenth century, Galileo, faithful Catholic that he was, ripped faith and reason apart, and in the seventeenth century Isaac Newton, the pious Anglican, saw no contradiction among his roles as architect of the modern scientific worldview, as author of a thoroughly medieval, allegorical commentary on the prophet Daniel, and as the practitioner of alchemy at the University of Cambridge.

Following in the footsteps of Galileo and Newton, the scholars of the Enlightenment took up the issue of the relationship between faith and reason. Their views careened wildly from the deists, such as John Toland in England, who wanted to interpret the Christian faith as one example of a universal religious impulse; to the skeptics, like David Hume in Scotland, who relentlessly pushed Christian thinkers to admit that there was no logical argument for the existence of God; to the pietists, who refused to admit that the game was up but who failed to do more than retread the classical and medieval arguments. Only John Locke, in positing a new psychology, made room for faith as a separate category of the mind through which experience with God could be accessed. John Wesley, one of my spiritual mentors, eagerly embraced Locke's solution and rejoiced, perhaps prematurely: "Let us unite the two so long divided — knowledge and vital piety."

But the nineteenth century was no kinder than the eighteenth to the claims of faith in a world awash in scientific materialistic determinism. When Hegel attempted to explicate the role of Absolute Spirit in the creation of the universe, Karl Marx rudely dethroned the new sovereign with the harsh realities of economic determinism and declared that religion was an opiate for the ills of the world. A decade later Charles Darwin pulled humankind from its place at the center of the earth's creation, just as Copernicus had removed the earth itself from the center of universe 300 years before. Meanwhile, Christian missionaries sailed triumphantly around the globe, bearing the cross as well as the national flags of the West. Revivalists crossed and recrossed the Atlantic Ocean, stirring multitudes with their evangelistic message. But at the end of the century Christian Fundamentalists, whether Protestants who demanded absolute obedience to the literal interpretation of Scripture or Roman Catholics who compelled the same authority for the magisterium of the church, drew ever smaller concentric defenses around their intellectual positions. Pentecostals imploded the use of the mind in a completely affective response to the modern world.

But autonomous reason was about to turn inward upon itself. Early in the twentieth century Albert Einstein projected a universe too vast for any single Newtonian system of understanding, and Sigmund Freud challenged the sacred principle of the objectivity of the human mind. Then, the political and economic industrial world was battered through half the century by the destruction of two world wars and the Great Depression. The horrors of the Stalinist purges and the efforts of Hitler to exterminate the Jews of Europe in the Holocaust called into question the Enlightenment sense of inevitable progress.

Meanwhile, the rational search for meaning led down the ever narrowing alleys of logical positivism and existentialism and deconstruction in an effort to salvage meaning out of the rubble and maintain some role for human reason. But, for many, the search seemed as fruitless as his own quest had to Matthew Arnold a century before when he walked the sands of Dover Beach:

the world...
Hath really neither joy, nor love, nor light,
Nor certitude, nor peace, nor help nor pain;
And we are here as on a darkling plain
Swept with confused alarms of struggle and flight,
Where ignorant armies clash by night.

Is it possible for us to renew the search for meaning from the perspective of faith? Jaroslav Pelikan proposes that we take Goethe's Faust as the metaphor of our dilemma. The drama opens, you may remember, on Easter morning, as the old philosopher laments his failure in his lifelong quest for meaning. As Faust hears the angelic choir chant the Easter anthem, "Christ is risen," he replies: "I hear the message all right; it is only the faith that I lack." To his servant he points out the shortcoming of inherited tradition: "What you have as heritage, now take as task, for thus you will make it your own." Gustav Mahler, in his Eighth Symphony, first performed in 1910, juxtaposed the closing lines of Faust with the ancient Christian hymn, the *Veni Creator Spiritu* — "Come, Holy Ghost, our hearts inspire, and lighten with celestial fire."[1]

If we had taken the critical temper of our religious tradition seriously, as Faust proposed, then we should not have been surprised that reason, ripped apart from faith and life and set on its own course, might well have asserted its own superiority and, then, unenlightened by revelation or uninformed by morality, would turn in upon itself. It is a display of what St. Augustine called concupiscence — or selfish desire; it was his definition of the doctrine of original sin.

Friederich Schleiermacher, the greatest Christian theologian of the nineteenth century, proposed that "the cultured despisers of religion" of his day look deep within themselves in order to discover not autonomy, but a "feeling of Absolute Dependence," the sense of the image of God in the human soul. So perhaps we can renew the search for meaning at the end of the twentieth century at the place St. Anselm pointed us toward in the eleventh — faith in search of understanding. Otherwise, like Faust, we only hear the words of the tradition or analyze their context without being grasped by the subject of faith. Only then can we move in our journey toward understanding.

Hopefully, however, we have learned some things in the last two centuries that will be helpful to us in the quest.

First, I suggest that we must put away once and for all the triumphalism of religious arrogance or intellectual superiority. Too many times persons of faith, as well as scholars, have been guilty of saying, "I have the truth; do it my way." Who dares assume the luxury of arrogance in the shadow of the death camps of Auschwitz, whose capture fifty years ago we mark this very week. D. T. Niles, the great Christian bishop of India, once defined evangelism as "one beggar showing another the way to bread." If the gospel means anything at all, it means that God has called those who were outcasts in the world and that God made himself known in the world through such events as the deliverance of the Hebrews from slavery in Egypt and the public execution of Jesus, not through learned argument and experiment in the comfort of a university setting. Consequently, our demeanor in seeking understanding ought to befit those who have been set free from the slave camps or granted pardon at the mount of execution in Jerusalem. There is no "royal road to learning" within in the context of faith.

Second, the person of faith is most likely to gain understanding in his or her encounter with persons and with the natural world. Martin Buber wrote about that encounter in what, for me, is perhaps the most important book in the twentieth century, *I and Thou*. That's your assignment, if you've never read it! In a way that mirrored his forebears, the ancient prophets of Israel, Buber reminds us that only in the encounter with one another as persons and with the world as our fellow creature can faith come to understanding. And that encounter includes all that humankind has thought and done.

That may sound great in the abstract, but how does Buber translate into the day's work, tomorrow's math assignment, an English paper, or a chemistry experiment? Josephine Humphreys, in her splendid novel, *Rich in Love*, works at finding meaning in history, for example. She has Lucille Odum, the narrator of the novel, say at one point:

> I liked history. Not the kind in the textbooks, the treaties and political parties and government shenanigans, all of which gave me a headache. There was more to history than that. There were things hidden in it, mysteries worth going after.... I wanted to know, to put it bluntly, the secrets of life. I believed they were to be found in the dusty corners of human history. Human history...I also felt that history was a category comprising not only famous men of bygone eras, but me, yesterday. Wasn't I as mysterious as John C. Calhoun, and my own history worth investigating? I had spent some time doing so.[2]

Neither Buber nor anyone else ever claimed such a task was easy. One of the greatest frauds perpetuated in the name of education is the notion that "learning is fun." Nonsense. Whether it is Faust earning four degrees, or Schleiermacher looking deeply within, or Lucille Odum searching "the dusty corners of human history," it may bring deep satisfaction, but it is not fun.

Third, the answers we gain in the search are always tentative. At no other time in human history should we be more aware than we are at the end of the twentieth century of human fallibility and the limits of reason. While we should know those things from faith, they are also clear from the experience of the last 100 years. Yet we do not seem to learn. It is rather amusing, if not down right alarming, to see a new generation of political leaders elected to office, assured that they now have the answers to the ills of society that have eluded generations before them. Perhaps a word from Koheleth will suffice: "Vanity of vanities," says the Teacher, "vanity of vanities! All is vanity."

The search for meaning proceeds from question to question, and the answers — the human paradigms we construct — satisfy us for awhile, until our reason — fed by new data — transcends the old answers, and the human soul cries out for greater insight. In 1903 an aspiring, nineteen-year-old German poet sent some of his work to Rainer Maria Rilke for his criticism. The two struck up a correspondence. Rilke's letter of July 16, 1903, contains some sage advice for faith in search of understanding:

> You are so young [Rilke writes] so before all beginning, and I want to beg you as much as I can, dear sir, to be patient towards all that is unsolved in your heart and try to love the questions themselves.... Do not seek the answers, that cannot be given you because you would not be able to live them. And the point is, to live everything. Live the question now. Perhaps you will then gradually, without noticing it, live along some distant day into the answer.[3]

Fourth and last, the hope that in "some distant day" we may live into the answer of our final question springs entirely from faith and not from reason. The vision of complete knowledge is a hope founded in faith. Scientists may theorize about the end of life as we know it on this planet or in this solar system, but the knowledge of the meaning of that life in its totality belongs to the realm of faith. St. Paul, in his first letter to the Corinthian church, speaks from such a perspective:

> As for [human] knowledge, it will come to an end. For we know only in part.... But when the complete comes, the partial will come to an end.... For now we see in a mirror, dimly, but then we will see face to face. Now I know only in part; then I will know fully, even as I have been fully known. (1 Corinthians 13:8-12, New Revised Standard Version)

In *The Pilgrim's Progress* Christian is directed to the Delectable Mountains where he is told that he and the other pilgrims will be able to see the gates of the Celestial City if they can use the "perspective glass," which belongs to the Shepherds. But they have been so frightened by their view into hell that, according to John Bunyan, "their hands shake; by means of which impediment they could not look steadily through the glass; yet they thought they saw something like the gate and also some of the glory of the place." As they were about to resume their journey, one of the Shepherds gave them a map of the way to the Celestial City. Another "bid them Godspeed."[4]

Unfortunately, I have no such map as Bunyan proposed, either for your journey, or for mine. Perhaps my view of the damage we have done to one another and to our world has made my hand shake. But the way lies before us. So this pilgrim simply bids you and all the rest "Godspeed."

## Notes

[1] Jaroslav Pelikan, *Christian Doctrine and Modern Culture (since 1700)*, Vol. 5 of *The Christian Tradition: A History of the Development of Doctrine* (Chicago, IL, 1989) 1-2.

[2] Josephine Humphreys, *Rich in Love* (New York, NY, 1987) 46.

[3] Rainer Maria Rilke, *Letters to a Young Poet* (New York, NY, 1934) 33-34.

[4] John Bunyan, *The Pilgrim's Progress* (New York, NY, 1957) 118-19.

# Linda A. Julian
## English
### October 9, 1995

In my tug of war to convince my students that Charles Dickens is one of the greatest writers ever — one still speaking truth today — I am discouraged and even pained to hear many of them complain that Dickens' characters are too villainous or too syrupy or too sentimental. Many of my students argue that especially Dickens' female characters fall too neatly into the camp of either angel or demon — Agnes Wickfield from *David Copperfield* or Florence Dombey from *Dombey and Son* in the camp of the good, for example, and Good Mrs. Brown from *Dombey and Son* and Charity Pecksniff from *Martin Chuzzlewit* in the camp of demons. Students cannot suppress groans of disgust when we read aloud such emotionally charged scenes as the death of Little Nell from *The Old Curiosity Shop* or the death of Little Paul Dombey from *Dombey and Son*. Few sophisticated readers today would deny that modern novels contain more realistic plot lines than those intricate plots found in Dickens' lengthy tomes, nor do they deny that twentieth-century novels contain more psychological complexity than Dickens' novels have. Nevertheless, these shortcomings do not evoke the impatience or ridicule that arises from students' reactions to the emotions motivating the characters in Dickens, impatience and ridicule from even those students disposed to like his work.

This ridicule often focuses, for example, on two of my favorite characters in all of literature, Captain Cuttle and Mr. Toots, both from Dickens' fabulous novel *Dombey and Son*. Like many of Dickens' virtuous characters, neither Captain Cuttle nor Mr. Toots is gifted intellectually, and although Mr. Toots is financially well off, no reader associates materialism with either character. Captain Cuttle, a retired sea captain who has a hook to replace one of his hands, is a naive, generous-hearted man whose sole concerns are the welfare of his friends and his commitments to others. He spends his Sunday evenings reading the Sermon on the Mount. Mr. Toots, who has been so force-fed by the educational system as to have exploded into a kind of good-natured, overgrown childlike adult, befriends Little Paul Dombey and, after his death, Little Paul's sister, Florence. His character is summed up in the way he dismisses his own feelings out of deference to other people's by constantly using the phrase "It's of no consequence," which in essence means, to him at least, "*I'm* of no consequence." The chief quality that these two characters share is kindness. My students, I have come to suspect, have trouble believing in or even liking Captain Cuttle or Mr. Toots very much because the students live in a world that does not place a high premium on such virtues as kindness. However, this underrated, undervalued minor virtue — kindness — is, however, what really matters.

To many of us, the word *kindness* suggests Sunday school lessons or precepts at our mother's knee: "Don't talk to strangers"; "Never wear safety pins in your underwear in case you're in a wreck"; "Be kind to others." "Be kind to others" always seemed to fall into the same category as the Golden Rule I learned at Sunday school, a category of low-priority items to try for once I had taken care of my more grievous faults like telling lies and giving my explosive temper free reign. Being kind was, I knew, a good thing, but not a great virtue like refraining from murdering my brother or obliterating the envy I had for the blonde curls and attention-getting dimples of my best friend. After all, the Ten Commandments said nothing about kindness, I reasoned. The fact that I was then, and have been thousands of times since, the beneficiary of kindnesses great and small, in no way made me grapple with the concept until fairly recently when my students' reactions to Dickens joined forces with a host of other worries about the differences in living in Dickens' world and in our own. These differences have convinced me that we need to rethink the concept of kindness.

The words *kind* and *kindness* have many meanings, some alive and some obsolete, but three especially contribute to my way of thinking about kindness these days. The most obvious thing that occurs to most of us when we hear the word *kindness* is, I suspect, tenderness or mercy in the way we treat people. But a now obsolete definition of *kindness* is more at the core of what I want to suggest as the view we ought to have, that *kindness* is "kinship; near relationship" with other human beings. I cannot help thinking that the loss of this meaning has paralleled the dwindling importance of the virtue *kindness* in our culture. This failure to identify with one's own kind surely is evident every time the newspaper or television accounts of teenage murderers report that the young killers feel no remorse for their crimes. This inability of a human being to identify with his or her kind means that bank robbers don't flinch as they open fire with semiautomatic weapons on unarmed customers and tellers. It means that children can be sexually abused and murdered by adults or even other children who have no feeling for the suffering of their small victims. It means that our culture is no longer shocked when high school or even middle school students open fire with semi-automatic weapons on their schoolmates. It means that our culture can give rise to a Jeffrey Dahmer, who tortured, killed, and cannibalized his victims. It means that the likes of Hannibal Lecter, in the books *The Silence of the Lambs* and *Hannibal*, have proliferated into killers and begetters of gratuitous violence for movie and television screens, which are inuring us and our children to the pain of suffering. Personal identification with humankind and its pain seems at an all-time low.

Some of you will no doubt argue that times have always been violent, that people have always been evil, that humankind is progressing, not regressing. Certainly the nineteenth century in England and in the United States saw as much, if not more, disease, violence, carnage, child abuse, and exploitation of human beings by slave owners and industrial giants as we have in our own age; but I believe the attitude about such suffering was less remote, less disengaged than it seems in our own. Even in an age that championed public executions and floggings and that witnessed child prostitution to a degree surpassing our own, an age that sanctioned mangling children in machines, if need be, to make a dollar, people seemed to empathize more with one another's pain than seems to be true today.

Of course, I am not so naive as to believe that everyone regards kindness as a virtue. In the often quoted speech from *Macbeth*, Lady Macbeth clearly views the "milk of human kindness" as a major weakness. In her famous soliloquy she says,

> Glamis thou art, and Cawdor; and shalt be
> What thou art promised: yet do I fear thy nature;
> It is too full o' the milk of human kindness
> To catch the nearest way: thou wouldst be great;
> Art not without ambition, but without
> The illness should attend it. (i.v.16-22)

This speech comes, of course, from the woman who reveals her own callused nature a few lines later in trying to convince her husband to overcome his scruples and cowardice so that he can murder the king, an act he has earlier vowed to commit. She says,

> I have given suck, and know
> How tender 'tis to love the babe that milks me:
> I would, while it was smiling in my face,
> Have pluck'd my nipple from his boneless gums,
> And dash'd the brains out, had I so sworn as you
> Have done to this. (i.vii.54-59)

Clearly, in Lady Macbeth's soliloquy, the "illness that should attend ambition" was — as it is today — the suppression of or utter stripping away of kindness. This ruthless suppression has given rise to such monsters of the twentieth century as the financial and personal exploitation of prison laborers and subsistence-level workers in third-world countries — not to mention in our own; the production and use of weapons of mass destruction; the starving of whole populations in the third world — and the toleration of such starvation by the rest of us; and genocide in many parts of the world. The phrase "the milk of human kindness" suggests that we human beings imbibe this virtue in our mother's milk, that it is basic to humanity; yet our actions speak of repression of kindness in the most profound sense, the denial that we belong to our kind. To act kindly toward others often convinces others that we are weak or cowardly. But being kind does not mean becoming a doormat to be trampled on by the go-getters of the world, nor does it mean lying by omission rather than telling someone the hard truths he or she needs to hear. Kindness certainly implies honesty in our dealings with others.

Another obsolete definition of *kindness* suggested by the phrase "the milk of human kindness" equates kind and *nature*. That is, *kindness* is "natural inclination," or doing "what is natural to one." This obsolete definition of *kind* means "nature in general, or in the abstract," according to the *Oxford English Dictionary*. In my mind, this definition conjures up images of a modern humankind that has mutated into a natural state in which interpersonal remoteness has become the status quo, a state in which doing "what is natural to one" may mean killing one's children or setting someone on fire. The objectification of other people has, to a large degree, replaced the natural sympathy and empathy of earlier times. This objectification of others is at the heart of one of the great books of the twentieth century, Martin Buber's *I and Thou*, a book written by a Jewish theologian following World War I and first translated into English in 1937 in the midst of the Holocaust. In it, Buber discusses the need to enter into complete dialogue with another human being in a relationship that he calls an *I-You* relationship, rather than an *I-It* relationship in which we make another person an object. Buber believed that the genuine *I-You* relationship is a way of seeing God. He believed that God is revealed in true human encounters. Buber wrote that "the basic word I-You can only be spoken with one's whole being. The basic word I-It can never be spoken with one's whole being" (54). Buber said that "Relation is reciprocity" (67), and he said, "without It a human being cannot live. But whoever lives only with that is not human" (85).

Buber also explains that true encounters between human beings require a kind of passivity. That is, by seeking too hard to suppress our own egos to achieve true relationships — true encounters — we are, in fact, making true relationships impossible. Buber strongly suggests that only the grace of God puts the person in dialogue who has refined her or his own nature enough always to be open to the possibility of genuine human interaction. To seek it otherwise is like wearing a banner that states "Ego suppressed." Pinning on the banner, however, indicates that we are shamming in our openness — that our own egos are being gratified by the gesture itself. I know that I am not in an *I-You* relationship when I fail to listen carefully to people, when I find myself putting their comments on automatic listen while I jump ahead to prepare my own witty comeback in this game of one-upmanship. I know that I am not in an *I-You* relationship when the time I spend deliberating what I will wear today is more important than the time my spouse or my friend needs me to listen to a problem or help with a solution. As a disciple of John Stuart Mill, I know that I am not in an *I-You* relationship when I fail to admit that another person's ideas are perhaps as valid as mine or perhaps, in their possibly half-baked state, that the ideas of others contain some kernel of truth, or perhaps that they have at least as much right as mine to be heard in rational discourse.

The kindness I'm trying to come to terms with is exemplified in an experience realized by Thomas Merton, a twentieth-century Trappist monk and poet. In his book *Conjectures of a Guilty Bystander*, Merton wrote:

> In Louisville, at the corner of Fourth and Walnut, in the center of the shopping district, I was suddenly overwhelmed with the realization that I loved all these people, that they were mine, and I theirs, that we could not be alien to one another even though we were total strangers. It was like waking from a dream of separateness, of spurious self-isolation in a special world, the world of renunciation and supposed holiness. (Qtd. in Cunningham 67)

This epiphany of identification with human beings we do not know illustrates the joy felt by those who experience the true sense of community found in kindness.

But, of all sources of wisdom on the question of *kindness*, the New Testament is central to our understanding. Although the word *kindness* appears infrequently in the Bible, the figure of Christ is the ultimate symbol of kindness. To enter into dialogue with humankind, Christ became one of us. He is both fully godhead and fully humankind. And, as one of us, Christ is clear in his teachings about how our identification with our own kind should affect the way in which we interact with others. In Matthew 25, in the events just before his crucifixion, Christ is teaching about the last judgment. He says,

Then the King will say to those at his right hand, 'Come, O blessed of my Father, inherit the kingdom prepared for you from the foundation of the world; for I was hungry and you gave me food, I was thirsty and you gave me drink, I was a stranger and you welcomed me, I was naked and you clothed me, I was sick and you visited me, I was in prison and you came to me.' Then the righteous will answer him, 'Lord, when did we see thee hungry and feed thee, or thirsty and give thee drink? And when did we see thee a stranger and welcome thee, or naked and clothe thee? And when did we see thee sick or in prison and visit thee?' And the King will answer them, 'Truly, I say to you, as you did it to one. of the least of these my brethren, you did it to me.' (Revised Standard Version)

In other words, God is so fully identified with humankind through his Son that all people can potentially encounter God in the kind acts that link them to other human beings. The story of the Good Samaritan also teaches us to be kind and to avoid seeking recognition for our kindness. Matthew 6 reminds us: "Beware of practicing your piety before men in order to be seen by them; for then you will have no reward from your Father who is in heaven." Thus, the New Testament teaches us to be kind without calling attention to ourselves as being kind. But even this brand of kindness is not without its pitfalls.

Oscar Wilde, one of my favorite sinners, once said that "one can always be kind to people about whom one cares nothing," and he was right. We like our kindness sanitized. Is it not a comparatively easy kindness to write a check to the United Way or the Red Cross? At tax time, don't we feel smug and self-righteous as we take the measure of our own kindness in the dollars and cents of a fat tax write-off? How much easier is it to write a check than to seek out a homeless person and minister to that person's need for food, clothing, and shelter? And how much easier is it to take care of these physical needs than to provide what may be the most critical need and the root of the greatest pain — the need for human interaction, human touch, and the sense of inclusiveness in humankind? Wilde was right that it is easier to be kind to those we don't care about — especially if we are kind in a general way that spares us the ordeal of looking into the face of true human suffering.

*Kindness* affects all dimensions of our lives, manifesting itself in actions ranging from the most profound circumstances to what Wordsworth, in the "Tintern Abbey Lines," calls "that best portion of a good man's life, / His little nameless, unremembered acts / Of kindness and of love." Filtered through true kindness, civil discourse could lead to solutions of global and national problems like war, civil unrest, racial conflict, and various kinds of discrimination. The racial problems highlighted by the O. J. Simpson trial seem to have come to a boiling point after simmering for years in a community where people do not seem capable of rational discourse. It seems to be a community in which two races have largely objectified each other rather than encountered each other in genuine dialogue.

On a much smaller scale, the "nameless, unremembered acts of kindness" often have a greater impact on people than would seem possible. Those of you who teach have no doubt had students tell you — well after the fact — that some little favor you did or personal interest you showed had a great significance in their lives far out of proportion to its seeming importance at the time. On more than one occasion, when an especially timid student has been in my office for help with a paper, I have asked about the student's roommate or social life in an attempt to create a warm atmosphere where learning can be nurtured. Instead, I have been sometimes overwhelmed when such questions invite tears and worries that have been dammed up, concerns about a sibling coming out of the closet, a parent with a terminal illness, or sexual abuse by a relative. In such cases, a little kindness is a dangerous thing, because it forces us to enter into dialogues we may not want to participate in to discuss problems that seem overwhelming. Such kindness can make us our brothers' and sisters' keepers in a way we may not be ready to undertake. My point here tonight is not to gloat over the fact that I have occasionally been kind to someone, but to suggest my real fears about the lost or mangled opportunities when I have been too busy or selfish or angry to care about someone else's life.

Although kindness can manifest itself simply in kind words and a pleasant demeanor toward others, these trappings are not really the essence of kindness. In fact, I know about these trappings first hand. Some of my closest friends have told me over the years that I am too nice, that I am too friendly, that I speak to too many people, that I smile at others too much — in short, that I must be an axe-murderer underneath a façade of cotton candy. Their suspicions are no doubt founded on the observation that sometimes those who are most unkind seem the most compassionate. It is true that I want desperately to be kind, in the fullest sense of the word, but I have come to realize that I am not always nice, kind, or compassionate. What I am is frustrated by the disjunction between the goals held out by modern society and what I know to be the goals for living a true life of the spirit. As my colleague Duncan McArthur told our team-taught class this week, the goals of an individual in society have remained rather constant over the last thousand years or so. These goals were — and are still — sex, money, and power. These goals require the objectification of others and the inflation of the ego.

In the 1980s I was intrigued by all the talk about the "me generation." But isn't the "me generation" still here in the guise of victimization and problems of low self-esteem. Not for a moment do I intend to denigrate any individual's quest for self-knowledge, for I believe completely that until we understand ourselves fully and accept the truth about ourselves — whatever that truth might be — we can never be fit partners for relationships of any sort. I believe that a healthy self-esteem is a solid building block for helping others, and I certainly do not underestimate the scars of victimization that many of us carry. Nevertheless, the proliferation of talk shows and self-help books and videos and encounter weekends suggests to me the same truth I find in the proliferation of books and tapes and art about angels — that we are groping for fulfillment and are looking in the wrong places for it.

Only in true community with other human beings can kindness flourish. And a condition of this community is a certain degree of self-abnegation. Instead of focusing on how we can kick others out of the way in our mad climb to the top of the heap, the truly kind person, it seems to me, is trying to pull everyone else to the top, too. No, unlike some of Dickens' characters, I am neither naive nor overly hopeful. Yet I do believe that what is happening in our time is not working and that kindness is perhaps a route we should explore in our efforts to redeem our opportunities as human beings. But I don't think we should explore frivolously in the vein of a recent Oprah Winfrey show. This show, on kindness, highlighted anonymously performed good deeds and the reactions of the recipients and observers. The sort of thing Oprah stage-managed was having a person at a toll booth pay the tolls for the next five cars or leaving an unusually large tip for an overworked server in a restaurant. About the same time that this show aired, one of the many catalogues delivered to my door offered for sale a sweatshirt on which was printed the slogan "Practice Random Acts of Kindness." At first glance, random acts of kindness sounded like a good idea, especially in a culture starved for kindness, but on closer examination, this slogan suggested to me that such an attitude toward kindness smacked of playing games and paying off our consciences.

No, kindness, when fully achieved, restores harmony to our own kind, humankind, and makes it possible for us to be fitting stewards of the other "kinds" of the creation. It allows us to mediate between the Ego and the You of the world.

Real kindness comes from genuine identification with and empathy for another human being. This kindness promotes real community, the sort advocated at Furman University and in the Greenville area as a whole by L. D. Johnson. When I came to Furman in 1980, L. D. and I did meet, but we never really knew each other, though I feel that I have come to know him somewhat through his legacy to the community. L. D. did have a great impact on my husband, Clark Brittain, who was a student here in the sixties. Clark tells me that L. D. taught him many truths, but none more important than the advice to avoid giving into depression and self-pity by getting up off his derriere (L. D.'s word was a bit stronger) and doing something for someone else. L. D. told him that a person can never expect to find happiness if he or she turns inward to worship at the shrine of the Self, but that true happiness comes from serving others — in other words, in paying attention to that minor virtue, kindness.

## Works Cited

Buber, Martin. *I and Thou.* Trans. Walter Kaufmann. New York: Charles Scribner's, 1970.

Cunningham, Lawrence. *The Meaning of Saints.* New York: Harper & Row, 1980.

# David W. Rutledge
## Religion
### January 29, 1996

The audience on an occasion like the L. D. Johnson lecture usually expects the speaker to be "morally uplifting," or "profound," or at least witty, to offer sage advice on living that is neatly packaged into forty-five minutes. The difficulty is that profundity and wisdom seldom come on demand, and it seems to be the same with humor. The comedian George Burns once confessed with some pride that he had bested Groucho Marx at a party when the two of them were entertaining the crowd by swapping jokes. Burns finally stopped and said, "All right, everyone listen up now; Groucho's going to be funny for the next five minutes." And, of course, with everyone waiting expectantly, Groucho was now speechless. Even though I've had a bit more time, I appreciate his plight.

And yet it is important that we try, that we have this lecture series that forces us as speakers and as listeners to attend for two nights a year to the weightier questions of our lives. We all have such questions — brought to the surface by being away from home for the first time; or perhaps by a sudden calamity; questions dealing with who we really are, or want to be; with our faith or lack of it; with friends or with loneliness. Though I am the one who gets to share his reflection this evening, I hope you will feel invited to think along with me, to try my ideas on for size and hopefully come up with better ones. So what have I found, as I pondered our topic?

1. I find first that deep within my bones is an appreciation for *civility* between people, for the showing of unspoken as well as spoken *consideration* toward those with whom we are dealing. Kenneth Clark once called courtesy "the ritual by which we avoid hurting other people's feelings by satisfying our own egos,"[1] and I value the reminder that I should not be so preoccupied with myself, that I should remember those around me. Now, it is obvious that rituals of courtesy can become stale and artificial, occasionally even cruel — anyone growing up in the South knows how insincere social rituals can be. But would any of us argue that spontaneous behavior is always more sensitive than ritual, that lack of restraint is a surer guide to treating people

justly than the patterns of social custom? *Any* behavior can become a vehicle for satisfying our own egos, and I appreciate habits that help to restrain that tendency.

2. I also find that I appreciate simple *competence* in people, the knowledge of what to do and how to do it well — without unnecessary fussing, without serious mistakes, and adequately for the need of the moment. Whether they are plumbers, musicians, or farmers, people who know their craft, their art, their business and evince a proper pride in this knowledge, fascinate and inspire me, especially when I think about how long it usually takes to become truly competent in any of these ways. My father owned a furniture store, and it was amazing to learn how much there was to know about furniture. Dad knew woods — could tell at a glance whether that was wild cherry, fir, mahogany, teak, poplar, red oak, birch, or maple. I, on the other hand, could usually tell *pine* (if it had large knots). He knew how furniture was made, being a good carpenter and having made some himself. He knew about fabrics and upholstery and different spring systems in sofas and chairs, how to level cabinet doors and repair finishes and fix tight drawers, tricks for moving heavy furniture easily, and a thousand other things that most people never learn about. I did not appreciate his competence fully until, in the years after his death, many former customers commented on how extraordinary his knowledge and his helpfulness were.

3. One of the signs, perhaps, that I am a child of my age is that I think *humor* matters, that an ability to laugh blesses anyone favored by it. Had I the money to pay for it, I would love to slip into the strategic plan for Furman's future the appointment of a professor of humor, who would teach no classes, but who would be expected to deliver a monologue at the *beginning* of every faculty meeting, and at the *end* of every committee meeting (the meeting furnishing the material for the comedy). What a difference that might make! Ten minutes of Robin Williams before faculty deliberations could change the entire tenor of Furman's educational program, mostly for the better.

And yet I remember the well-known fact that humor skates on thin ice, always threatening to plunge us into pain and disappointment. There is no humor if we are not also aware, at the dim edge of memory, of bitterness and suffering. A good example of this twin nature of humor can be heard in an actual letter that W. C. Fields received in 1940 from his Catholic relatives in Ireland:

> Your cousin Hughie Dougherty was hung in Londonderry last Friday for killing a policeman. May God rest his soul and may God's curse be on

Jimmy Rodger, the informer. May his soul burn in hell. God forgive me....

Times are not as bad as they might be. The herring is back...and the price of fish is good, thanks be to God. The Black and Tans are terrible.

They go through the country in their lorries and shoot the poor people down in the fields where they are working. God's curse on them.

Your uncle Danny took a shot at one of them yesterday from the hedge, but he had too much to drink and missed them. God's curse on drink....

Things might be worse than they are. Every police barrack and every Protestant church in the country has been burned down. Thanks be to God.

PS. Your Aunt Maggie, who has informed me that more Protestant churches have been burned to the ground, sends her love.[2]

Could it be that the unintended humor of this letter helps us to handle the terrible blindness it shows — of violence, of religious hatred, of alcoholism, of the thoughtlessness with which we kill one another? And yet the laughter I normally respond to, contrary to so much of what passes for "funny" in our society, is not savage, disguising a weapon as a joke, hiding a desire for revenge behind a quip. The humor I need pierces but leaves no wound; it pricks the skin without leaving a scar. (I think of the wonderful true story in *The Greenville News* yesterday of the hunter who was shot by his dog! Shades of *Bloom County*!) There are sound reasons for the instinct I feel for this sort of laughing, even amidst the pain: Krister Stendahl claims that "joy is closer to God than seriousness. Why? Because when I am serious I tend to be self-centered, but when I am joyful I tend to forget myself"[3] This is one of the warmest memories I have of our colleague Theron Price — his love of humor, his delight in stories that prevented us humans from taking ourselves too seriously. It matters that we laugh *at* ourselves, *with* each other.

4. And let me add to this short list of virtues one that is a bit harder to describe, one that I think of when I remember, again, my father. It is the virtue that gives one the strength to maintain one's dignity when life is hard, when one is not favored by inheritance, or looks, or great intellect, or social graces. Self-restraint or *forbearance* might capture it, or perhaps simply a kind of stoicism that refuses to whine when life is not comfortable or just or happy. I whine more than I should — about busyness, grading papers, unhelpful sales clerks, terrible referees — and my visceral regret when I do so tells me that I have forgotten something crucial to any human dignity.

The Bible gives us two wonderful stories that capture these contrasting types, the whiner and the man of patience. Jonah is the anti-hero of the book that bears his name, fleeing from God, misunderstanding his mission, —

furious that his mediocre talents are not better appreciated by the Divine. We last see him sweltering under the midday sun, pouting at his fate, whimpering "it is better for me to die than to live." The other story concerns Job, who, despite the goodness and justice of his life, watched it all be taken from him, piece by piece — children, home, health, the support of his wife. Job feels all of the rage and confusion that any of us would, but he refuses to whine. Even when his wife despairs and says those terrible words, "Curse God and die," Job simply answers, "Shall we receive the good at the hand of God, and not receive the bad?" He refuses to give in to the idea that his life has been meaningless, but he also refuses to simply accept his fate without questioning, without more understanding. And this tenacity, this steady holding on to what wisdom he knows, despite the vicissitudes of life, finally brings him peace. Price once called hope "the power of patience," and it is this sober but real hope that sustains Job as he waits for the meaning of it all to appear. Wisdom does not say life will be easy or clear; it does say that despite the difficulties, it is full of meaning.

So, being considerate of others, doing our work well, laughing freely, and enduring without complaint — these are important virtues that I commend to you. But Price, in the first lecture delivered in the name of his friend L. D., reminded us that "so many, many things are important. Perhaps few finally matter." Though the things I have mentioned are important, they do not go to the deepest level of our concern, and they also reflect a personal temperament that you may not share. So let me focus for the rest of this evening on one thing that certainly matters for each of us.

## Community Matters

Anyone standing in the midst of American culture today must be struck by the apparent unraveling of the social fabric that is occurring all around us, in racial, political, economic, and family settings. It would be natural to expect that in a time of such rapid change and fragmentation in basic American institutions, we should expect some "ripple effect" in our local situation here at Furman. How could we *not* be affected by some of the same forces that operate in the larger society, forces that have the centrifugal effect of pulling us apart, buffeting us about, making it difficult to sense a unity in the day-to-day activities of the college. I want to take this as a starting point — the way in which we are related to other people in this academic community at the foot of Paris Mountain.

My remarks will spiral through several topics connected to this theme of *community* in what may seem haphazard fashion. But it is important for me to keep this more a conversation than a systematic treatise, to keep from suggesting that I have worked it all out. I need to also explain that I will use the first personal pronoun often tonight, in imitation of E. B. White, who confessed that "the first person singular is the only grammatical implement I am able to use without cutting myself." It is also crucial to my argument, not to mention my sanity, that I constantly remind myself that the truth or falsity of what I say resides in my willingness to affirm these words as *my own* and no one else's.

Let me begin by presenting a proposition to you: We are much better at being individuals than we are at being members of a group, part of a community. We are much better at improving *ourselves* than in developing friendships. There is a huge world of self-help guidance out there in the bookstores, on the Internet, on television or radio talk shows that gives people answers to questions like "Who should I vote for?" or "How can I have a better sex life?" or "What's wrong with my car?" (Click and Clack!) or "How can I firm up my abs?" or even "Why is the government always making me mad?" With a trip to the bookstore and a couple of hours in front of the TV or the radio, one could gain all the information needed to be a fulfilled individual. And yet notice that all of these questions are self-referential, asking how *I* can improve, and notice that they are answered by people who are complete strangers to those they are helping. Though we can find a thousand people to help us improve our individual selves, we cannot find, without a great deal of hard searching or a good bit of luck, people who are interested in entering genuine community with us. Perhaps this is why television programs such as *Seinfeld* or *Friends* are so popular — they deal with the deep desire most of us feel for a "web of kindred spirits."

Of course, we can find groups that want us to *join* them as a member — political groups, hobby groups, entertainment groups, religious groups — but we rarely see such groups develop into a community that fills the deep need, the longing in us, for close relationships with people we like and respect.

One almost always gets a better purchase on a big question like this — "Why are we better at being individuals than friends?" — by dealing with it locally, and if I turn to my local experience at Furman University and in Greenville, I find surer footing. Surprisingly, for a former philosophy major nurtured on Kierkegaardian dread, Heideggerian anxiety, Sartrean bad faith, and Camusian alienation, I have concluded that here at Furman we still are relatively fortunate, that for some reason in the great scheme of things this little corner of South Carolina has escaped many of the worst influences of our society. When I think of the talent and dedication of my colleagues, the exhausting but exciting energy of our president, the eagerness of so many students, the improving character of our facilities, the beauty of the local country, and most of all an atmosphere of caring about people, education, and hard work, I feel blessed. Note that I *did* say we are "relatively" fortunate; this isn't the garden of Eden, and the bright surface of the Furman culture could always prove to be a veneer. Perhaps the reason our community is as intact as it is, is because we have had our head in the sand, *avoiding* challenges and controversy. Possibly. But I think honesty requires that we should not ignore our unique strengths, that we should not see dire crises where only problems exist.

And yet, for those of us who have chosen to spend our lives in universities, it is crucial that a college not simply look as a college ought to look — like something out of *Southern Living* — but that it be *real*, a plot of extraordinarily fertile ground where things are alive, even if it grows weeds as well as fruit. When the culture around us despairs over solving its problems, colleges and universities must remain, patiently and enduringly, places of genuine confidence in the power of imagination, in the reach of reason into the stars, places of real dialogue between people who care about understanding the world, themselves, and each other, and are determined to do what they can to contribute to a just and healthy future for everyone.

Amidst everything at Furman we can be grateful for, I doubt we would say that the dormitories vibrate with intellectual ferment; that eating in the dining hall always immerses one in serious discussions over healthcare reform, over the reasons for racism, over whether someone genuinely committed to justice can in good conscience spend four of the best years of her life in the Furman bubble. Is it important that each year we spend several times more on intercollegiate athletics than we spend on the library? When we hire new faculty, do we expect them to be loyal to this community or only to their professional discipline? Does Furman's Christian heritage mean that students and faculty do not have full academic freedom? Does hosting an ROTC unit on campus to train soldiers deny our stated commitment to "respect for the ethical and spiritual dimensions of human experience"? If Furman had a choice of being "one of the top twenty-five liberal arts colleges in the nation" according to all polls, *or* being a place where excellent education went on, virtually unknown, which would it choose? Many would try to wimp out of answering that question by saying "we are going to do both" — but is that possible? Is it possible to appeal to everyone and still have integrity? Perhaps. What really matters here is not absolute answers to these questions, and certainly not *my* answers, but that we live in and be committed to a community of people who honor such questions by engaging them with all the energy and honesty they can muster. Few things are sadder for a professor than a noble, imaginative idea obscured in a sloppy paper or by careless, monosyllabic speech. Few things are sadder for a student than to sit and listen day after day to a teacher who has lost any sense of transcendent purpose in what she is doing, and resents the students in the classroom for reminding her of that fact. It seems to me that Furman lies in the middle of these extremes, possessing all of the raw materials for an educational revolution, yet not having found the spark, the vision, that would put this revolution in gear. We are half-awake, perhaps, struggling with whether to get up and on with a new day, or to roll over and get some more sleep.

What are the causes of this kind of half-sleep, in which we sense educational excellence, but have not yet found the formula to get us there? Certainly there are many, and every facet of the university's environment could be blamed for keeping us from our goal. As a faculty member, however, I want to speak to faculty complicity in this situation, not because it is the only or the largest contributor to our *intellectual ennui*, but out of the conviction that the problem will not be solved without a change in my profession's attitudes.

## Professors and Their Calling

The philosopher Bruce Wilshire, in his book *The Moral Collapse of the University*, points to the elevation of professionalism and the degeneration of community as the twin causes of mediocrity, even deadness, in higher education. The relationship of the two is clear, Wilshire argues, for it is the obsession of university teachers with improving their status among other American professionals that has led gradually to the narrowing of disciplines, in order that they might provide specialized training that prepares people to become managers of the industrial economy. Though the sheer quantity of knowledge has contributed to the tendency of faculty to specialize, it seems a greater cause is the allegiance of scholars primarily to the academic discipline in which they are trained in graduate school, and their desire to make that discipline more visible in society. Out of the many subtle forces at work, Wilshire argues that the faculty's desire to improve its status, to set itself apart from less desirable classes in American life, is a determining motive in creating a professional elite with a narrow vision of education.

If we professors are ashamed to do the same things that high school teachers do — teach — then teaching will be replaced by research in our affections. If faculty are faintly embarrassed at how unsophisticated their out-of-date culture is, with its academic gowns and homecomings and degree ceremonies, then these community activities will be seen as inferior to professional meetings in far-away cities. If a faculty member sees himself or herself as an independent scholar, hired to do scholarship within a disciplinary guild, then he or she will resent local community activities as an infringement of their right to privacy and an impediment to the very scholarly work the university expects of them. If faculty are indignant that they do not make as much money as the other kind of doctor, then they will place greater and greater stress on the kind of productivity that the market honors: countable articles, books, reviews, speeches, chairing sessions — in short, "doing business" as an academic. All faculty know these tensions; they are real and palpable.

So the great stress in this country since the Second World War on improving one's economic condition and on becoming a part of the professional classes has led academics to copy the patterns and values of the economic world: One must be efficient, productive, up-to-date; one must use good marketing techniques, and "position oneself favorably" vis-à-vis the competition. This bureaucratic or corporate model of academia has not totally taken over, of course, but it is surprising and alarming how much of an impact it has made on faculty activity.

Where in this vision of professional life do we put advising a student about his or her career? Or where attending the university gathering scheduled for this Wednesday? Or where doing research in the library not for publication, but to answer a student's question? These are not efficient or productive, but aren't they important to an educational community? Now, some of my listeners might be hearing me say that what Furman needs is less research and more teaching, less professional activity and more sitting around feeling communal. That is not true. What I am arguing is that scholarly activity — which necessarily includes both first-rate research and excellent teaching — should not be governed by the economic marketplace or standards of social class, but by the demands of education. I am wondering if social forces unrelated to education have led us to ignore central values of the educational enterprise, *without realizing it.*

If we ask why collegiate faculty might have been seduced into defining themselves by an alien standard, I think we have to recognize that the assumptions about *knowledge* that the university encourages today make it all but impossible for a faculty member to be committed to knowing and teaching as a way of life. Our very standards of knowledge do not allow us *to commit* ourselves to it — commitment and knowledge are believed to be antithetical states of being.

Let me share with you an example of this attitude to knowledge that I have used in my classes. Irwin Fridovich, a biochemist at Duke University, once wrote that "big questions such as 'what is life?'...are futile because they are not approachable by measurement or experiment. If your purpose is serious and your commitment firm," he continues, "you will instead ask a series of much smaller questions," each of which is framed in a way "which permits an answer to be obtained by experiment or observation.... In this way, through the cumulative efforts of many workers, a body of verifiable facts will be built up.... We know of no other way for surely approaching truth." Now there is a good, clear statement of knowledge as a series of small facts, which we get clear and certain before pronouncing them "true." Fridovich then asks, "What about truth in cases where precise measurements and experiments are not yet feasible? The very best approach here is to remain uncommitted. If verifiable facts are not available, you do not have to choose sides. Judgment is suspended while the quest for verifiable facts continues."

Let's examine this for a moment: First note that early in his comments, Fridovich said, "If your purpose is serious and your commitment is firm," you will avoid asking big questions and ask little questions. Is asking little questions a serious purpose? How would we ever know? Can we put "asking little questions is a serious purpose" into an experiment? Can we measure it? Or to what should one be firmly committed? The truth of the scientific method, perhaps? Well, can we measure the scientific method? Can we put the scientific method into an experiment, that is, conduct an experiment which tests whether experiments are a valid way to knowledge? How would we know if the experiment failed, since only valid experimental results count as knowledge? It would seem that Dr. Fridovich, on his own grounds, must remain uncommitted to the truth or falsity of his work, of his vocation. He also, of course, would have nothing to say on most of the great social, moral, and political issues of our day, or to his students who were seeking advice about their careers, for none of these questions can be tested or measured experimentally, and so we can claim to know nothing about them.

Now, I do not think that Irwin Fridovich actually remains uncommitted on all these issues. I think Dr. Fridovich and others who agree with his views perform a sleight-of-hand by which they secretly import into their view of science certain values and commitments that cannot be established within science and that they therefore ignore or hide, but without which their entire enterprise would collapse. He is a deeply committed man, but he cannot prove the truth of his commitments by the only model of knowledge that he recognizes; therefore, he has to pretend he is *not* so committed.

It is interesting that most scientists ignore the contradictions present in this view of knowledge, since it is a philosophical claim, not a scientific premise; they have no need of it when doing science. But it is tragic that professors in other disciplines are not so fortunate or so wise, and they have often come to the conclusion that because knowledge of this empirical, verifiable, certain sort is so hard to come by that one cannot stand behind *any* claim to knowledge; one cannot be committed to know *anything*, and so one is reduced to rhetorical pronouncements, or political slogans, or assertions of power, rather than claims to truth.

By now we are familiar with these arguments of what, for simplicity's sake, I will call "postmodernism," and with the confusion they have caused among many of our contemporaries. On the one hand, postmodernists are *right*, I believe, in saying that the standards of knowledge that came to us from the Enlightenment, from Descartes, Hume, and Kant, cannot be sustained as adequate paths to certain or absolute truth. The great dream of putting all human knowledge on the same unquestionable foundation as the rules of mathematics has proved not only elusive, but profoundly misleading. On the other hand, I believe this postmodern critique to be *wrong* in its further claim that because the critical knowledge of the Enlightenment is flawed, *no* claims to a truth beyond our personal preferences are possible. *I* say, "I believe they are wrong," but many in our society do seem to accept their conclusion as unavoidable, even if distasteful.

Let's return for a moment to the question of why, from a faculty perspective, Furman's intellectual metabolism is so sluggish. Note that on Irwin Fridovich's grounds, intellectual ferment is impossible. If knowledge is the slow, steady accretion of facts, which are established by testing and measurement, then what is there to discuss — which yardstick to use, the purple one or the white one? If the only way to truth is through such objective standards, then no debate is necessary; one simply feeds in the data and reports the results. Remember, I have suggested that few scientists actually follow this picture when practicing their science; my impression is that research teams of students and faculty in Plyler Hall, doing undergraduate research, offer one place where exciting education often goes on. The tremendous prestige of science, however, has ensured that a view routinely ignored by science will have tremendous influence among nonscientists in the academic world, and so it has. We are sometimes reluctant to pursue the "big questions" — how is racial justice possible in the United States? how should we understand homosexuality? how could we know if there is a God? — because we secretly believe these are not matters of truth or knowledge, but only matters of personal opinion, of private judgment. So professors teach public facts and discussion of these facts, but do not encourage engagement with the living issues that confront and divide us, that are actually shaping us even as we decline to commit. Our students, then, subjected to tremendous pressures to get good grades and a good job, see few role models of people pursuing knowledge for its intrinsic value, for its bearing on reality.

Now, we cannot solve these problems tonight, but I would like to suggest some partial remedies, some directions in which we might move to begin restoring some health to our common enterprise. Such an effort must begin with the root of the problem, our lack of confidence in our claims to knowledge and truth, and move from there to the unavoidably communal, social character of education.

At least one of the problems in the picture of knowledge that people like Irwin Fridovich espouse is its suggestion, usually unnoticed, that people may have bodies, but knowing is solely a function of their minds. The dualism of mind and body, to which Descartes gave impetus, has led subsequent thinkers to describe thinking as a purely mental event, and ideas as statements with purely logical, abstract, mental properties. But, rather than beginning with an objective, impersonal standard of truth or knowledge, why not begin where we are, with the everyday thinkings and doings of people as they go about their lives? What do we find when we simply observe ourselves and others? That we use the words "know" and "true" all the time, without the slightest bit of trouble, and both we and our listeners usually understand perfectly what we mean. (Perhaps the only time, in fact, when things get tangled up is when we are within the ivied walls of the academy, where human speech is abstracted from its natural setting.) So I may say, "Better take the Honda, Dee — I know it's got gas" or "I know you're planning to feed the dog later, Adam, but you need to do it before supper" or "Okay, it's true I promised we could go to the Furman basketball game, Matt, but that was before they moved confirmation class." And so forth.

In thousands of ways each day we speak of truth and knowledge meaningfully, without any doubt ever arising. Our thinking hangs together in our speech precisely because we speak with*in* a world where speaker, hearer, bodily gestures, tone of voice, and context — body and mind together — all cohere. If we were to examine carefully enough, I think we could even assert that all order and meaning is ultimately rooted in the archaic implications that tie us to our bodies, to our language, and to those with whom we speak. Rather than ignoring this substratum of sureness and imposing some foreign test, such as the clarity and distinctness of a mathematical proof, why not simply accept this as our starting point? Knowledge is possible, and truth is real, because in the natural life of couples, friends, families, and communities, people know things, including the truth of some things. This does not mean people know everything they claim to know or that people are never wrong or that the truth or falsity of things people say is never in doubt. But it does mean that underlying such problems and questions is a ground of understanding and assurance that gives us the support needed, the traction, to ask our questions. It means that the burden of proof lies on those for whom nothing hangs together, for whom every statement is as true or false as any other, on those for whom the verities of the past are meaningless.

Now, you are probably thinking that Rutledge is a great disappointment if all he can recommend to solve the problems of higher education is common sense. But, without claiming to have seen the entire answer, I do indeed think that this is a big part of it. We have been so bewitched by theory, by abstraction, by formalisms and formulas, that we have almost forgotten where we firmly stand each day. In some ways we need to reverse the Enlightenment obsession with finding universal laws of reason, and become adept at uncovering the particular logic of ordinary life. It is also true, however, that it has taken me a great deal of reading of many people over many years to be satisfied that such a "common sense" approach is sound, that it can meet enough of the objections against it to commend itself to us. Sometimes when the doctor examines a patient and says, "Take two aspirin and call me in the morning," he is a charlatan. But sometimes when she gives this prescription, she is wise. A simple prescription is not necessarily a simple-minded cure.

Let me take another run at this, from a different direction. When we look at the etymology of the word "logic," we are led to the Greek *logos*, and find that its first meaning is "speaking," first human speech generally, and then speech about revelation by God, as both Greeks and early Christians used the word. So "logic" resides properly, appropriately, in the speech, the conversations of human beings. When there is an order, a pattern, a meaning in human speech, which we find when real communication occurs, then we say there is a "logic" to that speech. We do not go out and establish truth and then import it into our lives — it arises from the midst of life. Or, as H. Richard Niebuhr puts it, "The movement of life is not from idea to personality, but personality to idea."

But let me worry this bone a bit more. A moment ago, when I talked about how our everyday speech of knowing and truth hangs together, I mentioned the context in which such speaking occurs. Human thinking, including the knowledge that the university is concerned with, begins in conversation of the sort I had in mind, that is, normal conversation between people who are physically together, looking at one another as they speak, bound together by the language and bodily natures in which they are both implicated. The picture I am urging on you is one of knowing as a thoroughly social activity, and think of how much this differs from the picture of knowing that we find in Descartes, in Hume, or in Locke. There, the knower is imagined as a pure mind, autonomous, isolated, silent, receiving sense impressions from the world and categorizing them, then putting them together according to laws of inference — the "laws of logic" — patterned after the procedures of mathematics. This is the picture of a solitary researcher, and it differs dramatically from the understanding of knowledge that has been surfacing over the last thirty years. In widely separated fields, men and women are becoming aware of the importance of the role of *commitment* in knowing, that knowledge is gained by communities that share a common language, a common discourse to which all the members give allegiance. Ironically, many institutions of higher learning still assume a model of knowledge, the Enlightenment model of the solitary researcher, that is being radically, rapidly modified.

When we look at any field of knowledge, we find that it begins with students *listening with confidence* to their teachers, *believing in* the information and the picture of reality they are given, *trusting* their textbooks and their equipment, *relying on* the help of their classmates to understand difficult points, *assuming* that the special language of the discipline that is used has a meaning that the student can eventually discover. Do you remember your own excitement when you realized for the first time that you could understand complex knowledge? That you could also use the vocabulary of an arcane branch of study, and impress your friends with casual references to "oscillation" or "prolegomenon," to "transfer functions" or "eschatology"? As the student demonstrates in conversations and writings that she grasps more and more of the knowledge of the field, that she can begin to "speak the language," she is introduced to other parts of the community — to upper-level courses, perhaps to a majors club, to lab procedures, to internships, to research teams or programs, to honorary societies, to professional meetings, to disciplinary journals, and perhaps eventually to graduate school or a job in the field, where the process begins again, at a more advanced level. At every stage, the student's *knowing* is conditioned by her *believing*. Without trust in the persons who initiate us into a field of knowledge, we could not get started; without a community to mentor us, to show us "how it is done" in sociology, or music, or geology, we would wander around for a long time clueless.

Some people, upon hearing such talk, see an abyss of relativism open up before them, and instinctively pull back from the brink, rejecting any social dimension to knowing. But this fear is misplaced. To say that knowledge is social does not mean that we must be skeptics, that we must give up "hard knowledge" of the world for some kind of mushy social consensus. An important part of conversations, after all, is correcting and improving our speech, and this applies to the dialogue with nature — science — as well as the dialogue with other cultures, with history, or with art. Indeed, to read earlier conversations, whether Galileo on sunspots, or Luther on obedience to the state, or Samuel Johnson on Milton, reminds us that judgments of knowledge have changed considerably even in the modern period. So to know something reliably is to believe in persons, and in the relations between persons that we call community. Knowledge is acknowledgment.

The suppression or forgetting of this simple fact contributes to the fragmentation of the university, for no single discipline can claim to have a corner on all of knowledge, to understand everything. And, therefore, other communities, other languages and conversations, are necessary to complete our picture of the world, or even to suggest new perspectives within our own discipline. We have become more aware in this century of how different languages shape our understanding in different ways, one of the most famous examples being Benjamin Whorf's study of the language of the Hopi Indians. While the English language might describe a topography as "hills and valleys," the Hopi would render it as something like "ground in motion," which is an altogether different way of seeing the world.[4] Conversations about mathematics and conversations about poetry tell us different things about experience, and both are needed for "whole vision."

Not only investigations into language, but even the varied disciplines that share the name "ecology" contribute to our understanding at this point. Perhaps the central claim of ecology is that, as John Muir put it, "Everything in the universe is hitched to everything else"; everything is connected and interrelated. This fact of the natural order has become a powerful heuristic in the human and social sciences for reenvisioning human knowing. We cannot understand anything in isolation, by itself, which is how the process of analysis normally renders things. Phenomena, be they chemical compounds in the brain or a population of wrens in the Appalachian Mountains or wealthy landowners in Central America, are the nexus of a large number of forces and factors that extend out in every direction. To ignore this rich net of meaning in order to focus on a highly specialized part of the process is to leave a great deal out, and so to misunderstand the whole. "We murder to dissect." One lesson here for academia is that our compartmentalization, our departmental structures, may be seen in just a few years as dinosaurs, as archaic survivors of a primitive stage of human education, because the world does not come departmentalized; it comes connected, and only an *inter*disciplinary understanding, an ecological awareness, will be adequate to comprehend it.

Thus, I want to suggest that an appropriate image of academic life, generally, one in keeping with the nature of reality and the nature of human understanding as we now see them, is *the college as a Great Conversation*, a grand colloquy carried on by countless partners, most living, some dead, most here, some in other parts of the world, some speaking more fluently than others, but everyone respecting both their partners and the conversation itself, all equal in access to the discussion, but each different in the resources they bring to this free-for-all pursuit of truth. When such a conversation gets going, it seems to me, then education follows, and the better the conversation, the better the education. The conversation will be multilingual, not only in French and Japanese and German, but in the languages of music and computer programs. Its aim will be dialogue, not monologue. It also will respect times of silence as part of the larger conversation.

If you will entertain my image for a moment, the question then becomes "How can we improve our conversations?" We might be helped simply by thinking of good conversations we have had — perhaps roommates sitting on their beds late at night; or family members around a dinner table; or faculty members over lunch; or friends gathered in our homes or at the beach or in a restaurant. Perhaps good conversation even happens occasionally in a committee meeting (imagine!) or in an advising session between professor and student. Whatever the setting, think to yourself of what is required for the conversation to be good: unhurried time, no fear, a feeling of acceptance and respect from the others, enough shared experiences or commitments so that everything we say doesn't have to be explained. Such ingredients establish a framework, open up a space, in which real sharing of minds and education may occur. In effect, they establish a community, which is the normal and proper home of education. (Note: It is community and not the department that is education's natural home! Perhaps our goal should be to turn our departments into part of the larger community.) In the last part of my remarks, let me pursue this topic of community a bit with the help of H. Richard Niebuhr's wonderful book, *Faith on Earth*.[5]

A crucial element of the social character of knowledge is that our relation to other knowers with whom we are in dialogue is necessarily one of trust, for we do not see the other person as simply a knower, or a subject, but as a self, a person, "one who is bound by promises and as such can betray me, can tell a lie, or can speak truth" (p. 41). I do not trust the other — my teachers, my fellow students, my colleagues — simply because I have decided on the evidence that they will not make many mistakes in their thinking. For they are not just "thinking machines," giving me feedback about data. They can say few words to me or be patient as I struggle to grasp a difficult point. They may deliberately mislead me to win a competition for grades, or they may give their time even at the expense of their own work. Niebuhr writes, "When we believe a person we acknowledge that there is present to us a moral self...who has bound himself to us by explicit or implicit promises not to deceive us but to be faithful in telling us the truth about what he knows" (p. 41). Here, we find a deeper ground for the "hanging together" of things, the logic that establishes knowledge and truth in the various disciplines. Such knowledge is rooted not only in the language of communities of scholars, but also in the personal relationships of knowers who trust one another, who believe one another to be moral beings.

This introduces yet another dimension to our picture, for we see that the conversational situation is not just two people talking, say a student and a teacher, or two partners in dialogue. There is also a third element in the relation, namely a common object or goal in which both partners are interested and about which they speak. In every conversation there is this third element, the subject of our common speech, the shared world to which our speech refers. In the university this is the thing that we are investigating, the aspect of the world or life that we want to know or make clearer or understand at a deeper level. Though normally unvoiced, all of our conversations are a triad of self, other, and object; as Niebuhr puts it, "I know you or acknowledge you in my act of believing your statements about a common third" (p. 40). Students and professor do not simply speak randomly about experience; they try to clarify particular realities. Did the arrival of humans in western America some 12,000 years ago cause the disappearance of large animals that occurred about the same time? Or to what degree will an increase in interest rates affect unemployment? Or was the Reformation essentially a medieval or a modern event? Even if the "reality" discussed is a symbol system, as in mathematics, or a linguistic convention, as it might be in literature or philosophy, there is still a third object in even the simplest conversation that binds the speakers together in a common venture.

If these reflections on community are sound, then we may conclude that the problem with the vitality of an intellectual community, of a college like Furman, is not ignorance, but distrust. The obstacle to better education is not brighter students or more productive professors, but the absence of a structure of mutual trust and shared goals that can nurture lively conversations. What can I say to you, or you to me, if when I talk I am rehearsing the lecture I will give later to a professional society, while when you speak you are rehearsing the speech you will give later at your job interview? I am displaying my professorial expertise, and you are trying to impress me for a better grade. We may talk in the same room, but no community is established, because we do not relate to one another as moral selves; that is, we do not really listen to one another, and we do not share a common vision of what it is we are talking about.

Thus, our original proposition, that our culture helps us more to be individuals than to be friends, has led to a deeper awareness of the challenges that face us here at Furman. How can we create the great conversation, the lively dialogue about things that matter, that can sustain interest and hope in the coming years? We can find ways to help community, of course, and a number of people have been working to do just this with improvements to the residential and social environment, with a more open, inclusive administrative style, with more occasions to get together and share thoughts and questions. But another need is for us to begin to talk about that common goal, that shared reference point that will join together all of our smaller conversations into a complete education. There are many possibilities here, depending first upon whether we envisage this common purpose as a goal to be worked toward, a vision of who we want to be, a map of where we are going, a list of resources that will fuel our journey, and so on. Perhaps the only possibility for a complex and diverse community like Furman is a cluster of distinct but related values that give voice to the different facets of this college. We can easily see some of the possibilities by looking at what other good institutions have said they are about, and certainly a central, shared value for most, if not all such places, is the free, untrammeled pursuit of truth that we mentioned earlier in introducing the image of a great conversation.

But after we survey the options among our peers, I suggest that we return to also consider the unique possibilities that Furman already offers, that come naturally from her past, and that continue to be affirmed by most of the present community. These possibilities reside, of course, in a Christian perspective on the world, grounded in biblical wisdom and in the experiences of religious communities and individual Christians throughout Western history. I suggest that it is time for this community to articulate just what this commitment should mean for us, and that the results of such a process could provide the overarching vision of purpose that our conversation needs. Now, what I have just done, of course, is not *just* invite misunderstanding, not to mention suspicion and even hostility, but I have also committed a social gaffe of monumental proportions; one of the subjects that urbane people cannot talk about in polite conversation is their religious commitments, or lack of them, or their confusion or uncertainty or ignorance about them. We acknowledge that they exist, perhaps — Furman's institutional statements affirm our continued loyalty to a Christian view of the world — but we refuse to speak about what that might mean, for fear perhaps that others will mean by it something that we don't. Thus, at a crucial juncture of institutional history, on a central question of our identity, we are silent — not the silence of peace, of repose, but of uneasiness. Actually, what I've just said is not *quite* true — these Johnson lectures have been one place where such matters have occasionally been explored, and I remember several occasions that the Philosophy department sponsored for discussing religious issues. But it is not enough for one or two departments to raise these issues — they must be explored more widely by faculty and students and the administration if the conversation is to be healthy and to have good effects. We owe such discussion especially to new faculty and to new students, but it is important for us all.

I am undaunted by the prospect for conflict that this opens up, for if anything becomes clear in our culture's experience, it is that no achievement of any worth ever comes without a certain amount of strife and struggle. Perhaps this is the other side of the coin of "intellectual ferment and vitality." A conversation about Furman's Christian commitment should be lively, because it will be about things that matter, ultimately, both to individuals as well as to the institution.

So, what common vision could arise from this community's roots in the biblical tradition that gave rise to both Judaism and Christianity? Let me leave you with a few to start the conversation off:

• that truth is God's self-revelation, and therefore infinitely valuable and not to be feared;

• that "the universe is on the side of justice," as Martin Luther King liked to say, not as an interested observer, but as a passionate partisan for the poor, the forgotten, the oppressed. In Jesus of Nazareth we see this character of God at work.

• that human beings should refuse to give complete loyalty to any penultimate idea or principle, such as the state or a political ideology or a racial or economic group, that is, that we should be ceaselessly critical of pretensions to divinity, whether in secular or religious life;

• that the creation is good and important, that nature can be understood and nurtured, and that humans have a duty to do so;

• that human reason is a divine gift meant to be used not as an end in itself, but as the means for better understanding of the world, ourselves, and God. Thus, reason operates as part of a larger context of meaning, rather than as isolated, autonomous mind; though it is free to question everything ceaselessly, we remember that there may be mysteries that reason alone cannot solve.

• that human beings are fallible creatures, tending to pride and self-absorption, denying their potential fulfillment in favor of complete autonomy.

Such a list could go on, of course, or it could be condensed, and my list certainly can stand improvement and correction. It goes without saying that we are talking of a liberating Christianity that is open to the world, without giving it allegiance; that no one has suggested that Furman should be turned into a church or a congregation, rather than a college; that no one has dreamed that there should be some kind of religious test for everyone; that no one would advocate that our adherence to the principle of freedom of thought and conscience should be limited in any way. What I *do* say, however, is that Furman will acquire an identity, whether we give any thought to it or not, and if we do not, then our identity will be completely nondescript, made up of the lowest common denominators of the views that end up here. I believe that anyone who has studied the full range of Christian life in the history of the West must acknowledge that, despite its flaws, it contains great resources for both nurturing and protecting an academic community — surely greater than those resources that have appeared in research universities over the past 100 years. One of the greatest benefits of acknowledging our Christian commitments is that precisely their difference from modern academic culture may do us a great service by providing an independent perspective on what we do, a prophetic criticism when the academy begins to forget that it is not the only thinking community in the world. My hope is that we can choose how to articulate our Christian identity in a way that supports and strengthens what we all want to do, rather than limiting it. One of the interesting things about inviting a discussion of Christian commitments is that some of the brightest people at Furman will take radically different positions on these matters, and some of the people I admire most will be adamantly opposed to my suggestions, and that too is good. Everyone is welcome to the conversation, as long as they are genuinely committed to it, trusting their partners to speak honestly and respectfully.

For those of you who are uneasy at this suggestion, let me simply end by posing these questions outside of any reference to religious faith: "What do *you* really believe? Does it relate to your beliefs about education? And what common ground can we stand on as we work together at Furman?"

# Notes

[1]Kenneth Clark, *Civilization, A Personal View* (New York: Harper & Row, 1969) 347.

[2]Printed in Conrad Hyers, *The Comic Vision and the Christian Faith* (New York: Pilgrim Press, 1981) 9.

[3]Krister Stendahl, "To Think and To Pray," *Harvard Divinity Bulletin*, XV:2 (Dec. 1984–Jan. 1985) 16.

[4]See H. Richard Niebuhr, *Faith on Earth, An Inquiry into the Structure of Human Faith*, ed. R. R. Niebuhr (New Haven: Yale University Press, 1989) 36-38.

[5]Ibid.

# Robert McNamara
## Sociology
*October 14, 1996*

In trying to answer the question of what really matters, my first reaction as a sociologist was that this was the kind of question we are trained to avoid. After all, one of the first rules of sociology is to describe what *is* not what *ought* to be. And it seemed to me that this question has quite a few "ought" statements in it. For by telling you what really matters, I am telling you what ought to really matter. Consequently, I felt that my training did not allow for such ponderings; rather, they were better left to philosophers. On a personal level, I think everyone who has been asked to participate in this exercise has struggled with it because we feel it is very presumptuous to tell other people what is important. I thought to myself, "Who am I to tell a group of educated and talented people what is important? They already know what is important to them. And if not, what makes what I think more significant than their own conclusions?" I was always taught, "Never offer unsolicited advice," yet here I am doing exactly that.

Then, I realized that the basis of this lecture series has quite a bit of sociology attached to it. For what really matters is subjective and, in some cases, changes over time. This is sometimes referred to the *social construction of reality*. Peter Berger and Thomas Luckman's text describes this process in that what is important in a society is constructed by the members of that particular group as they interact with each other.

At the same time, as I alluded to a moment ago, the question "What really matters?" implies what really matters to *me*. This, too, is grounded in sociology. C. Wright Mills once wrote an article titled "The Promise," in which he discussed how ideas are a result of the intersection between biography and history. In other words, a person's perspective, point of view, or theory of the world is often a function of who they are, at what point in time they have lived, and what experiences they have encountered. It seems to me that this intersection is an important element if I am to tell you what really matters.

With all this in mind, let me begin to try answering this perplexing question. *City Slickers* is a movie about a middle-aged man, Mitch Robbins, played by comedian Billy Crystal, who tries to find the meaning of his life and what will make him happy. In an attempt to discover the answers to these compelling questions, he and two of his friends embark on a cattle drive in the plains of the Midwest. They are assisted by experienced cowboys and a trail boss named Curly, played by Jack Palance. In perhaps the most important scene in the movie, Mitch and Curly are riding along a dusty trail, and Mitch asks him about the meaning of life.

> Curly: A cowboy leads a different kind of life…when there were cowboys. We're a dyin' breed. Still means something to me, though…. There's nothin' like bringin' in the herd.
>
> Mitch: See, now that's great. Your life makes sense to you.
>
> Curly: You city folk, you worry about a lotta garbage, don't ya? You're all the same age with the same problems. You spend fifty weeks a year gettin' knots in your ropes, and then you think two weeks up here will untie 'em for you. None of you get it…. You know what the secret to life is?
>
> Mitch: No, what?
>
> Curly: This. [Holds up one finger.]
>
> Mitch: Your finger?
>
> Curly: One thing. Just one thing…. You stick to that and everything else don't mean nothin'.
>
> Mitch: That's great, but what's the one thing?
>
> Curly: That's what you've got to figure out.

The movie *Bull Durham*, starring Kevin Costner, offers us a similar view of life. Unlike Mitch, who struggles to understand life, his role in it, and what really matters to him, Costner's character, Crash Davis, a minor league baseball catcher, has no illusions about what is truly important. In perhaps the most noteworthy scene in *that* movie, Susan Sarandon, who plays the owner of the baseball team, describes the way in which people form relationships and how life evolves. She talks about how we never really choose one another — that it really has to do with quantum physics, molecular structure and timing. This is Costner's response:

Well, I believe in the soul, the dawn, the night, the small of a woman's back, the hanging curve ball, high fiber, good scotch, that the novels of Susan Sontag are self-indulgent, overrated crap. I believe Lee Harvey Oswald acted alone; I believe that there should be a constitutional amendment outlawing astroturf and the designated hitter. I believe in the sweet spot, soft-core pornography, opening your presents on Christmas morning rather than Christmas Eve, and I believe in long, slow, deep, soft, wet kisses that last three days.

I am not certain I have Curly's wisdom, nor do I feel I understand the world sufficiently to state what is really important as emphatically as Crash Davis, although I do believe in opening your presents on Christmas morning rather than Christmas Eve. I think it involves four things: an anchor, a scale, a cheerleader, and soul food.

## An Anchor

I am currently working on a book that tries to intersect many of the problems that our society faces, such as poverty, racism, crime, and the decline of the family, with a personal narrative that offers the reader an insider's glimpse of how these large-scale problems influence the individual. In many ways it is an autobiographical account juxtaposed with a discussion of the research on these topics. I can tell you that it has been a very painful experience, and it has taken me a long time to feel strong enough to write about these events. As I put the finishing commas and semicolons on this book, along with last-minute clarifications, I realized that in the process, I have determined what is really important, at least to me.

My early childhood was spent in the Hill section of New Haven, Connecticut, historically and currently one of the poorest sections of the city and one of the worst neighborhoods in the entire state. At a young age I was exposed to the violent, ruthless, and racist side of life. My early adolescent years were marked by periods of living on the street and by frequent stays with various families, what might broadly be called foster homes, although it was not until years later that the state intervened to ensure adequate standards of care were being met. Most of the families performed their duties with the hopes of making a profit rather than out of a sense of compassion and concern for others. In many ways, while the address had changed, the living conditions remained the same.

Although no records were kept until the state intervened, my best estimate of the number of families was approximately nineteen. I literally lived out of one small suitcase, which contained a pair of pants, three shirts, a few pairs of undergarments, and a couple of books I managed to secure. I tell you this because my story is not unlike thousands of other children and is more common than we like to believe. The problems I and other children encounter is also very similar to the need in many of us as adults to alleviate feelings of isolation and insecurity in our lives.

My colleague David Rutledge has said that we are much better at being individuals than we are at being members of a group, and that one of our quests in life is to feel, as he puts it, a part of a "web of kindred spirits." I think this is true: Man *is* a social being who needs to feel a part of something greater than himself. However, this can only occur if the person has some sort of anchor, a mooring, a place to call home — a sense of place. Without one, I think we lose a part of ourselves, and it renders us incapable of seeing other things that are important.

To borrow from Maslow for a moment, while our physical needs must be met, we also need to feel that there is a place where we are safe and cared for. In this way, an anchor also involves a social or emotional component. And, to be honest, it has only been since I have come to Furman that I have felt this sense of place: physically, with the purchase of a home, but emotionally and socially by becoming a part of the "Furman family."

## A Scale

Second, and related, is a solid sense of fairness and equity in dealing with each other. In the process of interacting with others, we struggle to find out who we are at different points in our lives. As adolescents, we struggle with our identities since we are caught between being a child and being an adult. As adults, we often try to define ourselves by our careers and occupations, although this is not always possible. And, finally, many people struggle with who they are in their later years, such as the unpredictable and sometimes bizarre behavior of men during a midlife crisis, or the struggle for an identity after we retire.

The development of who we are is essential if we are to be fair to others. Unfortunately, we are consumed with getting ahead without having any real sense of who we are or what we want. We have relied on society to define ourselves and to be satisfied with what makes other people happy rather than what makes ourselves happy. If we have a large home, new automobiles, and the ability to take exotic vacations, we *are* somebody. We don't seem that concerned about others because we are too preoccupied with ourselves. And if our objectives lead us to take advantage of others, we seem very willing to do so without much thought to the implications or the consequences.

In short, we have lost sight of the notion of fairness and have forgotten that with the privilege of opportunity comes the responsibility to help others. Thus, in addition to having a secure sense of self, what really matters is what one does with it. There is a large body of research that tells us that many of the problems of the poor and other minorities involve issues of being treated unfairly and of not being given the opportunities to succeed. This introduces the controversy over poverty, welfare reform, and things like affirmative action. Let me take a moment to frame the debate from a sociological perspective.

## Fairness and Poverty: The Debate

A moment ago I mentioned how we seem preoccupied with our own interests and that we often look upon the problems others encounter as somehow a result of their lack of effort or talent. This is often referred to as the culture of poverty explanation. For instance, in *The Negro Family, The Case for National Action*, or what is commonly known as the Moynihan Report (1965), Daniel Moynihan viewed single female-headed households, crime rates in certain black communities, and substance abuse as common features among African Americans. He explains the cause of these behaviors and attitudes in a distinct black culture with its own value systems.

A related school of thought argues that welfare actually creates and perpetuates poverty. In *Losing Ground*, Charles Murray (1984) claims that the poor see no need to care for themselves because they know that the state will do it for them. According to this view, poor people *choose* their "lifestyle" because doing otherwise would require working hard and participating in mainstream culture. Thus, poor people are more interested in leisure activities and unconcerned with the consequences or the future.

Murray goes on to argue that every individual is responsible for improving their own position in life, and as such, we cannot hold the state responsible for making these changes for them. In his view, people are poor simply because they are either lazy and unwilling to take control of their lives or they do not possess any type of work ethic.

As evidence of the validity of their claims, culturalists like Murray often point to the purchasing practices of some poor families. They contend that poor African Americans and Hispanics own too many leisure items like expensive clothes, stereo equipment, televisions, and luxury automobiles. Those who buy these types of things are considered wasteful and ungrateful for the financial support they receive. They are too present-oriented and therefore uninterested in changing their current status. Those who only buy the basic necessities are characterized as committed to changing their poverty status because they "appreciate the value of the dollar."

What is interesting about the cultural evaluation of the poor is that it does not account for the fact that we are clearly a materialistic society. We are so insecure that we feel we must flaunt our affluence through status symbols and what Thorsten Veblen referred to as "conspicuous consumption." Another way of looking at this, then, is to say that the poor, like the rich, are simply trying to attain part of the "American Dream" through what they own. As such, they are subscribing to mainstream societal values. Perhaps more importantly, the cultural perspective provides an exaggerated view of the poor in general. While there is indeed a small percentage of people in poverty who abuse the system, the vast majority are referred to as the "working poor." They have full-time jobs and work hard. And most people who use the welfare system benefit from it as a short-term strategy — as it was originally intended.

## What Does All This Tell Us?

The issues surrounding race and poverty, namely, policy decisions like affirmative action and welfare reform, are far from clear. With regard to programs like affirmative action, many conservatives, such as former Governor of California Pete Wilson, argue that the issue should be based on merit, not on race or other factors. This has a certain appeal to most people. After all, it is based on the idea that has a ring of authenticity to it: fairness. If the person is the most qualified for the job, then they should be the one hired. What could be more American than that?

Wilson and other conservatives are also quick to point out that the increase in the number of middle-class African Americans is an indicator that we no longer need to "set aside" programs for businesses, and we no longer need strategies such as affirmative action because they have accomplished what they were intended to do: to give people of color and other minorities the opportunities to gain a foothold in the labor market.

People who espouse this view also frequently point to African-American conservatives such as Thomas Sowell or William Raspberry as if they somehow have a greater understanding of the issue because they are black. Thus, if an African American espouses conservative views, that means we should give greater weight to what they are saying. While the number of middle-class African Americans has increased somewhat, and there remains a good deal of debate about this, what this argument ignores is those at the very bottom of the labor pile.

Let's consider the conservative point of view a bit further. With regard to the last point, the only reason some minorities have been able to make the strides of success is *because* of programs such as affirmative action. While the conservatives argue that we have achieved equality, they have not accurately assessed what this really means, and they have failed to recognize that it was forced upon them. They had not and would not have done so willingly. This, it seems to me, is the crux of the issue.

We all know that people are given jobs because of who they know, are related to, or for some reason other than merit. But when legislation was passed prohibiting nepotism and patronage — with the jobs going to unknown minorities instead of friends, relatives, or college mates — suddenly the issue becomes one of merit. Do minorities get jobs for which they are unqualified? Sometimes, but so does the boss's son who is put into an executive position when he knows little about the business. And there are countless other examples where unqualified people get the job over a qualified applicant simply because they know someone in the company. This is not surprising. We often hear the phrase "Life is about networks." The issue of merit is not the reason for the concern.

I think the real issue is one of power. Our history shows us that we will never simply "do the right thing" when it comes to including minorities in the work force. This was the reason legislation was enacted in the first place. We are interested in helping ourselves, our friends, and people we like — people who are similar to us. As such, we will never be able to achieve equality unless we make it a priority.

A second and related point can also be made. If we as a society are honestly interested in giving minorities a legitimate chance to become qualified candidates, why have we continued to perpetuate the class distinctions in education? The sociological literature on the relationship between education, income, and occupation is well known, especially concerning life chances of parents and their ability to pass those opportunities on to their children. Those who are able to obtain a good education can expect many lucrative career opportunities, and the same is true in reverse as well. Those with substandard educations will likely occupy jobs in the lowest paying sectors of the market. Thus, the best predictor of one's life chances in our society is the social class one is born into and that despite claims of an "open" class system, most people reproduce their parents' social class standing.

Since minorities are usually found at the lower end of the educational continuum, how will they ever be given a chance to compete on an equal footing? If we abolish programs that require employers to give minorities a chance to become a part of the system, how will they do it on their own?

You might say, "They can do it if they get the same or similar types of education." Okay, great. Yet there are clear differences in the amount of money spent in education between social classes. As Jonathan Kozol points out in his book *Savage Inequalities*, tying educational spending to property taxes only perpetuates the kind of class-based educational opportunities that have existed for decades. And despite the Supreme Court's charge to desegregate the schools with "all deliberate speed," this type of system has led to the segregation in many public school districts across the country. Perhaps even more disquieting is the attack on educational programs by conservatives during the latest round of budget hearings. Eliminating programs for inner city children only exacerbates the problem. Substandard education makes it even more difficult for minorities to compete, which in turn will shunt them out of the job market since someone else will be "more qualified."

Again, this is not about merit. We can all agree that the most qualified person should get the job. However, what has happened is that we have made it nearly impossible for minorities and the poor to obtain the necessary credentials to compete. But the end result is the same: very few minorities. However, in this instance the argument is that there are no qualified minorities to do the job. Of course not.

So how do we make the playing field even and try to minimize the head start many already have? How do we balance the scale so that people have a legitimate chance at success? If you think about it, if we wanted to give minorities an honest chance to compete without programs like affirmative action, we would have to spend a great deal *more* on education and other programs targeting minorities than we would spend on affluent children. This is because so many poor children are behind in virtually all phases of learning. How likely is it that affluent parents are going to be willing to pay more taxes to give minorities a chance to compete? Not very likely at all.

In sum, we seem to want it both ways. We say we want equality, but what that really means is we want equality for us, not for everyone else. We will provide special advantages for our children, but we resent it when we are forced to give those similar opportunities to others. We say the basis should be merit, but what we are really saying is that we do not want the choice taken out of our hands. We say everyone should be on an equal footing, but our behavior and social policies continue to exclude minorities from their chances for success.

With regard to opportunities, I think it is fair to say that we all have opportunities that we squander. Some of us are better than others at taking advantage of them, but I think we can all agree that there have been times when we are presented with an opportunity but, for a variety of reasons, have done nothing with it or have not maximized its potential. Yet when people from less privileged backgrounds do the same thing, we are often very critical of them. In essence, they are doing the same things all of us do, but somehow they are held to a higher standard of accountability than we are.

A similar approach relates to spending patterns. As I mentioned, we expect people to live in a materialist society, where certain products are considered evidence of success. For those who have limited resources, priorities are made of sacrificing other necessities in order to purchase those products. Again, it is similar to our own spending habits and our attempts to live the American dream. Yet certain groups are considered negligent or wasteful while others are simply aspiring to live life at a certain standard. But most of us are unable to maintain this standard, as is evidenced by a recent news report that the balance on the average American credit card is $2,000 and have an average of two cards per person.

Thus, we have not provided certain groups with a fair chance to compete in the marketplace; we are unwilling to offer them those chances, and then we have held them to an unreasonable standard of conduct. And the history of race and ethnic relations in our society has shown that we have done this even for those groups that have desperately wanted to assimilate into our society. And when some of those groups have been successful, such as some Asian Americans, our response has been to castigate them for their success.

Thus, we continue to forget that tipping the scale in our favor only leads to additional, more complicated problems for us. We have forgotten that one of the things that really matters is to treat people with dignity, respect, and, above all, fairness. In the process, opportunities will be offered, some of which will be squandered, but more will be accepted and maximized if the recipients feel as though they have a chance to succeed.

## A Cheerleader

Related to this is the topic of role models. As any teacher will tell you, the confidence level of a student, even the most talented and gifted, hangs in a delicate balance. One of the primary functions of the teacher, then, is to encourage, to inspire, to elicit in students a belief in themselves and in their abilities so they may achieve whatever objective for which they strive.

If this is true, and I believe it is, then the same premise must also apply to others as well. If people are provided with an adequate support network, where they are encouraged to strive for lofty goals and know that failure is an acceptable part of learning, the feats they can achieve are often nothing short of remarkable. Moreover, this is not simply the moralizing of a young scholar. There is a great deal of research that supports this notion.

Speaking on a personal level, as a young boy growing up in the inner city, the exposure to drugs, crime, and various forms of deviant behavior was very, very pervasive. The individuals who were looked upon as leaders in this community were not the most upstanding our society had to offer: the pimps, drug dealers, fences, bookies, loan sharks, and gang leaders. *They* set the standards of behavior — *they* were admired. The lessons learned and the advice given by these individuals translated into the behavior of everyone I knew. A few examples: My best friend Arthur Gilmore tested his newly learned techniques of how to hot wire a car, which he then tried to teach to me; or Marquette, who started out selling cartoon stickers laced with LSD and eventually became a midlevel dealer in cocaine; or Eddie, who joined a gang and became a rather prolific and well-known armed robber in our neighborhood.

Then there is Val, the Italian immigrant who spent a lot of time as a numbers runner and learned the finer points of bookmaking operations from his adult mentors. And finally there was James, a good friend, who watched older kids sniff glue out of a paper bag and quickly moved on to using and injecting heroin. In 1992, after almost twenty years of IV drug use and sharing needles, an important part of the drug-using culture, he was diagnosed HIV-positive and died a year later.

Like them, I too was on my way to a criminal career. Had I not gotten out of that neighborhood and been directed in life by some greater force, who knows what kind of life I would have had? What I can say is that it would be highly unlikely I would be here with you this evening. It is not hyperbole when I tell you that many of the people I grew up with are now drug addicts, in prison, deceased, or on their way to one of those outcomes. In fact, I had the opportunity a few years ago to return to my old neighborhood as part of a study sponsored by the Center for Disease Control of heroin addicts. I found quite a few of my old schoolmates in methadone clinics, in shooting galleries, and on the street, and learned of the fate of many others. It was a difficult time, especially when questions were asked about my life and what I had done with it. There have been many nights, then and since, where I have sat and wondered why things happened the way they did. Why me? Was it luck? Motivation? What? But the fact of the matter is that I got out. They stayed. And, as I mentioned, the research supports the notion of how mentors or role models are an important factor in shaping the attitudes, values, beliefs, as well as the behavior of today's youth. But what do we really know? Let me probe into this body of knowledge for just a minute to give you an idea.

## Role Models and the Poor

In the 1980s, perhaps the most prominent theoretical explanation for inner-city problems emphasized the increased levels of poverty in poor neighborhoods. The main thrust of this explanation was the shift in the economy, specifically the tendency for factory jobs to move out of the city and to areas where costs of production were cheaper. In perhaps the most influential work on the subject, William Julius Wilson's *The Truly Disadvantaged* (1987) focuses on the large numbers of working- and middle-class blacks leaving the inner city, which exacerbates the social isolation of those who are forced to remain. Thus, the problems of a changing economy have led to an increase in residential segregation for the poor.

Wilson also argues that the departure of working- and middle-class African Americans from cities also leads to a decline in the number and quality of role models. This further intensifies the overall problems in the inner city. Similarly, Elijah Anderson's (1991) work in Philadelphia, titled *Streetwise*, echoes Wilson's earlier point. Anderson argues that these groups served the community as visible symbols of "success, and moral value, living examples of the fruits of hard work, perseverance, decency and propriety" (p. 58). Thus, he argues that the people who left the inner city "were effective, meaningful role models lending the community a certain moral integrity" (p. 59).

Anderson underscores this point with his discussion of the increase in teenage pregnancy. He argues that the number of traditional adult *female* role models, who often exerted a considerable amount of social control over their younger counterparts, lost much of their ability to influence young women. This is due, as Wilson argues, largely to the deterioration of inner city neighborhoods. In this type of environment, Anderson argues that even the adult role models have been taxed to the breaking point. They, too, have become demoralized, and many have left these neighborhoods.

The same is true with regard to employment. As meaningful jobs become increasingly scarce, the traditional male role models — who emphasize the importance of hard work, determination, and a belief in the American dream — become irrelevant, largely because they are no longer possible. Thus, while some will remain and continue to attempt to have a positive influence on the next generation, many have decided the conditions in these neighborhoods have reached an unacceptable level. Like their female counterparts, these "old heads" typically move out of the area. In their wake, however, a new role model emerges: one that is involved in criminal activity and scorns mainstream society and its rules of acceptable behavior.

********

It seems obvious, then, that most of the research on the subject of role models calls attention to the importance of having a positive influence on a young person, which in turn shapes their outlook on life, their confidence, and their belief in themselves. There are success stories, even in the worst of neighborhoods, where young adults who should have succumbed to the street did not. They were somehow able to resist the temptations of unacceptable behavior such as crime, gang life, and drug use and to somehow square their self-images with those of their peers. But we cannot use them as evidence of success — the odds of them making it are so great, and they are so few in number that the ones who escape are quite rare. Yet we continue to point to them as evidence that anyone can do it if they work hard enough or want it badly enough. I will not discount the work ethic or the motivation aspect of this argument. I think it is important to remember that *anyone* who wants to succeed must possess these characteristics and use them. However, there are many talented people who will never reach their goals because they will not get the chance to do so. Far more do not make it out of the inner city than the few who do.

For those who do succeed, in virtually all of these instances there was someone who was instrumental in putting and keeping them on the right path. They served as mentors, taught by example, and acted as cheerleaders to provide encouragement and tried to instill in the person the belief that they were important, that they really mattered. In my case, it was my junior high school football coach and his wife who saw what was happening to me and, despite considerable costs to themselves, chose to literally and figuratively save my life. To this day, they give balance to my life and serve as my emotional and social anchor.

Thus, if we really want to do something about the problems of poverty, delinquency, unemployment, and the like, it begins with providing opportunities and helping people come to the realization that many of their dreams are in fact possible. In my view, that is essentially what really matters.

## Soul Food

Many of the things I have discussed this evening have an external focus. This one is much more internally directed. In many ways, this has been the most difficult for me and it has only been recently that I have identified it. So what is soul food?

It is the thing or things that feed your soul — what sustains you and gives your life a sense of meaning and purpose. It consists of those activities that fill you with a deep sense of gratification and help you understand why you are here. For many years I have not reflected on what my soul food was because other more pressing needs were being addressed. I felt that I had to reach a particular point before I could allow myself such ponderings. What feeds mine can be captured in the simple concept of sharing.

In the past few months I have finally come to realize that I derive a tremendous sense of satisfaction by giving to others and seeing them benefit from it. Whether it be enlightenment through information in a course, showing students the fun and excitement of research and then watching them grow intellectually, or offering advice or insight that helps them solve a personal problem, or economic sharing to those who need it, or simply sharing my life with my best friend — my wife — this feeds my soul. It is as simple and, at the same time, as complicated as that.

As I struggle even now to define what really matters and to reconsider if what I have said in this article is satisfactory in my own mind, perhaps I can end with a parting shot that parallels life according to Crash Davis' world-views:

I believe in the quiet of a New England snowfall; the frenzy of a busy Manhattan street; the excitement of beating your father at Nintendo for the first time, even when he cheats; hockey players who teach rather than injure; and novels that keep you up all night because you simply can't put them down. I believe in room service, good pizza, and long naps at Thanksgiving while watching football with your family. I believe Anita Hill was telling the truth, that honesty and politics are impossible companions, and that Shannon Faulkner is the Rosa Parks of the 1990s. I believe in belly laughs from small children, rooting for the long shot, and never ever forgetting where you came from.

# James B. Leavell
## History and Asian Studies
### October 14, 1997

"All composite things must pass away. Strive onward vigilantly." According to tradition these were the final words uttered by Siddhartha Gautama, Shakayamuni, "The Awakened One," the historical Buddha. Wisdom seems to begin with the proper definition of the human condition. Understanding the essence of the problem is a vital prerequisite for achieving the problem's solution. The Buddha's analysis of our human condition is incredibly powerful.

I first encountered the Buddha's teaching, not as part of any academic endeavor, but in the midst of the dark night of my soul. I was a sophomore. Cultural Christianity, my crib faith, had become utterly unacceptable. That stage of my spiritual struggle ended many months later with something of a Damascus road experience I was ultimately to interpret with the help of Kierkegaard and, oddly enough, D. T. Suzuki, the first great interpreter of Zen for the English-speaking world. Though my leap of faith focused on the Christ, my debt to the Buddha has deepened through the years. My contact with Buddhists, particularly Japanese Buddhists, has helped clarify my basic understanding of life and periodically reenergized my spiritual life for almost forty years now. My comments tonight would hardly be authentic if I failed to acknowledge this part of my history.

History — this is another significant element in tonight's remarks. In my view, ideas, feelings, and insights are not disembodied entities. They have context — histories. To disregard the context of particular ideas is to risk misunderstanding their essence. We historians are uncompromising about this. For this reason we demand that our students probe the biographies of authors whose works we assign. Professional historians often research and write to exorcise personal demons. It is helpful for the reader to know just what those demons are before ingesting a work of "non-fiction." We call this, in the trade, understanding the author's bias. What is the author's personal history? How does it color the ideas? You will get some of that kind of background tonight, hopefully not so much that you will be made uncomfortable. "All composite things must pass away."

Tonight's exercise is something like an intellectual and spiritual striptease. This is one reason accepting this task is so chilling. It is also probably the main reason some of you come to this lecture series on a regular basis. Let me hasten to say that, being a Baptist preacher's son, my knowledge of the metaphor I am using is scanty indeed. I have not even seen Demi Moore's recent, highly advertised exposé of the subject.[1] I am using the metaphor striptease in a shameless attempt to regain the attention of any undergraduate male who has wandered in here thinking he was going to get CLP (Cultural Life Program) credit and is already mentally anesthetized by references to Buddha, Jesus, and that greatest of all cures for insomnia — history. Incidentally, I am convinced the striptease metaphor would have been greatly appreciated by the Right Reverend, and often irreverent, L. D. Johnson, in whose memory this lectureship was inaugurated. He was an earthy man. During his first conversation with me, he employed language most unbecoming to a university chaplain as he discussed the character flaws of my immediate male relatives against whom he had played basketball at Southern Baptist Theological Seminary. I seem to recall something about their unchristian use of elbows under the basket. As his descriptive words became increasingly more colorful, it was evident that my father and uncle had used such unloving tactics as their only means of defeating Johnson and his teammates. The fact that the Baylor mafia trounced the Johnson crew regularly could apparently only be explained by the regular employment of foul play. Johnson seemed convinced I must have inherited a serious genetic flaw. Despite this shaky beginning to our relationship, L. D. willingly served as one of my mentors during my early Furman years. Team teaching with him on Furman's 1978 Middle East foreign study trip was an incredibly exciting experience.

Back to the striptease metaphor, L. D. would have liked it. I am told that the art of the striptease is primarily in the teasing rather than the stripping. This general approach was what I took to be the import of a colleague's suggestion to keep this evening's tone light. With the first scarves already floating in the air and a dark night of the soul already exposed, let me reiterate that "all composite things must pass away." Change happens.

"Ceaselessly the river flows, and yet the water is never the same, while in the still pools the shifting foam gathers and is gone, never staying for a moment. Even so is man...unenduring as the foam on the water."[2]

---

[1] *Striptease.*

[2] Kamo no Chomei, *Hojoki* in *Ten Foot Square Hut and Tales of the Heike* (trans. A. L. Sadler). Tokyo: Charles E. Tuttle Co., 1972, p. 1.

These are obviously the words of a man in his sixties without a retirement plan. Kamo no Chomei spent most of his life as a Shinto priest serving Kyoto's Kamo Shrine until he was victimized by clerical downsizing. With a deep sense of institutional betrayal, he became a hermit, took solace in Pure Land Buddhism, and ultimately produced the *Hojoki*, translated as *The Ten Foot Square*. This small, painfully honest literary masterpiece chronicled Chomei's progress toward divesting himself of worldly attachments — of the things he was convinced did not really matter. His ultimate assessment was that we and our possessions are as "unenduring as the foam on the water."

My initial observation this evening is about as safe as I can utter aloud. There is not much behind this veil to shock you. Here it is — "what matters" changes, depending on our constantly evolving life circumstances. What matters depends on which river current has caught our bit of foam at a given moment. "All composite things must pass away."

Another thirteenth-century Japanese classic, the *Heike monogatari* (*Tales of the Heike Clan*), begins as follows: "The sound of the [temple] bell of Jetavana echoes the impermanence of all things. The hue of the flowers of the teak tree declares that they who flourish must be brought low. Yea, the proud ones are but for a moment, like an evening dream in springtime. The mighty are destroyed at the last, they are but as the dust before the wind."[3]

Every Japanese school child memorizes these opening lines of the *Heike monogatari* the way many of us in this room were forced to learn the Gettysburg Address and Mark Antony's funeral oration. History is about change. As a historian I spend a lot of time thinking about and discussing the accomplishments of dead people. Old-fashioned historians like me rarely, if ever, devote time to discussing dead people who did not accomplish something. For my professional colleagues present, my fellow academic historians who also teach undergraduate students, let me acknowledge that I am aware that the strongest *current* river current, the most active bubbles of foam in our pool at present, revolve around the difficult task of finding something to say that will be meaningful to eighteen to twenty-two-year-olds about *un*accomplished dead people. Social history is much in vogue.

Stepping back from the often exciting narrative of who killed whom, when, where, and why, we hear undeniable wisdom in the opening lines of *Tales of the Heike Clan*: "The sound of the [temple] bell of Jetavana echoes the impermanence of all things. The hue of the flowers of the teak tree declares that they who flourish must be brought low." No empire, nation, or

---

[3]A. L. Sadler (trans.). *Ten Foot Square Hut and Tales of the Heike.* Tokyo: Charles E. Tuttle Co., 1972, p. 22.

clan has ever remained on top. Edward Gibbon was so disturbed by this thought he devoted a sizable chunk of his life to investigating how England's imperial leadership might be sustained by avoiding the mistakes of the Romans. Forests were cut down to print his analysis. Despite his efforts, all of Hong Kong's current administrators speak fluent Chinese. No empire, nation, or clan has ever remained on top. "They who flourish must be brought low."

I got some inkling of this depressing truth in Sunday school, but certainly not from my early social studies training in grammar school. There in Mrs. Brock's fourth-grade class I was introduced to the stirring tales of my own national heritage — the saga of the Republic of Texas and its absorption of the United States. I continue to be appalled each year when I discover how few Furman students in my Western civilization classes have never heard of Cabaza de Vaca, the first white man to explore Texas. Even the politically correct undergraduates (I encounter one every year or so), who might be forgiven for having overlooked the exploits of this dead white man, seem to know nothing of the Korankawa or Tejas Indians. Ignorance of Texas seems profound here in the East. Mrs. Brock never once suggested that "they who flourish [*Texans* and their American associates] must be brought low." The Alamo was simply a prelude to greatness.

I received more advanced civics training in the 1950s from a Yankee outlander who called herself Miss Zerex. Within her worldview, the medieval Japanese wisdom words under consideration here would have seemed in no way applicable to America. Our nation, according to Miss Zerex of Robert E. Lee, Jr., High School, is the most powerful the world has ever seen, and since it stands for what is good, true, and beautiful — all eternal values — then America, too, will shine eternally. To be honest, what mattered to me during those years was whether I would make the football team, somehow grow as tall as Margo Kirkham (girl of my dreams), and be able to buy enough Clearasil to make a difference. At that point in my life I believe the words "all composite things must pass away" would have been a comfort.

Mentioning my early civics training in the 1950s is my opening for the "when I was a boy" part of the address. This is the extremely self-indulgent part of "the strip," but I also recognize that it has its dangers. There are young people here who will begin to yawn, and there are elders present who can easily "harumph" and mutter uncomplimentary remarks about my generation. But I proceed — cautiously.

Any one whose childhood included participation in a religious community has been encouraged to consider not just what matters, but what *really* matters. In my case, this encouragement began as early as I can remember. I received the usual informal parental guidance of the sort you would expect from a Mississippi father and Kentucky mother. Right away I know that those of you steeped in the lore of Southern regional culture recognize me as the product of a mixed marriage. Add to this unstable alliance a paternal grandmother reared in Ming dynasty China by missionary parents and you are going to have to concede the likelihood of my having some passing contact with discussions of what *really* matters. I must confess my most powerful recollections are of my grandmother's injunctions. I do not know how many Christian converts were produced through her parents' ministry, but I am certain the Chinese made a dedicated Confucian of this ramrod straight, red-headed barbarian woman. Favorite injunctions: "Remember who you are" (uttered routinely as I headed out the door on Friday night, bent on a wild, flaps-down, full-throttle, two-fisted binge at the Dairy Queen). In my mind she was really saying, "You represent the ancestors. Do not bring shame to the name of the clan." That generally took the "ha" out of my "yee-haaa." I had seen pictures of some of those ancestors. Now, how about *this* grandmotherly admonition: "Do not do to others what you would not want others to do to you." Sooooo. Even Jesus borrowed from Confucius. Yes, yes I know Jesus turned the negative into a positive, but neither version did anything to inflate the fun factor.

Now, I have been discussing the informal parental instructional sessions about what really matters. My father had a special bonus afforded few patriarchs. He got a formal shot at me three times a week — twice on Sunday and then again every Wednesday night. As I revealed earlier, I was a preacher's kid. Incidentally, having already negotiated our arranged marriage with my mother, even my future wife's parents had a crack at me every Sunday evening for several of my impressionable adolescent years through a well-organized Baptist catechism class called Training Union or BTU. The fact that my wife and I had an arranged marriage has always fascinated our Japanese friends. What mattered in my mid twenties was marrying the right girl. Those of you who know Judy regularly acknowledge that my mother could really pick 'um! Ah, Confucianism.

I must admit that those early experiences living in the parsonage with the church community, a constant larger presence was in some ways painful, but they have remained at the core of my value system. As I, along with many of you, listened to Prime Minister Tony Blair read 1 Corinthians 13 at Diana's memorial service, I acknowledged again what *really* matters and even toyed with the idea of simply reading that biblical passage for you tonight and inviting us all to adjourn downstairs for cookies. Clearly, I do not have that much good sense. Not enough strip or tease in that.

What mattered in the early sixties was the selection of a college major and whether Baylor could somehow beat the University of Texas in football.

What really mattered was whether Judy liked me as much as her parents did. (I suppose most of the young unmarried men present here tonight are already well aware of the danger to a significant relationship when "her mother likes you.")

Religious or not, in love or not, many males reaching young adulthood during the mid to late 1960s were forced to consider what mattered. The one individual chosen to represent the Vietnam era in the official Washington Memorial Day program last summer was Marine Captain Bill Griffis, my schoolmate from first through the twelfth grades. Professor Duncan McArthur knew him at the University of the South. I vividly recall that Bill's attitudes on issues that would later define him were already diverging from mine by the time we reached the eighth grade. If the film *Forrest Gump* describes my generation, and I believe in many ways it does, Bill was for me Lt. Dan — a difference being that there was no Forrest Gump to drag him out of the line of fire. What mattered in the late sixties and into the early seventies were questions about free-fire zones, Cambodia, and the ethics of national leaders. "All composite things must pass away."

Eligible for the draft or not, young adults of the sixties were challenged by the Civil Rights movement to consider what *really* mattered. Shortly after the notorious Little Rock Central High School incident, my West Texas hometown school board voted to integrate. Somehow, those choices seemed easy on the frontier. It was not until I entered college at Jerusalem-on-the-Brazos, Baylor University, the Baptist Notre Dame, that I experienced the institutional struggle for equal opportunity. My most vivid memories are of students from Mississippi, like Ted Estes (now Dean of the Honors College at the University of Houston) and Milburn Price (later to be Chair of Furman's music department). Their personal moral outrage about Baylor's reluctance to admit black students was fueled by long years of ethical and spiritual nurturing in Southern Baptist churches, which in the early sixties seemed blind to the obviously immoral social practices of the pervasive secular and religious culture we mistakenly saw at the time to be uniquely Southern. My grandmother was right, whether she was quoting Confucius or Jesus, whether it's the do or do not version, it really matters how we treat each other.

I want to confess a suspicion. I have the sneaky feeling that the title of this series of lectures (check the front of your programs) was conceived out of the mind of a middle-aged individual. I consider myself in this age bracket and have been there, it seems, for some time now. During my undergraduate senior year, I recall a university chaplain remarking that I was the youngest forty-year-old he had ever met. He did not really mean this as a compliment, but then he was one of the first adults I had known well who lived by the adage that you can get older, but you can be immature all your life! When the reality of actually being middle aged hit me, I was depressed. I now find that I fervently embrace being middle aged as I look in the mirror and begin to suspect I may be about to shift into the next category. "All composite things must pass away."

What matters evolves. Not having hair like John Shelley actually matters less to me now than it did last year. Being confused with Bill Lavery matters more. But looking back on my early middle-age years, I recall an intensified concern about what matters, particularly with regard to career priorities. I remember raising questions about what mattered around the time T. C. Smith, Theron Price, and Gerda McCahan were retiring from Furman. I saw myself at a crossroads. The number and variety of opportunities struck me as multitudinous. I was also aware that I did not have the energy to do all of them. I was going to have to choose. What I wanted to know from my colleagues who had come to the end of their Furman careers was "If you had it to do over again, what would you have spent your energy doing?" I wanted each of these individuals to give me their honest evaluation of the various aspects of their Furman experience and guide me in making my choices. That such questions are less pressing now suggests to me I am moving out of middle age. My bit of foam may be about to shift currents in the river.

A story for those of us who are foaming up together in our late fifties. Elder heads may simply care to nod. You younger folk better listen *real* sharp, here! In 1973–74 I was serving on the faculty of Seinan Gakuin University in Fukuoka, Japan. During that same year Roger Kirk, a psychology professor of Baylor University, was on campus using his sabbatical to update his popular psychology text on statistical methods. (Popular text on statistical methods — is this what is meant by an oxymoron?) The book had brought Roger both professional attention and a tidy extra income. Roger was and still is an incredibly disciplined workaholic. I began to observe his habits carefully as I struggled with the early chapters of my doctoral dissertation. On a number of weekends, Judy and I were able to lure him to join us in search of folk pottery kilns, which were scattered among the mountain villages of Japan's large southern island. These outings gave me opportunities to tap the man's wisdom. According to him, *energy*, rather than time, is the primary commodity one must budget. I was thirty-two at the time and must admit the comment took me by surprise. At forty-two it made perfect sense. At fifty-six it has become a personal mantra. What matters changes with our life stages. Finding ways to optimize energy is certainly a key issue from middle age onward. This matters, but is not what *really* matters.

Change is built into the fundamental nature of all things. "Ceaselessly the river flows, and yet the water is never the same." Shakyamuni, the historical Buddha, said this quite succinctly. "All composite things must pass away." It was further his understanding that change is painful, painful because we tend to become attached to a particular transitory configuration of circumstances — a Furman lake with water in it; a roommate who really cares about you, an e-mail system that works most of the time, having hair on your head, being considered smarter, more beautiful, or just plain nicer than anyone you know, having parents to depend on, close friends who are vigorous, a body free of serious disease. We suffer a sense of loss, even betrayal, when these elements display their true nature by reconfiguring. These transitory configurations seem to me to dictate for us what matters, and I have tried to suggest that what matters changes. It also seems to me that what *really* matters is how we face inevitable change, particularly the kind over which we have absolutely no control. What *really* matters is *attitude*. Again, the words of the Buddha, and this time the entire quote, with which I began: "All composite things must pass away. Strive onward vigilantly." Change happens. Deal with it. *How* you deal with it is what *really* matters.

# Susan S. D'Amato
## Physics
*October 26, 1998*

As other speakers in this series have noted, it's both an honor and a challenge to be asked to ponder the question of "what really matters?" from the perspective of our academic disciplines and life experiences and to share our reflections with this audience. While I well understood the honor when the invitation was first extended, I did not fully appreciate the challenge until some months later, when I first tried to put pen to paper.

To collect some thoughts, I began paying attention to the events of daily living and scribbling phrases on a Post-It note whenever inspiration occurred. I observed that getting to work safely in the morning does matter; beating the red lights in Travelers Rest does not. Accomplishing an important task during the day does matter; leaving my desk in a clutter-free state does not. Asking my child how her day went does matter; persuading her not to put stickers on the dog does not. Gathering the family for the evening meal, lighting the dinner candle, and saying a blessing — these things matter — but serving food that hasn't seen the inside of a microwave most decidedly does not. The hard part began when I finally reviewed these accumulated lists of "things that matter" and "things that don't" and struggled to find some organizing principle to help make sense of it all.

It was in this state of mind that I was watching a newsmagazine show on network television late in the summer. The story that caught my attention focused on a young mother who, on learning that she has a serious case of breast cancer, has begun to methodically fashion a remarkable legacy for her six-year-old daughter to inherit in the event of her death. She is creating a series of videotapes filled with motherly advice, instruction, and loving encouragement, designed to be viewed by her daughter as she reaches different life stages over the years. Several clips from the tapes were shown during the story. The advice ranges from pragmatic to profound. In one scene, the mother stresses the importance of a good credit history. In another, she shows her daughter how to apply makeup to her face in a way that won't leave a distinct line at the jaw. In another, very touching scene, she gives her blessing for her husband to remarry and for her daughter to love her future stepmother, saying, "I'll always be your mommy. I'll always be watching over you from heaven."

My reaction to this story was mixed. One part of me wondered why anyone would be willing to discuss such sensitive and intimate matters on national television. Another part of me criticized these obsessive preparations for death, which might well be interfering with the relationship between mother and daughter in the here and now. For example, it hurt me to hear that this mother doesn't tuck her little girl into bed at night anymore. She has given this important responsibility over entirely to the father, reasoning that at the time of her demise, there will be no disruption of the bedtime ritual.

But, by far, the predominant component of my reaction to this news story was a sense of revelation. Sensitized by my own struggles to prepare this lecture, I realized with a shock that for this woman, thinking about *what really matters* is no mere exercise in the theoretical, but a practical imperative. Threatened with imminent, permanent separation from her family, she has searched her mind and heart and reached her own conclusions about what values are worth passing on to her daughter — and then has taken extraordinary steps to ensure that this sharing of values will not be interrupted even by her own death.

Her clear-sightedness in this task has inspired me to take up this theme for my talk here today. For the rest of the evening, I will share with you some tentative but deeply felt answers to a question I can easily imagine framing for my own two-year-old daughter: "Alexis, what really matters?" These will be values that I hope to share with her in the years ahead, not by legacy from the grave as might well be the other mother's sad necessity, but through our conversations, shared experiences, and all the thousand interactions that comprise the day-to-day realities of our living relationship.

At this point, I feel the need to state a disclaimer. In what follows, there will be instances where I will delineate values that I believe are worth living by, in full recognition that I am not being true to those values in my own life. Those of you who know me well will probably recognize these discrepancies. It has certainly been a painful experience for me to uncover and acknowledge them. But, nevertheless, I have welcomed the opportunity to articulate some principles that I believe really do matter, and I will gladly accept the challenge of renewing (or in some cases redefining) a personal commitment to the ideals that I'll share with you this evening.

Let's go forward, then. What is it that I hope my daughter will learn in life? In simplest terms it is this: *Know yourself — first, by understanding your connection to the many human communities to which you belong, and secondly, by understanding your connection to the whole of creation. From this self-knowledge will spring an understanding of your responsibilities to self, community, and creation — and a mandate to live in fulfillment of these responsibilities.*

## Connection in Community

First, let us speak of community. We belong to many communities. The most immediate and intimate of these is our family. Families are a source of joy, comfort, and many forms of sustenance. They teach us about our origins and personal history, and they introduce us to the larger communities to which we belong. If we are fortunate, we grow up in loving, stable homes with parents who nurture and challenge us and with siblings who understand and accept us as only someone who has shared our life circumstances can do. If our good fortune continues, we meet and marry our life partner and take on the challenge of raising our own young ones, who may be natural or adopted children or may be nieces, nephews, the children of good friends, beloved pets, or some combination of the above.

Our own (very crowded) household currently consists of two adults, a toddler, a cat, and eight dogs ranging in age from two to twelve years and ranging in weight from fifteen to 115 pounds. We all share the house, the yard, the washing machine, and a family motto — "Don't let Bailey get it!" — referring to our playfully destructive youngest canine. One of our special blessings has been to live in the same city as my parents and my grandmother. Not only has this been enjoyable — not to mention helpful! — for Jim and me, but it has put young Alexis in the enviable position of spending the entire work week with two doting grandparents who offer a seemingly endless supply of stories, music, bubbles, picnics, visits to the zoo, and other delightful experiences concocted through a special magic of wisdom and devotion. Alexis adores them. And she also adores my grandmother, her great-grandmother, which would surprise me, in view of the almost 80-year difference in their ages, if I didn't remember clearly from my own childhood how well this special person knows the heart of a child.

Unfortunately, except for these three people — plus a close neighbor who is a dear family friend and "honorary grandparent" for Alexis — the members of our family are separated by vast physical distances. Jim's mother, father, and grandmother, our brothers and their loved ones, our aunts, uncles, and cousins all live in cities that span half a continent. For Alexis' sake as well as for our own, it's essential that we maintain connections with our distant kin, as difficult as that might be. In the years ahead, there will be times at which she will need their strength and they hers, for family members are our partners in adversity as well as good fortune. When we experience pain or grief or despair, they offer solace and assistance, and when adversity is overcome, they share our joy.

Of course, family represents only the first circle of community. A widening circle encompasses, in turn, good friends, neighbors, schoolmates, fellow citizens of our city, state, and nation, and fellow citizens of the world.

Good workplaces provide a form of community, if they are places where we can do work that is meaningful, side by side with colleagues whom we respect and with whom we share many fundamental values. I think Furman is this kind of workplace. From four different vantage points, first as the daughter of a faculty member, then a student, then a faculty member, and then an administrator, I've come to know Furman as a place where students, faculty, and staff bring a healthy diversity of skills and ideas to classrooms, committee meetings, group discussions, and individual conferences. In such an environment, differences of opinion — even strong differences of opinion — are inevitable. But the work goes forward; good things are accomplished because we all share a commitment to creating and sustaining a place where learning can flourish, and we respect each other as indispensable partners in this worthy endeavor.

Religious communities provide one final and very important example of a community based on shared values and commitments. Rabbi Nancy Fuchs writes about the defining characteristics of community in *Our Share of Night, Our Share of Morning: Parenting as a Spiritual Journey*.[1] Though she is attempting to describe the value of community in any form, Fuchs repeatedly illustrates her points with examples drawn specifically from healthy religious communities.[2] This made sense to me, since my own experiences in religious communities have validated all the strengths of community that Fuchs describes. I grew up in First Baptist Church, here in Greenville. Jim and I were married there, and for many years after we moved back to Greenville, we sang in the First Baptist choir. In more recent years we have attended the Greenville Unitarian-Universalist Fellowship. Last winter we became members of the Fellowship, and this past summer, Alexis was dedicated there in a ceremony that was very meaningful to us. We have found in the Fellowship a diverse community of people united by a common core of values, a respect for and acceptance of one another, and a commitment to service through continuous active involvement in issues of social justice. The Fellowship embodies for us all the characteristics of a healthy religious community that will both nurture and challenge us in the years ahead.

We've examined many examples of community, but we have not yet addressed the question of how communities — at least those we shall define as "good communities" — foster self-knowledge, and from self-knowledge, an understanding of principles worth living by. Good communities foster self-knowledge in several important ways. First, they simply provide each of us a place to *be* the person that we are. Fuchs points out that communities provide a diverse array of people with whom we can interact and from whom we can learn "about the varieties of human nature and the vagaries of human existence."[3] They provide us with "a safe place to mourn," in contrast to other places "where expressions of sadness and grief are generally unwelcome."[4] She implies but doesn't state the corollary — that communities also provide us a place to celebrate weddings, births, and other occasions of joy. In these and other ways, according to Fuchs, communities offer "the gift of acceptance": "A good community, in the words of Mr. Rogers, 'likes you just the way you are.' "[5]

Secondly, good communities teach us about our origins and history and about where we fit in the here and now. Just as families convey to each child a sense of personal history and family history through stories, pictures, movies, letters, and family rituals and traditions, communities use texts, songs, and community rituals and traditions to instill in each member a sense of the community's origin and history.

The analogy between community and family is apt and has one other important dimension. Families and communities alike not only accept us *as* we are, while teaching us *where* we are and where we've come from; they also challenge us with visions of who we can become. Families and communities teach values to their members[6] and then challenge them to live in concert with those values.

Here are some values that I have learned from my family and communities that I believe are worth passing on. *Respect others. Acknowledge and appreciate each person's unique gifts and the qualities that make that person different from you, as well as like you. Have empathy for others; be sensitive to their fears and sorrows, and offer whatever kindness and comfort you can. Help others. Belonging to the same community — the human community — imposes on each of us the obligations of love and service to those who need our assistance. And, finally, respect all living things. Humans have an obligation to care for fellow creatures humanely, to protect their well-being individually and as species, and to abhor any form of exploitation or cruelty toward them.*

To recapitulate, I have claimed that good communities foster self-knowledge. From this knowledge comes an understanding of the obligations of love and service. From this understanding must come action. Good communities unite their members not only in acceptance of one another but also in active service to each other and to others in the world.

Before we leave the subject of community entirely, it's worthwhile to mention that there are examples of "bad community" as well as good — that is, there are communities that do nothing to foster the healthy growth of their members and in fact may actively undermine it. Mary Pipher, a clinical psychologist who has also studied anthropology, has focused scholarly attention on the negative impact of community on families and individuals. In *The Shelter of Each Other: Rebuilding Our Families*, Pipher asserts that American culture in the late twentieth century has created a false community that is not only unfriendly toward families but is overtly hostile. "Our culture is at war with families. Families in America have been invaded by technology, mocked or 'kitschified' by the media, isolated by demographic changes, pounded by economic forces, and hurt by corporate values."[7] Pipher goes on to develop each of these points, dwelling at length on the subjects of technology and media. She characterizes electronic media — specifically television and the Internet — as both pernicious and invasive. These media dissolve the walls of the home, allowing violence, sexuality, and an ethic of consumerism to invade the living rooms of families whose personal values are at odds with those of the media. So, not only does the electronically-mediated community fail to reinforce the family's values; it defines a competing set of values and actively insinuates these directly into the defenseless family home.[8] Pipher concludes that rather than raising children with the goal of introducing them to the broader culture and encouraging their participation in it, parents must now actively work to protect their children from the culture outside the home.[9]

As if these conclusions were not alarming enough, in another work, titled *Reviving Ophelia: Saving the Selves of Adolescent Girls*, Pipher delineates in detail the poisonous effects of modern American culture on women and particularly on adolescent girls. Via case studies and personal anecdotes, and informed by her particular interest in the effect of culture on individuals, Pipher develops her thesis that in imposing its false values of sexuality, violence, and consumerism, our culture pressures adolescent girls "to split into true and false selves...to put aside their authentic selves and to display only a small portion of their gifts."[10] Furthermore, it pressures them to withdraw from their families, who might otherwise protect them, and to bond only with peers whose own poisoning by the culture makes them unreliable sources of strength and assistance.[11] According to Pipher, girls express grief at the loss of their true selves and react by conforming, withdrawing, getting depressed, or getting angry.[12] Her case studies illustrate all these modes of reaction.

Though disturbing, Pipher's book does offer hope for helping girls learn to protect themselves from the cultural influences that threaten their mental and emotional integrity, and she supports these with case studies of healthy girls and of clients who have regained their emotional health. The positive factors she cites include homes that offer affection and structure, contact with extended families, positive peer relations with well-adjusted friends, travel, spending time in the outdoors, opportunities for acts of altruism,[13] respect for the parts of themselves that are spiritual, and encouragement to work for the betterment of the world.[14] Her summary at the book's conclusion could be a recipe for emotional health in any individual:

> In order to keep their true selves and grow into healthy adults, girls need love from family and friends, meaningful work, respect, challenges, and physical and psychological safety. They need identities based on talents or interests rather than appearance, popularity, or sexuality. They need good habits for coping with stress, self-nurturing skills, and a sense of purpose and perspective. They need quiet places and times. They need to feel that they are part of something larger than their own lives and that they are emotionally connected to a whole.[15]

## Connection and Creation

Pipher alludes to an essential connection between *knowing* the world (that is, the natural world) and *understanding one's place* in the world (that is, one's place in the cosmos). Since my own disciplinary background is in the natural sciences, this thought resonates strongly with me. The idea that I want to explore with you in the remainder of our time together is this: By studying nature, we learn about ourselves, and from this self-knowledge comes an understanding of our responsibility to live in a way that acknowledges that we leave our mark on creation, just as it leaves its mark on us.

How is it that we study nature? At the simplest level, we explore it with our five senses. We can be physicists while enjoying the beauty of a sunset, a rainbow, or a peaceful snowfall, geologists while digging our toes into the sandy beaches of the Atlantic Ocean, and biologists while hiking a pine-scented mountain trail, sampling a vine-ripe tomato, or listening to the summertime music of crickets, cicadas, and frogs.

At the next level of study, we can use modern scientific instrumentation to extend our senses down into the realm of the very small and out into the realm of the very distant. School children can use an inexpensive classroom microscope to see tiny one-celled plants and animals; college students with access to a tunneling scanning microscope can see individual carbon atoms in a thin layer of graphite. Binoculars and telescopes let us see mountains and craters on the moon, sunspots on the sun, the rings of Saturn, the great Red Spot of Jupiter, comets in the inner solar system, gas clouds in nearby regions of our Milky Way, neighboring galaxies such as Andromeda, and more distant galaxies and clusters of galaxies.

But observation alone does not probe nature deeply enough to lead to understanding. We must extend the process of observation to include testing, inference, and mathematical analysis, in order to build models of nature that explain what we have observed and predict what we might yet observe. We construct these models by trial and error and by listening to critiques from other members of the scientific community. We must regard these models as ever tentative and be ready to discard them if new empirical information discredits them.

I've given this thumbnail sketch of the methodology of science for two reasons. First, some of the lessons of science are counterintuitive; nature doesn't always work in ways that we've come to expect on the basis of our everyday scale of experience. When I mention some of these interesting findings in a few minutes, it will be good to remember that they were not dreamed up at random, but were arrived at in a relatively systematic fashion, and that they have stood the test of time, at least until now. A second reason to talk about the methodology of science here is to illustrate that science is a way, one way, of seeking answers about our world. In contrast, religious faith provides a different way of framing questions and answers about the world around us. Science focuses its attention on creation — on describing and understanding the universe that we inhabit. Many of the world's great religious traditions focus attention on the Creator and on the interaction between Creator and created. Some people see these two modes of inquiry as being in competition or even in conflict with each other, but I agree with those who believe that they provide parallel and complementary ways of probing and understanding the world. To me, dialogue, not debate, characterizes the nature of the communication between these two very different ways of knowing.

To be sure, it's a fair question to ask how individual scientists hold this dialogue in their own minds and hearts. Just two weeks ago, Furman hosted a visit by the Pulitzer Prize winning scholar Edward J. Larson, Professor of History and Law at the University of Georgia. One of Larson's campus lectures focused on two recent studies of "the strength of religious belief in an era of ascendant science." In *Nature*, Larson and his co-author cited their findings that almost forty percent of scientists surveyed in 1996 affirmed belief in a personal God and in personal immortality.[16]

Though not cited explicitly, Larson's study may have provided the inspiration for a lengthy feature article in *Newsweek* last summer, titled "Science Finds God."[17] The article profiled statements of religious belief among modern physicists and astronomers, including prominent figures Allan Sandage, Jocelyn Bell Burnell, and Charles Townes. The point of the article was that many scientists find harmony, not conflict, between science and faith. Some see the Big Bang theory of the origin of the universe as evidence that the world was created with intelligence and purposefulness. Others speak of experiencing worshipful reverence in response to the beauty and mystery that a close study of nature reveals, echoing a passage from Fuchs' book: "Judaism prescribes blessings for ordinary events and blessings for extraordinary ones.... When it comes to extraordinary events, there is...a blessing...to be said 'upon seeing lightning, comets, falling stars, vast deserts, great rivers, high mountains...or...a strikingly clear morning after an all-night rainstorm.' It reads, 'We praise you God who provides us with moments reminiscent of creation.' "[18]

Now that we have spent a little time discussing science as a way of knowing that is distinct from, but in dialogue with, religious ways of knowing, let's return to the question at hand. What do we learn from a close study of the natural world? What are the lessons of science that lead us to self-understanding and an understanding of our responsibilities in the world we inhabit?

The first lesson is one of history, a perspective of where we belong in space and time. Astrophysics teaches us about the current state of our universe, its probable history, and its possible futures. Here is the fascinating story that we learn from the sky.[19]

When we look out at distant galaxies and clusters of galaxies, we have means of measuring their distances from us and their velocities with respect to us. Edwin Hubble, working at Mount Wilson Observatory in California in the 1920s, discovered that clusters of galaxies outside our own galactic cluster are traveling away from us at high speeds, and that the farther their distance from us, the higher their speed of recession. Why is this significant? Just as raisins in a loaf of raisin bread move away from each other as the dough rises and bakes, Hubble's discovery of the mutual recession of the galaxies implies that our universe is expanding — space itself is expanding — carrying the galaxies farther and farther apart. Now imagine that we have a "movie" of this expanding universe — and we run the film backward. If clusters of galaxies are currently moving away from each other, then they must have been closer together in the past. If the universe is now expanding, it must have originated in a much more compressed state. As incredible as this may sound, the currently accepted model of the origin of the universe holds that our universe began in a cataclysmic event known as the Big Bang. The Big Bang gave birth to certain forms of energy and to certain elementary particles. As the primeval universe expanded and cooled, some of the original elementary particles combined to form atoms of the lightest chemical elements — hydrogen, helium, and lithium.

If we could watch the young universe expand and cool further, over enormous expanses of time, we would see atoms collect in local regions that we can think of as giant clouds of gas. In pockets of the gas clouds, atoms begin to move together as a result of their mutual gravitational attraction. Eventually, these local concentrations of gaseous material condense into balls of gas hot enough and dense enough for the process of nuclear fusion to begin. At this point, the balls of gas become true stars. In their early stages, stars produce energy by fusing hydrogen into helium, but as time progresses, their nuclear furnaces become increasingly energetic and begin to form heavier nuclei, such as carbon, nitrogen, oxygen, and so on. Eventually, every star runs out of nuclear "fuel," and its core undergoes a massive gravitational collapse. Depending on how massive the star is and how energetic its collapse, the death of the star's core might result in a shockwave that causes the outer layers of the star to explode in what we call a supernova event. The supernova explosion allows even heavier atomic nuclei to be formed, and it disperses the nuclear materials throughout the dying star's galactic neighborhood in the form of gas and dust. This material will be recycled in the next generation of stars.

During the formation period, some stars acquire planetary systems. The same swirling cloud of gas and dust that can give birth to a new star at its center can also allow planets, moons, asteroids, and comets to build through collisions and accretion over hundreds of millions of years.

What about the origins of life? Biochemical models claim that microscopic forms of life originated on the primeval earth from the chemical building blocks and energy that were available on the young planet. Life began in simple forms and evolved into more complex forms. Each generation of life was constructed from the chemical elements available to its progenitors, and in turn recycled its own materials for use by the next generation.

To me, the significance of this history lesson is this: The hydrogen, carbon, nitrogen, and oxygen atoms that are in our bodies today originated in the Big Bang or in the fiery furnaces of distant stars — and have been on the earth since our planet formed four billion years ago. In this direct, physical sense, each of us has a personal connection to the rest of the cosmos and to the moment of creation.

Another lesson to be drawn from science — this time from the quantum theory — tells us something significant about the very act of observing the natural world. Contrary to our expectation that a person or device can observe and record a natural phenomenon without affecting the system being studied, quantum theory tells us that the observer and observed become inextricably entangled by the act of observation. In other words, to observe nature is to change it, to give it a shape it would not have had if the observation had not been performed. When we talk about this in a physics or astronomy class, students invariably say, "Well, you don't disturb a system by just looking at it!" But, of course, you do, because to look at something, you have to shine a beam of light on it, and the photons in that beam of light interact with the system in complex ways before light eventually enters your eyes and triggers a physiological reaction that translates into your perception of the object's appearance. This disturbance-effect has been known for hundreds of years. But physicists never considered it a problem, for two reasons: First, the disturbance was considered to be small, and secondly, it was believed that the effect of the disturbance could be quantified and corrected for mathematically. The problem only became obvious when we began probing the microscopic world, as we did in the late nineteenth and early twentieth centuries, because there our measuring devices produce disturbances that are as large as the system being studied. Furthermore, according to Heisenberg's Uncertainty Principle, the disturbance is by its very nature uncontrollable, and thus it cannot be corrected for.

The interaction between observer and observed has another, more subtle dimension. Observing a natural system disturbs it — but observing it is the only way we can learn anything about it. Therefore, all we can learn of nature is what we see in interaction with it. We are forced to abandon any attempts to talk about the behavior that nature *would* manifest, absent our interaction with it. We're not allowed to speculate about the tree in the forest that falls with no listener nearby. Reality unobserved is not a reality that can be known. Observer and observed are forever entangled, forging a new reality with each interaction.

What is the point of this lesson from science? Just this: *It really matters* that we understand that we have an irreversible effect on the world. For each of us, being here changes the shape of things. We make a difference. We change reality by our very presence and by our every action.

George Bailey learned this lesson in the movie *It's a Wonderful Life*. In a moment of despair, while he was contemplating suicide, he was given the gift of seeing the shape the world would have had if he had never been born. Isak Dinesen, writing wistfully of life on her coffee plantation in Kenya in *Out of Africa*, asks:

> If I know a song of Africa…of the Giraffe, and the African new moon lying on her back, of the ploughs in the fields and the sweaty faces of the coffee pickers, does Africa know a song of me? Would the air over the plain quiver with a colour that I had had on, or the children invent a game in which my name was, or the full moon throw a shadow over the gravel of the drive that was like me, or would the eagles of the Ngong look out for me?[20]

We can answer her now with "yes."

I began this evening by saying that I wanted to share with you the values that I hope my daughter will learn. It's time to summarize those, and to close. What is the essence of what I want to say to her, to myself, and to you?

*Learn your values; then, live your values. Spending time on what really matters is what really matters. You will leave your mark on creation, just as it will leave its mark on you. Your life will touch many other lives and events, in ways you can't even imagine. Whether intentional or not, you do leave your imprint on the world — both on the natural world and on the many human communities to which you belong. Choose wisely what that imprint will be. Let it represent the completion of your best and truest self. Let it be a shape you are proud of.*

## Notes

[1]Nancy Fuchs, *Our Share of Night, Our Share of Morning: Parenting as a Spiritual Journey* (New York: HarperSanFrancisco, 1996) 45-56.

[2]Fuchs, *Our Share of Night*, 45-50.

[3]Fuchs, *Our Share of Night*, 48.

[4]Fuchs, *Our Share of Night*, 48.

[5]Fuchs, *Our Share of Night*, 49.

[6]Fuchs, *Our Share of Night*, 47. She points out that the community reinforces the values taught by the family.

[7]Mary Pipher, *The Shelter of Each Other: Rebuilding Our Families* (New York: Ballantine Books, 1996) 9.

[8]Pipher, *Shelter*, 10-15.

[9]Pipher, *Shelter*, 11.

[10]Mary Pipher, *Reviving Ophelia: Saving the Selves of Adolescent Girls* (New York: Ballantine Books, 1994) 22.

[11]Pipher, *Ophelia*, 23.

[12]Pipher, *Ophelia*, 43.

[13]Pipher, *Ophelia*, 280-289.

[14]Pipher, *Ophelia*, 72.

[15]Pipher, *Ophelia*, 283-284.

[16]Edward J. Larson and Larry Witham, "Scientists Are Still Keeping the Faith," *Nature* 386 (3 April 1997) 435-436.

[17]Sharon Begley, "Science Finds God," *Newsweek* (20 July 1998) 46-51.

[18]Fuchs, *Our Share of Night*, 17.

[19]Accounts of the Big Bang theory can be found in many astronomy and astrophysics texts and books written for the layman; I have drawn on the particular account given by Alan Lightman in *Ancient Light: Our Changing View of the Universe* (Cambridge MA: Harvard University Press, 1991) 15-50.

[20]Isak Dinesen, *Out of Africa* (New York: Vintage Books, 1985) 83.

# James M. Pitts
## Religion and University Chaplain
### February 8, 1999

A year ago yesterday, my father-in-law, Furman Stewart, died. He was eighty-nine years of age. This good man had been a significant part of all my adult life. That is, if you agree that adulthood begins at eighteen. For forty-two years, Furman Stewart had been an encouraging and supportive friend, partner in projects, supplier of beef from his pasture and produce from his garden. He was a wise counselor, welcoming grandfather, churchman, and all-around good and gentle man.

Among the gifts he and Lillian granted me was the hand of their daughter, my wife Nancy, and a good gene pool. Our two sons, Stewart and Jonathan, are evidence of this legacy. Mr. Stewart's success in business was earned, literally, the hard way. He was a cotton ginner, lumberman, fertilizer, and feed dealer. Regardless of the season, he was busy and productively involved in life.

During the last few years of his life, his energy was not what it used to be. So he spent more time on the porch and in the den. Occasionally, as his generation is prone to do, he would enjoy reminiscing about days gone by and giving us instruction and insight into what we should know and remember.

Being a survivor of the Great Depression, Pa Pa thought it wise to have some cash on hand or literally buried in the ground. You know, "Just in case, you need a little silver or gold for an emergency." Not wanting to appear too crass about cash, we would tune out and turn away when he talked about his buried treasure — that is, Mason jars filled with silver dollars buried in the barn.

Following his death, especially on rainy days when sitting around the house at Six Mile, our conversation would drift back to the location of the buried coins. Various members of the family were confident they knew exactly where they were hidden. With shovels in hand, in and near the barn, we have dug here and then there. We should have listened more carefully to the wisdom and guidance of that old man. Being modern and enamored with technology, we brought in a metal detector. We discovered and dug up nails, sheets of tin, a child's ring, but no glass containers of silver.

On a blustery winter day before Christmas this year, we were digging inside a stall area of the barn. Confident that this would be the day of discovery, Stewart, who is always full of energy and ideas, brought his video camera. Lights were placed on tripods. Jonathan dug, then Stewart dug, and Dad supervised. Nancy and her mother watched and offered their direction. Observing this scene, I got tickled and started to laugh. "We've found it," I announced. The family wondered what I was talking about and shot me an incredulous look.

The treasure, I concluded and announced, was not silver, even though that would be nice to have. The treasure was what we were experiencing: young and old, hand in hand, laboring together in a common cause. If Mr. Stewart were observing, I am sure he would have smiled. We should have listened more carefully. I know that he would have enjoyed that scene. And then he would have grown impatient, and taking shovel in hand, he would say, "Let me show you!"

"What really matters" is not silver or success, power or prestige, or any of the other proximate concerns to which we devote inordinate amounts of time and energy. This treasure is not so much hidden as forgotten or simply taken for granted. What really matters is relationships. That's the treasure that I want to celebrate tonight.

In my conversation about "what really matters." I have chosen to deal with this enduring and continuing question in a personal and autobiographical manner. Therefore, it will be subjective. Hopefully there will be themes and allusions that will resonate with your own story.

For those who are busy declaring their autonomy and independence, focusing on relationships may seem quaint and regressive. This topic is not nearly as salacious as the current campaign for condoms on campus. Nor does it present the fervor of underage, adolescent alcohol consumption. However, as any casual observer of contemporary collegiate life can see, belonging, finding acceptance, experiencing approval by peers is vitally important. Without relationships, there would be nowhere to sit in the dining hall, no fraternity or sorority in which to belong, or person to date, or group with whom to party or pray.

In our contemporary love affair with technology, relationships get in the way of efficiency, detached objectivity, and management by the numbers. Some assume that relationships interfere with the bottom line. However, sooner or later, when all is said and done, relationships are at the core of all that is true, all that is noble, all that is just and pure, all that is lovable and attractive, excellent and admirable.

*Relationships* refer to our interpersonal interaction with significant others, with our selves, and with our God. How we view ourselves, and either approach or avoid God is conditioned by our relationship with others. The formation of faith is caught more than it is taught. Entrance into the believing community is an invitational process, into which we are spiritually birthed, then nurtured, and matured as generative members.

*Relationships begin before birth.* The other evening, my daughter-in-law Jackie and son Jonathan invited Nancy and me for dinner and to see a video. The video, four months in the making, was of our grandchild-to-be. Nurtured in Jackie's womb, the baby tossed and turned, putting on a show for the ultrasound image. Then, a freeze frame technique was used to measure and monitor. With a sense of humor, since inquiring minds wanted to know, the medical videographer drew an arrow to a vital point and printed out on the screen, "boy parts." Nurtured in the protective stillness of his mother's body, the baby is being fashioned by a genetic pool, combining streams of ancestry that will provide a foundation for lifetime. Children are a family's greatest treasure.

Come early June 1999, or whenever the child chooses, he will make his dramatic entrance into the world and be cradled by family arms. I know that Jonathan and Jackie will be great parents. None of this formative process will be consciously remembered by the child, but will serve as bequeathed bedrock as he encounters and embraces life. Birth parents are a given; they are not a child's personal choice. One day in an adolescent rage, I stormed out at my Dad, "Listen, I didn't ask to be born!" Never at a loss for words, my father paused, "I know; that's what bothers me!" As I observed inscribed on an elderly woman's pillow, puffed beside her beautiful white hair, "Old age is a way of getting back at your children."

Unlike friends who claim to remember everything, I cannot remember being born. I have seen the papers, little footprints and parental fingerprints and signatures, an etching of the hospital and baptismal medals. But all of it is simply required to be taken at face value.

Our older son, Stewart, used to enjoy hiding his brother's birth certificate in order to terrorize him and tell him that he was not really a member of the family, but was adopted. Jonathan's curly blond hair and blue eyes dipped deeper into the family genetic pool than the brown eyes and brown hair of his brother. Jonathan looked into the mirror and was genuinely worried. However, upon reflection, perhaps he may have been pleased and relieved there was a possibility he was not related to his brother by blood.

My earliest relational memories are murky. They revolve around licking the icing off of a spoon that my mother had used to ice a cake; experiencing her warm and protective embrace as we traveled overnight by train in a

Pullman sleeper; eating Jell-O in the diner, because my throat was sore; playing in my father's shop, raising and lowering the barber's chair, spinning it around and around until my father ordered me to stop.

I remember being impeccably dressed — shoes shined, hair combed — posing for portraits in my mother' studio; having a Mexican Chihuahua named Choo-Choo. (The name was chosen because the dog chased his tail, like a toy train circling the Christmas tree.) Choo-Choo in my young eyes and heart was a more significant support and companion than any adults. Whatever occurred, he was there, accepting, affirming, and full of affection. In my formative years, Choo-Choo's love was a significant and important relationship. He even taught me how to chew my food. I am not sure if he helped me with toilet training. However, a rolled-up newspaper still prompts me to jump off the couch.

Early in my life, a larger than life influence and certainly the bringer of blessing was my paternal grandmother. Her major influence on my life came about through a family crisis. My parents were having marital difficulty because of my mother's inability to control her drinking. In retrospect, all of the disintegrating and destructive signs of alcoholism were present. My grandmother, who had already raised ten children of her own, welcomed my brother and me into her home and heart.

Only in retrospect and with maturity can I see that was a centering moment of personal identity and faith formation. Grandmother's hospitable relationship provided a gift that was joyfully received. Only in time did I appreciate its sacrificial cost and transforming value.

As you may know, when a child's mother is an alcoholic, there is no immediate and obvious refuge. The intended nurturer and biological protector is caught up in her own sick storm of emotions. A child's dependency is just another overwhelming demand on a person drowning in a sea of substance abuse and denial. Tossed from grandiosity to disgust, creating waves of chemical highs and sinking into troughs of depression, the addicted person and family members drift out into the depths. Everyone connected — parent and child, relatives and neighbors — is negatively affected and is drawn into the family trap.

With such a relational heritage of unreliability and instability, developing trust is difficult. For, in such settings, promises are rarely, if ever, kept. The baseline of "normal" family relationships is an unknown reference. Compensating for the deficit in missed loving and learning (for the child of an alcoholic) is a lifelong recovery process.

Thanks to my father's request and my grandmother's response, for me the way up and out of that drowning pool was a sheer gift of God's grace. It came in the person of my grandmother. She offered shelter and security, loving warmth, and the limits of reasonable discipline. She offered herself in relationship. As a youngster in the second grade, along with my younger brother, I was invited into her life and heart. Later, I want to come back and reflect with you about enduring spiritual significance of that grandparent/grandchild relationship.

Relationships are not just warm "fuzzies," goosebumps and "touchy-feely" moments. Likewise, relationships that really matter are not all always positive. Most all of us could relate stories of relationships that were bad and went worse. They, too, can offer life-changing insights, value clarification, and serve as the catalyst for better choices. Have you observed that, often, it is the adult children of alcoholics who are running the world? Where would we get preachers and politicians, nurses and other sacrificial caregivers, if it were not for dysfunctional families? The challenge for persons with such a heritage is to make their history work *for* them instead of *against* them. The trick is to transform a negative into a positive addiction.

One of the first challenges is to distinguish between healthy and sick relationships. This is a continuing and lifelong assignment. Relationships bless or curse, promote or poison, affirm or abuse. Relationships are complex and ever changing. Some are given. Others are chosen. Most mature. Some deteriorate, become brittle and break, and blow away like a dusty powder. Some relationships are finite, so shallow with only a momentary touch they shatter. There are relationships to which we aspire and work hard to establish, yet are denied. Others relational connections literally become eternal, deep, and all-encompassing.

*Relationships that are healthy* are optimistic, respectful, trustful, and intentionally inviting. They are freeing and complementing. They are filled with love and laughter. People in healthy relationships have the ability to listen, to really listen with ears and eyes, to discern and perceive before responding with word or in action. Their focus is on life and others. They are givers. Healthy relationships are filled with faith and freedom, humility and honesty, affirmation and praise.

*Relationships that are sick* are primarily pessimistic, abusive, suspicious, and secretive. They are filled with discord regarding power and control, conflictive and complaining, full of disease or anxiety and anger. Their focus is on depression and self. They are selfish takers, promoters of uproar and division. They are not generous givers. Sick relationships employ fear, coercion, aggression, duplicity, seduction, embarrassment, sarcasm, subversions, and punishment. Such relationships produce pain rather than pleasure.

Friends that know us and love us, and really like us, can help us work through some of the glandular excitement, rationalizing denial, and romantic flights from reality that are often present in the initial stage of a relationship. A willingness to be open to the perspective and assessment of a caring and trusting other is a sign of maturity.

Among my teachers who have helped me better understand the core value of relationships are: Wayne Oates, my mentor and supervising professor in pastoral care and counseling; Bill Glasser, psychiatrist and author of *Reality Therapy*, and Tom Cloer, colleague and friend, who genuinely cares for people. Tom is more than a reading specialist; he is expert in reading people. More than anyone else I know, he has the gift of encouragement. With self-effacing humor, Tom helps us to laugh at our pretentiousness and invites "children of all ages" into the learning process.

Also, my chaplaincy colleagues and personal friends, Vic Greene, Jr., and Shirley Smith, mirror health and a holistic perspective that unites heart and mind, body and soul. In addition to being competent colleagues, they are genuine friends who love God, like people, and are at ease with themselves. Shirley's husband, the late John Smith (who was chaplain and administrator of the Greenville Hospital System), and I shared a friendship that began here at Furman. Our lives literally paralleled both professionally and personally.

Relationships that are positive first and foremost value people. The institution, program, the agenda, the bottom line, the mission, the strategy, while important, are secondary to people. When all is said and done, people remain our greatest asset. The strength of any organization, enterprise, or partnership is its people. Our strength and power are not measured by property or body counts, wealth or endowment, but by the nature of our community. What is the quality of our life together? How we invite and retain, encourage and educate, genuinely care and support one another is ultimately the way we are evaluated.

Deceptions abound in the relationship area. Relationships are not found on the world wide web at <relationships.com>. There is not a touch-tone vend-a-buddy service, psychic hotline, or an automated help line with a synthesized voice. Locally, we have a broadcast conglomerate claiming to be "Your Friend Four." Friends, none of these fulfills the reality test of relationships. Such deceptions deny genuine relationships and are a phony pretense. Such dishonesty reveals basic flaws in character and values. They slide toward the sociopathic and indicate a love of things over people. Such pretense pollutes pools of good will, creates chasms of cynicism, and amplifies human alienation.

In healthy relationship people have names and faces; they are not just numbers and functionaries. Health management organizations — as well as governmental, educational, ecclesiastical and related institutional bureaucracies — are enamored by the contemporary rush to outsourcing. Their combined outcome promotes depersonalization and societal fragmentation, frustrates loyalty, and demeans people.

In human resource jargon, a person is simply another disposable unit in the production cycle. The greatest value trumpeted is cost-containment, efficiency, and bonuses for the "slash and burn" priesthood of executive management. As in Pharaoh's Egypt, the mandate is for more bricks with less straw. No wonder in a society that is literally "going postal," people are cheering *Patch Adams* and other films promoting the value of personal relationships over detached professionalism.

People are primarily people; they are demeaned and diminished when they are seen primarily as patients and cases, clients and customers. A college should be a face-to-face place, where adults of all ages — young, middle age, and mature — gather to engage in learning and serving, growing and becoming the persons that God intends each of us to be.

A college, especially which expresses Christian ideals, does not relegate students to consumers or use industrial models for management. A college is not a factory, but a distinct academic community with a unique philosophical heritage and educational mission. In a world with a pragmatic push, a college is a somewhat arcane, idealistic, and useless place. In a hard-sell environment enamored by technological specialists and dazzled by multimedia glitter, generalists in life and interpreters of the "good life" are not in great demand.

The official symbol of the university, affixed on the front of the library, emblazoned on the podium during convocations and at commencement, and engraved on every diploma, states in classic Latin *Christo et doctrinae*..."Christ and Learning." The spirit of this place is not narrow and dogmatic, but inclusive and ecumenical. Furman's tradition is excellence in education, reverence toward God and respect for all people.

I am grateful that Furman aspires to be a community of gracious civility and acceptance of personal diversity. We stand united in opposition to religious bigotry, racial prejudice, and abusive behavior. We are not appreciative of outrageous posturing, but in favor of thoughtful dialogue. Here, it is important that people not only talk, but actually take time to really listen, empathetically striving to understand one another. Taking our religious heritage seriously, we affirm openness to truth, respect for individuals, and religious freedom. All of these are integral parts of our church-related tradition.

Despite occasional sneers from critics, who must be kin to Cinderella's stepsisters, at our "quaintness" and provincialism, we take pride in referring to ourselves as a community. We are the "Furman University Family." This is a place in which people know one another, like and respect each another, and genuinely care that each and all become the person that God would have them be.

Beginning with my student days and continuing to the present, literally my life, to use a biblical metaphor, has been surrounded and supported by a great cloud of witnesses. The roll call of past and present students and staff, faculty and administrators is an endless scroll. As a student, there were faculty who became mentors and friends. Some became big brothers and older sisters. They were prepared and present and very real. They were great character studies, academically demanding, at times boring, willing to laugh with you, and believed that I was capable, worthy, and that there was reason for hope. They genuinely cared and worked very hard.

One such person in my life was Joe M. King. Thanks to Joe, we stayed in touch following my graduation. It was Joe who gave my name to L. D. Johnson in the summer of 1967. By September, I was back home at Furman and L. D.'s associate. Also, none of this would have been possible without the vision and friendship of President Gordon Blackwell and Provost and Academic Dean Frank Bonner, who invited L. D. in the spring of 1967 to become Furman's first full-time university chaplain and a member of the religion faculty. Talk about networking and the value of relationships. Having such an opportunity was beyond my imagination and has offered a career that has been a source of professional fulfillment and personal joy.

Since the rniversity chaplain serves at the pleasure of the president, I will always be indebted to John Johns for offering me the opportunity to succeed L. D. Johnson. John and Martha, in my view, are the epitome of people persons. If there was anything that President Johns wanted at Furman, it was for everyone to feel a strong sense of community on campus. I am grateful that Johns Hall continues that tradition with a focus on personal interaction. This magnificent structure was designed for informal gatherings and conversation. It encourages everyone — students, faculty, and staff — to share ideas, to work together, and especially to find ways to enjoy and appreciate each other.

I am appreciative of the energy and vision of President Shi. I knew David as an undergraduate. As a matter of fact, he was a contemporary of my colleague in chaplaincy, Vic Greene, Jr. When David was named president, I told him that transition made me feel very finite. Since he was also my new boss, I told him I hoped that I would not feel terminal.

On I could go identifying colleagues past and present, those who are at the peak of their careers, others who are just beginning their college sojourn, and those who are no longer with us. I remember with great affection Theron Price, Tank Hardaway, Sandy Molnar, Howard Wheeler, Bob Gray, Junius Gladney, and Roosevelt Richardson.

Continuing relationships with former students, such as Cecil Staton, Jr., Carlton Allen, Ron Singleton, John Adams, Bill Bellinger, Peggy Haymes, Mary Mitchell Campbell, and Melissa Sexton are a source of pride and friendship. Alumni and the present generation of students continue to inform and inspire.

I am thankful for the presence and participation of Susan Bennett, Caroll Huff, and Mary Babb, who share a common commitment to ensure that the chapel is a place of hospitality.

I would be remiss not to mention the religion faculty, including retired colleagues T. C. and Ellen Smith, Bob and Dovie Crapps, David and Clara Smith, Edgar and Shirley McKnight. Another constant in this dynamic place has been my colleague and friend for thirty years, now Vice-president for Academic Affairs, A. V. Huff. On a desk I read this serious jest: "Do you want to speak to the man in charge, or to the woman who really runs things?" Such persons as we all know are Peggy Parks and Kay Hudson, Priscilla Foreman, Beth Rice, and Carol Daniels.

Meeting here in the University Center, I am grateful for my relationship with Betty Alverson, Nancy Cooper, and Dave Thomsen. Each in their own distinct way has underscored the importance of breaking bread together and being a friend. As you know, Betty's untiring devotion and promotion both initiated and sustains this lecture series. Besides being a former classmate with Betty, I was privileged to preach the sermon upon her ordination to the ministry.

Until our move in December 1996 to the Charles Ezra Daniel Memorial Chapel, Betty was my landlord. The namesake of the "Queen Alverson" has always run a very tight ship in facilities management. Now that I have a similar administrative responsibility with the chapel, I can more fully appreciate the scope and complexity of that task. Along with the larger Furman community, I congratulate Betty on completion of the renovation and expansion of the University Center.

*Relationship with self.* The ability to be at home with oneself is a gift. This means that in our conversation with self, we must still those voices that seem to emanate from endless audio loops of criticism. Many simply "should" all over themselves. I should have done this. I should have done that. They voice no word of grace and acceptance and forgiveness to themselves. They quickly excuse others, but constantly blame and abuse themselves. As the Scripture teaches, we are to love others as we love ourselves. Too often, when it comes to graceful acceptance, we are the last in line to forgive ourselves. Caring for oneself is crucial for personal survival and health.

Several years ago, I was preaching in Belgium. The primary languages in that small country are Flemish and French. Therefore, whenever I spoke, an interpreter stood next to me. Always, this was a woman. One evening, I referenced that here in the South there is some controversy about women in the pulpit. However, I told the congregation that I was comfortable and accustomed to such partnership because I am married. Throughout my forty plus years of marriage, I am grateful for the covenant I have shared with my wife, Nancy. Continually, she has been an encourager and supporter, challenger and stabilizer, and my interpreter. On more than one occasion, she has stepped forward to rescue and tell others, and me, what I really meant to say. In this special relationship, I have been truly blessed. My wife and our sons have taught and continue to teach me much.

Our image of self is a reflection mirrored in the eyes of others. We learn from genograms that relationships often assign our roles and establish the rules that govern our life. They give us a name, a place, and define both who we are and to whom we are related. Our vocation or our calling may be assigned rather than chosen. Expectations and responsibilities are often fashioned by others before they are internalized and personally affirmed.

*Relationship with God.* I have come to believe that our basic relationship to God is initially conditioned by our relationship with significant others. If trust is present in primary relationships, then we will project a similar positive image of the Divine. If not, the image of God is clouded with distrust and shrouded with cynical despair.

Within the community of faith, we are introduced to God. A God of love or a God of hate, a picture of God as grace or law is developed in basic life orientation experiences/faith formation stages. This picture of God as one who loves and forgives, comforts and empowers, is foundational. These basic relationships provide a bold outline and a context to color with life's crayons both in and outside the lines.

This solid rock offers a place to stand, an anchor for life storms, and foundation for living. This vital relationship is informed, guided, and sustained through Scripture and prayer, the work of the Spirit and participation in the rituals of our faith tradition.

To paraphrase Hebrews 11:1, *God has spoken in many and various ways,* through creation, the wisdom tradition, by prophetic voices, the poetry and prose of the Hebrew Scripture, but in these last days he has spoken to us by a Son. As a believer in the Christian tradition, the crowning point of revelation is in and through Jesus Christ.

Jesus came to clarify and correct our negative images of God. Jesus did not come to give answers and to defend theological presuppositions, but came to offer a relationship of love. Jesus reveals God with a human face and invites us into a direct experience with the Almighty. Through this revelatory encounter, the Christian's relationship centers in Christ. In Christ, we are called to repentance and faith. In Christ, there is a centering point, offering perspective to view all of life through the eyes of Christ.

This incarnational perspective of God becoming flesh and dwelling among us full of grace and truth lays a foundation for Christian humanism. This is a counterpoint to strident dogmatism and suffocating legalism. I am affirming a faith that is dynamic and alive, growing and graceful. This Christian humanism affirms the value of persons, their autonomy and freedom, and their God-given right and responsibility to freely respond or ignore a divine presence and imperative. A relationship with God should be a personal choice, not manipulated and coerced. The believing community should offer a warm and welcoming witness that is underscored by civility and respect that graciously affirms diversity.

Remember Grandmother Pitts? When I was a young refugee being led by my father out of domestic dysfunction to a better life, he brought me with confidence to his mother's home. Through that relationship, I experienced a good word, literally, a gospel word that became flesh in a grandmother. Through her, I was introduced to another…the Significant Other, who could be trusted.

Grandmother had known him most of her life. He had provided for her, even when her husband's heart failed, leaving her as a forty-four-year-old widow with seven out of their ten children to raise. He was the forerunner who went ahead on our behalf. He went all the way. He entered behind the curtain into the heart of God by way of Calvary's cross and an empty tomb. He is the sure and steadfast anchor of the soul. He is God's promise and our eternal hope.

All the saints through the ages, including my grandmother, bear witness to his name. They call him Jesus — the one who walks with us, talks with us, calls us his own, promises never to leave us, and in God's good time will bring us into our eternal home.

Our relationships with others, self, and God are crucial to change and growth. These primary relationships offer comfort and challenge, acceptance and inspiration.

Being number thirty-four in this semi-annual procession called the L. D. Johnson Memorial Lecture, I know that I certainly don't have the first, and hopefully not the last, word on our common query, "What Really Matters?" As you may know, this theme and question was inspired by one of L. D.'s newspaper columns. In a succinct way, it represents the essence of what he continually stressed. He constantly challenged not only with word, but also through his life. He knew the importance of focusing on the basics of what it means to be a person with a positive relationship to community, the importance of possessing a healthy appreciation for oneself, and to be a child of God.

A native of Oklahoma, L. D. lost both his parents when he was a young child. His grandparents and his two brothers raised him. As a person who loved God and liked people, his various and many talents drew L. D. to ministry. An effective communicator both as a public speaker and writer, L. D. was capable of addressing complex and controversial issues with a graceful directness and respectful simplicity.

An incident in early life helped shape L. D.'s understanding of what really matters. When he was six years old, their house burned. The family was sitting at the dinner table. His grandmother, who was in a wheelchair, was serving the meal. Neighbors burst in to announce that flames and smoke were billowing out of the upstairs windows. His grandfather ran to the hall door of the small frame house and saw the fire descending down the stairs. In the excitement, someone yelled "Fire!" Grandmother jumped up from her wheelchair and ran out of the house. Her wheelchair was left to burn up.

With the children outside, men from the community began to carry things out into the yard before the roof of the house caved in. With much huffing and puffing, the prize rescued from the inferno was an old iron cook stove that L. D. said must have weighed a half a ton. Out of all the motley assortment of odds and ends, the iron cook stove was the one item that would have survived the fire. In excitement, we sometimes become disoriented to what really matters.

L. D. used that story to illuminate that the house of our culture is on fire. Instead of becoming hysterical and running away, he suggested that we "develop a greater measure of integrity in our relationships." We need to seek to hear what each other is saying and ask ourselves more searching questions about the moral directions of our families, our churches, our businesses.

We need to examine our own priorities in the light of the nation's welfare. Can no one inspire us to put the welfare of the country above our personal gain and private enjoyment? Have we as a people lost the capacity for moral indignation and unselfish decisions?

He concluded, "the word from God's word is that we humans do not learn much from experience. We tend to make the same mistakes again and again. But the word is not of despair; it is a word of hope, for God has the last word. He makes even the wrath of humanity praise him." (L. D. Johnson, *Moments of Reflection*, Nashville, TN: Broadman Press, 1980. p. 65)

For a person who once worked as an elevator operator, L. D.'s life literally had its ups and downs, valleys shadowed with loss and mountaintops of recognition. From the death of a college-age daughter and a young son, L.

D., along with his wife of forty-four years, Marion, was painfully familiar with grief. Times of affirmation included his receiving the George Washington Medal of Honor for a newspaper column he wrote and being named the William R. Kenan, Jr., Professor of Religion here at Furman.

L. D. Johnson was an effective minister and preacher, chaplain and pastoral counselor, professor and author. Part of his legacy transcends his death and continues with us in his writings, *An Introduction to the Bible*, *Out of the Whirlwind*, *Israel's Wisdom*, and *The Morning After Death*. I am grateful that the trustees made possible a new edition of *The Morning After Death*, which was published by Smyth & Helwys in 1995.

From the summer of 1967 until his death in December 1981, I was privileged to be L. D.'s associate and true friend. I am grateful that we who comprise the Furman community can perpetuate his memory and celebrate his continuing influence among us with this lecture series.

I hope that the question posed by this lecture series will be a reminder for us to consider again and again "what really matters." In a season of sex, lies, and videotapes; political theater and power games; tabloid television and media hype; horrific acts of abuse and betrayal; and crass commercialization; such a question is not simply a quaint academic exercise. "What really matters" cuts to the core of our values and reveals our true character.

As partners and participants in this ongoing educational mission "For Christ and Learning," perhaps in some small ways we can influence our larger society. More immediately, I hope it will help Furman to focus anew and be committed to "what really matters." Our policies and procedures, our actions and attitudes, underscore what we believe really matters. "What really matters" concerns the bottom line and the non-negotiable, the ends to which we aspire, the price we are willing to pay, and the means we are willing to employ to get there.

Should it be your turn to speak in this lecture series, how would you answer the question "What really matters?" It is more than something to think about; it's a question that we flesh out and answer daily in thought, word, and deed.

I am grateful to the One who came and lived among us full of grace and truth,
    whose birth and life we celebrate,
    and whose death and resurrection we reverence.
    In this revelation we find both clear example and eternal hope.

I am thankful for teachable moments that help us clarify
    between the good and the best,

between what is fashionable and what is lasting,
between what is trivial and what is treasure.

It is my prayer that our shared life experience and increasing maturity in faith
will provide us with discerning wisdom,
will empower us to be courageous,
will humble us to be open,
grace us with a teachable spirit, so that we can genuinely trust one another,
and acknowledge that all of us are smarter than any one of us.

May the Lord watch over us, guide, and empower us to do those noble things that are right and true, just and pure, lovable and attractive, excellent and admirable.

My last word is a succinct quote from my good friend Frank Espey, a retired neurosurgeon who served as counselor and confidant to L. D. In a personal note received on Saturday, he echoed the ending of a letter written by an old friend to Albert Einstein. His note closes with advice about securing longevity. "I urge you to strive daily for the perfect exercise, sleep, diet and elimination."

With increasing age, I am sure that we all can add our "Amen" to my good physician's practical advice. Exercise, sleep, diet, and elimination also really matter!

# Reflections

What do these essays say to you? Two thoughts strike me as I reflect on these deeply personal statements by my colleagues. First, something important occurs when good questions are asked. Second, though the answers given are diverse, common themes weave among them. Considering the first thought, what does occur when a good question is asked?

The questions an institution asks significantly influence the answers an institution gives. The answers guide its practice. For example, if one asks what are the most efficient and effective techniques for administering an institution, one will probably examine different types of administrative styles. The answers will most likely assume some form of survival, as assumed by many strategic plans. The answer may involve some form of satisfying the customer, as assumed by such plans as Deming's. The question calls for a discussion of the procedures an institution may adopt. It can be answered without facing the issue whether a procedural scheme is morally or religiously good for the institution. However, the answer will be in terms of the moral and/or religious dimension of the institution, if one is interested in determining what the institution believes matters beyond all else. The question requests a discussion of values and obligations.

Questions are not asked in a vacuum. They are asked in the light of a background. Consider persons for a moment. Particularly at a liberal arts college, the lives of the persons who teach and work there — the faculty, administration, and staff — are central to but not exhaustive of the college's conduct. What is taught and the way the administration conducts the school's affairs are important, but the way of life of the people is broader and more inclusive than the practice of an academic discipline or performing an administrative role.

The lives of the leaders of a college are guided by their deepest commitments, both moral and religious, which form the horizons lived out in administrative and educational work. Look to the lives of the people who live in it to grasp what is central to a college, to grasp the value commitments that guide the educational and administrative work of the institution.

Though autobiographical narratives are important in themselves, reflective narratives go beyond mere descriptions and chronicles. They lay bare the deepest value commitments that guide lives.

Since that is the case, we can also say that the question underlying these essays, "What really matters?", prompts us to consider our deepest value commitments. Guided by this question, the techno-managerial aspects of a college are not ignored. Rather, one is guided quickly to the value commitments on which the aspects rest. We are led by the question to consider why one ought to adopt a particular management system or an educational method.

It is important to note that the question does not lead to a particular, individual answer, even though the question guides the inquiry and frames the answers one gives to the question. It does not determine the particular answers, but the question deeply influences the kind of answers given. This implies a freedom of conscience, an openness of inquiry, a respect for the persons seeking and finding answers to the question, and an appreciation for the answers given to the question. This encourages rich diversity.

Finally, questions are asked in a context. No questions are simply rational, objective, and value-free. One's questions arise in the context of an ongoing way of life, one that is guided by deep value horizons. Those value horizons have historically become traditions. Ours is the Christian tradition, rooted in beliefs and practices of historical Christianity. When we ask "What really matters?", we focus on the deep value commitments of Christianity. We may not agree on the particular understanding of those commitments even though we find the commitments to be satisfactory answers to the question. Indeed, some find answers to the question outside that tradition. That is an implication of raising the question in a context of freedom. We must respect the persons and appreciate their answers, though we may deeply disagree with them.

A constructive critical conversation centered on the question "What really matters?" allows us to lay bare the value core of the institution. The value core truly unifies us. Though we may differ in our disciplinary practice and our administrative styles, we share in common the question and a background out of which the question arises. But is that all? Do we share common values? A careful reading of these highly personal essays indicates that we do.

One can find four themes common to these essays: the life of the mind, the development of the individual, community, and God. Furman is primarily an academic place. Our reason for being is the education of students who choose to spend their college years here. Our central focus is on the mind and helping it to learn. We seek to educate through teaching and practicing both the various academic disciplines and the particular kinds of engagements required by different kinds of learning and areas of knowledge. An important aspect of educating the mind is learning to live with ambiguity. And another is learning to respect the freedom and dignity of each person. Persons are free to decide on the answers they give to the central questions of life. As you have read, the authors do not agree on some issues. Central to the exercise of freedom, the whole person — students, faculty, administration, and staff — must be respected. We encourage each other to exercise that freedom responsibly. Though we emphasize the development of the mind through learning, we recognize that persons are whole, and not bifurcated into minds and bodies. Whole persons learn, not simply minds only. Since its inception, Furman University has emphasized the dignity and value of the individual, the whole person. Being person-centered, we emphasize the development of the individual as a whole person. Character, knowing oneself, artistic taste, openness to traditions other than one's own, and emotional well-being are some of the many areas emphasized in the daily life of the people who live and work at Furman University.

Community runs deep in Furman's life. Thinking of Furman as a community may be elusive; nevertheless, there is a way of life here. It is found in the common values, such as those you and I find on reading the personal reflections of some Furman people. But Furman is also communities within a community. From academic departments to social organizations, to athletic programs, many communities compose our life together. Within them we ask questions and find our own answers. Fundamental to the Furman community is God. Our environment is God, which is periodically recognized and reaffirmed, most recently by Furman's Board of Trustees in its statement of character and values. However, how the environment is best understood and what it means for the university is under continuous discussion.

Furman is a university community of persons within the Baptist Christian tradition devoted to asking searching questions and to disciplined, free, respectful inquiry into them. We ask you to join the inquiry, to be a part of the Furman way. How do you answer "What really matters?"

Thomas O. Buford
Editor